Backpacking Idaho

Help Us Keep This Guide Up to Date

Every effort has been made by the authors and editors to make this guide as accurate and useful as possible. However, many things can change after a guide is published—trails are rerouted, regulations change, techniques evolve, facilities come under new management, and so on.

We would appreciate hearing from you concerning your experiences with this guide and how you feel it could be improved and kept up to date. While we may not be able to respond to all comments and suggestions, we'll take them to heart, and we'll also make certain to share them with the authors. Please send your comments and suggestions to the following address:

FalconGuides
Reader Response/Editorial Department
Guilford, CT 06437

Or you may e-mail us at: editorial@falcon.com

Thanks for your input, and happy trails!

Backpacking
Idaho

A Guide to the State's Best Backpacking Adventures

Edited by FalconGuides

FALCONGUIDES

GUILFORD, CONNECTICUT
HELENA, MONTANA

FALCONGUIDES®

An imprint of Rowman & Littlefield
Falcon, FalconGuides, and Outfit Your Mind are registered trademarks of Rowman & Littlefield.

Distributed by NATIONAL BOOK NETWORK

Copyright © 2015 by Rowman & Littlefield
Text contributed by Ralph and Jackie J. Maughan and Luke Kratz

Maps by Design Maps Inc.

British Library Cataloguing-in-Publication Information Available

Library of Congress Cataloging-in-Publication Data
Backpacking Idaho : a guide to the state's greatest backpacking adventures / edited by FalconGuides.
    pages cm
  ISBN 978-1-4930-1311-1 (pbk.) — ISBN 978-1-4930-1424-8 (e-book)
  1. Backpacking—Idaho-Guidebooks. 2. Idaho—Guidebooks. I. FalconGuides (Publisher) issuing body.
  GV199.42.I2B34 2015
  796.5109796—dc23

                                                                2015005616

∞™ The paper used in this publication meets the minimum requirements of American National Standard for Information Sciences—Permanence of Paper for Printed Library Materials, ANSI/NISO Z39.48-1992.

CONTENTS

ACKNOWLEDGMENTS

The editors of FalconGuides would like to thank Ralph and Jackie J. Maughan and Luke Kratz, the authors of *Hiking Idaho*, from which this book was derived. Also thanks to Ric Bailey, Phil Blomquist, Don Crawford, Katie Fite, Gwen Gerber, Josh Keeley, Anne Kratz, Catherine Kratz, John Kratz, Lawrence Kratz, Mary Kratz, Mark Leininger, John McCarthy, Lee Mercer, Chris Murphy, Jamie Dewey, Cecile Perez, and Lindsey Tucker.

The East Fork of the Wood River trail #50 begins in rugged terrain at more than 8,000 feet.
Photo by Luke Kratz

INTRODUCTION

Welcome!

Idaho is one the most diverse states for hiking, backpacking, and exploring new landscapes. It is truly a gem, where you can find places to get away and explore without paying exorbitant amounts for guides, lodging, or transportation. There is great variety in the landscape, as well as in creating backpacking excursions that work for your time and abilities.

This book has two simple goals:

- To provide supplementary information to backpackers as to the locations of various trips throughout the state and general descriptions of the hikes.
- To introduce people to the diverse natural settings found in Idaho so they may enjoy, respect, and help protect these areas for future generations.

Idaho's Backcountry

As citizens of a beautiful green planet, we must act as stewards to use the land appropriately but preserve natural places for the flora and fauna we will share the earth with well into the distant future. In a fast-paced world of exponentially growing technology and pressures, it is also a relief to know that wild places of healing and recuperation still exist.

Idaho has more undeveloped backcountry than any other state except Alaska. The percentage of accessible and inhabitable scenic country that remains roadless and untamed by humans within the state's borders could be among the highest anywhere in the planet. Recreational use of wilderness areas has been increasing through the years, and in some places has doubled or even quadrupled. While recreational use such as hiking and backpacking poses less of a threat than development, there are still measures all visitors should take. It is becoming ever more crucial that users touch the land only lightly.

The wilderness is available to the public to share and will be further preserved if we all follow some general guidelines.

Litter: Pack out what you packed in. All items, including perishables such as toilet paper and sanitary napkins, should be either burned or carried out. Human waste should be buried deep in the humus layer of the soil, and latrines should be located at least 200 feet away from watercourses.

Backcountry camping: Most backpacking trails have many places available for camping that have been previously used. If at all possible, camp below timberline at least 200 feet from a lake or stream and at least 100 feet away from the trail. This is to ensure less impact on the area and a more enjoyable experience for campers. In this book we rarely suggest specific campsites in an effort to spread out the impact. Please use existing fire rings, and do not build new fire rings.

Fires: Make sure all aluminum or cooking debris is packed out of fire rings. Save campfires for campsites with existing fire rings. Make sure a fire is completely out before you rest or leave the site.

Cleaning: Do all cleaning of dishes, clothes, and so on with soap (including "biodegradable" soap) away from water sources such as lakes, rivers, springs, streams, or creeks. Dispose of the dirty water away from the water source.

Off-trail hiking: Stay on the trail and avoid "shortcuts" through switchbacks; these contribute to erosion and damage plant growth. When you're hiking off-trail, use good judgment to avoid disturbing fragile areas, especially in pristine alpine country where natural vegetation is fragile.

History of Wilderness

Once all the earth was wild, but now only fragments of its four billion years of history before humankind are left, some protected by the National Wilderness Preservation System, more in national parks and monuments, and much protected informally by the continual struggle of folks who love the land and fight off recurring attempts to damage it.

In 1964, after years of political struggle, the US Congress recognized the value of pristine undeveloped land and passed the Wilderness Act. The act empowers Congress to protect select parts of roadless public lands. It allows for permanently setting aside exceptional undeveloped public lands. The designation of undeveloped public land as wilderness prohibits the use of recreational motorized vehicles, construction of roads and buildings, logging, and most mining activity within its boundaries. It does not exclude livestock grazing that was in place before the wilderness designation. Pack animals, hunting, fishing, camping, and hiking are encouraged by the Wilderness Act. Wilderness designation is a very powerful tool for protecting pristine public lands. Unfortunately, it is a form of protection that is increasingly difficult to achieve because Congress has become more and more anti-wilderness since the late 1980s.

As of 2000, about 3,900,000 acres (6,100 square miles) of wild public land in Idaho have been permanently protected as part of the National Wilderness Preservation System. There are five designated wilderness areas that are all, or partially, in Idaho: the Selway–Bitterroot, the Frank Church–River of No Return, the Sawtooth, Hells Canyon, Gospel–Hump, and Craters of the Moon National Monument Wilderness. The Salmo–Priest Wilderness adjoins roadless land in Idaho, but the legal wilderness is in Washington state.

Most of Idaho's roadless country has no strong legal protection. Each year hundreds of square miles of this "de facto" wilderness falls to the ax and bulldozer. The pace of wilderness destruction accelerated when Congress passed the "timber salvage rider" in 1996. Called the worst piece of public lands legislation ever to become law by prominent columnist Jessica Matthews, this law suspended all environmental protections governing logging on national forest lands. Conservation groups referred to it as "Logging Without Laws."

The justification given by the supporters of the law was the emergency need to "salvage" the wood in dead and dying forests. The reality of this law is that *salvage* is defined in such a way that most of the logging taking place is of perfectly healthy, large, green trees. Most sales of burned and dead trees have no bidders. It is estimated that the law will cost American taxpayers about $1 billion because revenues received don't come close to the costs of administering the salvage sales.

In Idaho this law was used to destroy several hundred thousand acres of roadless land. The most severely affected national forests were the Boise and the Payette, but national forests throughout the United States felt the sting of this legislation. After the bill expired in 1997, the Clinton administration set about to prevent further damage by reducing the timber cut in the national forests, and in 2000 President Clinton took steps to protect all remaining roadless national forest land, not as wilderness but at least without any new permanent roads. Whether this effort prevails still depends on future politics.

In all, about ten million acres of de facto wilderness still exist on public lands in Idaho. For years most Idaho conservationists advocated a compromise that would protect about four million acres of this as designated wilderness. Despite many congressional attempts, no more wilderness has been designated in Idaho since 1980, when the Frank Church–River of No Return Wilderness was established.

Many wilderness supporters have come to believe that compromise has yielded no benefits in Idaho. As a result, in the last several years, most of the major groups favoring wilderness have come to advocate that all land still wild in Idaho be kept that way.

The immediate prospects for change in Idaho appear dim. The League of Conservation Voters yearly rates Idaho's congressional delegation as among the worst in the country. Several of Idaho's congressional members are supporting legislation to give management of America's public land in Idaho to the Idaho State Land Board or to the timber corporations.

Cherish your trips into Idaho's backcountry. This opportunity could disappear. That any of Idaho is left is entirely the result of a time when Idaho public officials, both Republicans and Democrats, cherished protecting the outdoors; of the constant efforts of local and national conservation groups; and of an environmentally friendly administration in Washington from 1993 to 2000.

—Ralph Maughan and Jackie Johnson Maughan, 2001

In recent years we have developed the technology to view the world from satellite images and see how limited the space on the planet is. Protection of wilderness is a growing concern, with many philosophies on how and why to preserve certain areas. Many people are still of the mind-set that the earth is for the taking and its enjoyment is at its own expense. Growing trends toward using off-road machinery and developing lands for housing and business encroach upon truly natural settings. We need to find ways to gently persuade others how important true wilderness is.

Become educated about what is truly best for people and the environment. If there are imminent threats to places sacred to you, then please e-mail representatives or organizations your concerns to make your voice heard. Check out the conservation organizations that have been listed in appendix A of this book and get involved today!

Several areas in the Owyhee Desert have become protected wildernesses. Currently two potential national monuments are under review. The long-awaited Boulder/White Clouds monument and the Caldera monument, which encompasses more than 700,000 acres in the Island Park area, have potential to become protected. If enough voices are heard these land can be kept wild for many generations.

The hiker believes in minimal impact to the earth. As you lightly tread along trails into wild places full of life and adventure, it is my hope that you find a sense of peace and gratitude for the opportunity to fully connect with natural surroundings.

—Luke Kratz, 2014

HOW TO USE THIS GUIDE

Each backpacking trip in this book starts with a brief overview paragraph, then contains a number of "hike specs" that break down the important elements of the trip.

Type of Hike

Backpacking trips consist of at least one night spent in the backcountry. In this book the trips have been split into the following categories:

Overnight backpack: A one-night backpacking trip that doesn't have as many options for base camp and day hiking possibilities (although there's nothing wrong with just hanging out a few days and fishing or reading). These are often best for families with young children who are being introduced to backpacking.

Multiday backpack: A backpacking trip that either requires or is best served by spending at least two nights and three days in the backcountry; could require up to a week or even more. Only experienced backpackers with good stamina should undertake these trips.

Loop: Starts and finishes at the same trailhead with no (or very little) retracing of your steps. Sometimes the definition of a *loop* is stretched to include creative shapes (like a figure eight or a lollipop), and sometimes the hike requires a short walk on a dirt road to get you back to the trailhead.

Out-and-back: A hike that travels the same route coming and going. The route back will feel different, with new sights and vantage points.

Shuttle: A point-to-point trip that requires two vehicles (one at each end of the trail) or a prearranged pickup at a designated time and place. One effective way to manage the logistical difficulties of shuttles is to arrange for a second party to start at the other end of the trail. The two parties then rendezvous at a predetermined time and place along the trail, trade keys, and meet later.

Options: Also available on many of the hikes for additional nights in the backcountry and exploration of nearby areas as long as you have the ambition and knowledge of the area.

We did not feel it necessary to point you in the direction of every campsite along each hike—finding a suitable campsite is part of the fun and adventure of backpacking. Almost any backcountry lake you visit will have established campsites and fire rings; please use these rather than creating new ones. In addition, you will find many campsites along rivers and creeks where the country levels off. If somehow you end up camping at a spot that doesn't appear to have been camped in before, please remove all sign of your stay before leaving.

Distance

The distances given in the hike specs are round-trip distances.

Measuring trail distances is an inexact science. In this book most distances have been taken from map measurements and from in-the-field estimates. Most trail signs in the backcountry do not include distances, and when they do you can bet they are just someone's best guess. Policy in many wilderness areas has become to minimize the number of signs and the information they give.

Some of the distances are based on "as the crow flies" rather than actual hiking mileage. As GPS units become more common and technically advanced, exact distances will become available.

Keep in mind that distance is often less important than difficulty. A steep 2-mile climb on rocky tread can take longer than a 5-mile stroll through a gentle river valley. It may be helpful to note that most hikers average about 2 miles an hour on relatively level ground.

Approximate Hiking Time

Backpacking trips are typically measured in days rather than hours. These estimates don't account for extra days you may choose to spend at a particular campsite (always a nice, relaxing option) or exploring nearby areas from a basecamp. They also don't include the time it takes to drive to the trailhead.

Difficulty

Difficulty ratings are inherently flawed: What's easy for you might be difficult for someone else. A heavy backpack with several days' worth of food and gear will be a factor as well. Still, such ratings serve as a general guide and give an approximation of a hike's challenge. Remember that ratings are not the final word, and that the most important factor is to be honest about your own fitness level when planning your trip. In this guidebook difficulty ratings consider both how long and how strenuous a hike is. Here are general guidelines for the ratings:

Easy: Suitable for any hiker—young or old. Expect no serious elevation gain, hazards, or navigation problems.

Moderate: Suitable for hikers who have at least some experience and an average fitness level. Likely includes some elevation change and may have places where the trail is faint.

Strenuous: Suitable only for experienced hikers with above-average fitness levels. May feature hazardous trail sections, navigation difficulties, and serious elevation change.

Best Season

This heading tells you the best months of the year to venture out on the given trail. Many trails have only a short window of "hiking season" due to spring runoff and fall hunting season. If you're backpacking during any other times of the year, please take the necessary precautions. Remember that in the high country snow is possible just about any time of year, so be prepared with warm, waterproof clothing and good waterproof boots.

Trail Surface

Nearly all of the trails in this guide have normal trail surfaces of dirt, with rock, gravel, or stones found along or in the trail. Good footwear is a must for any trail. This is one of those you-get-what-you pay-for situations: Good boots and careful hiking helps avoid blisters and ankle sprains, which can, sadly, lead to months or more without hiking.

Land Status

This indicates the name of the agency or organization managing the land where the trails are located. Most of the trails are on USDA Forest Service land or lands governed by the Bureau of Land Management.

More information on national forests of Idaho can be found at www.fs.fed.us.

Canine Compatibility

Dogs can be great hiking companions and enjoy the outdoors as much as hikers. However, our furry friends can also wreak havoc on the land, native critters, and other hikers. Because of this most land agencies insist that pets be under control or leashed, and they are not allowed in designated wilderness areas. The headings used are: **Voice control, On leash,** or **Not allowed.**

Fees and Permits

These may vary from year to year. As of early 2015 a permit was not needed for trails in the Sawtooth National Recreation Area, but that could change. In some wilderness areas a permit is required, but that is usually available upon entrance into the wilderness. Fees for backcountry permits and campground parking are also needed in some areas. If in doubt, check in with the nearest forest service ranger station.

Maps

The maps in this book serve as a general guide to get you started. It is always better to have more maps of the area, in addition to consulting with the forest service about your planned route. Remember, trail conditions can change on a dime.

Forest service maps: The forest service has maps of all of the national forests, and over time these maps have become more detailed and more accurate. Nevertheless, they are usually not sufficient for a hike that is the slightest bit complicated. Most wilderness areas have their own forest service maps available for purchase, and a number of private groups have created maps of selected wilderness or prime backcountry areas that are available for purchase.

USGS maps: Usually the very best maps are the topographic quadrangles of the United States Geological Survey. They come in a number of degrees of detail, but we recommend the most detailed, the 1:24,000, 7.5-minute scale. All of Idaho is mapped to the 7.5-minute scale. However, don't count on these maps being completely accurate. They are revised on a ten- to thirty-year schedule, so recent changes in trails, roads, fires, timbering, rivers, and lakes may not appear.

Maps can be purchased at outdoor specialty stores in Idaho cities and in most of the tourist towns near the hike locations. Maps are also available from many sources on the Internet, including the USGS site (www.usgs.gov) and www.trails.idaho.gov.

Many hikers and backpackers these days like to use a GPS unit. That's great, but you should always still carry a paper map (in a sealed plastic bag) and a compass in case the GPS runs out of batteries or somehow gets broken. It can happen! Always have a paper map and compass as a backup.

Trail Contact

This is the contact information for the given trail's land governing agency. The people here are quite willing to assist, provide updates on the trails, and answer any questions you may have.

Some websites that may help include:
USDA Forest Service: www.fs.fed.us
Bureau of Land Management in Idaho: www.blm.gov/id
trails.idaho.gov
wilderness.net

Natural History and Geography of Idaho

Idaho has a more diverse natural topography within its borders than most places. It has oceans of basalt-covered lava flows and semi-arid deserts, fertile rolling hills, temperate rain forests, and perhaps a greater percentage of land area covered by mountains than any other state. It hosts the deepest canyon on the continent as well as the highest sand dunes. It also has the most wild waterways and natural hot springs in the lower forty-eight. Altitude ranges from 700 feet to well over 12,000 feet.

Topography and mountain ranges: When you drive across the state of Idaho, it seems like a relatively flat agricultural land dotted with cities and towns. This is because most people in Idaho live along or near the Snake River Plain, from the

Boise area to Idaho Falls. Even northern Idaho cities are far from the vast wilderness areas. What people rarely see is the miles and miles of mountainous country that cover the state.

In eastern Idaho, near Wyoming, are ranges termed the Middle Rocky Mountains. The various long strips of mountain ranges in the south are part of the Basin and Range physiographic province, a vast area that covers all of Nevada and parts of Utah and Arizona. Southwest Idaho is part of the Columbia Plateau. Most of Idaho north of the Snake River Plain consists of the Northern Rocky Mountains, including the Great Divide along the border with Montana. You could walk from the Boise Front all the way to Canada, or along the divide, and be in mountains all the way!

Idaho has wet and dry areas and everything in between. Storms from the Pacific water the western slopes and especially the north, where large trees grow and temperate rain forest ecology is present. As the storms head eastward, less moisture is sucked out and the mountains on the eastern side of the state—some of the highest in Idaho—are semi-arid. Idaho's narrow southern ranges appear to be dry at their bases, but their upper elevations form small "sky islands" that are quite moist and lush. The Middle Rocky Mountains receive intermediate amounts of moisture and are especially prone to summer thunderstorms.

Forests: More than 40 percent of Idaho is forested. Climate, latitude, and elevation all impact soils of the various woodlands. The forest types are most easily understood when broken down into the different ecological life zones where certain tree species thrive.

Lower Sonoran Zone: In lower elevations much of Idaho's land is either sagebrush deserts or prairies of tall or short grasses. Cottonwood trees dominate the lowland forests alongside rivers.

Upper Sonoran Zone: This is where the expanses of the Great Basin Desert give way to sporadic forests of junipers and occasional pinyon and limber pines. These areas are quite dry and found primarily at elevations of 5,000 to 7,000 feet in southern Idaho and on the Snake River Plain.

Transition Zone: The transition from arid to lush mountain country normally is found at 5,500 to 8,000 feet. In Idaho, the western slopes are usually dominated by forests of ponderosa pine; the east are Douglas fir. Aspen groves begin here as well.

Canadian Zone: Also known as the Montane Zone, this area receives more yearly precipitation and snowfall. These forests usually begin at around 7,000 feet but are at much lower elevations in the north, where they become the temperate rain forests of the Pacific Northwest. These north Idaho forests are full of western red cedar, Douglas fir, white pine, hemlock, and larch trees. In most parts of the state, however, this zone is defined by forests of Douglas fir, lodgepole pine, and Engelmann spruce. In the forest of the Middle Rockies, groves of quaking aspen thrive due to moisture and fertile sedimentary rock. These two factors also contribute to the abundance of many varieties of wildflowers in this zone.

The largest of all deer, the moose is commonly found in Idaho's backcountry.
PHOTO BY ANNE KRATZ

Hudsonian Zone: In most parts of the state, this is where the forest begins thinning at upper elevations around 8,000 to 9,000 feet. Whitebark pines, subalpine firs, and subalpine spruce are begin to appear here, with occasional groves of lodgepoles and Engelmann spruce. The trees become smaller, and the winters are harsher.

Wildlife: The wildlife of Idaho still consists of all the large North American animals present before settlement by Euro-Americans, except the great bison herds. Idaho has populations of rare animals such as the grizzly bear, desert bighorn sheep, and a small herd of woodland caribou. Idaho is also a stronghold for the threatened lynx and the rare wolverine. Wolves were reintroduced to the state in 1995. More common predators include black bear, badger, bobcat, coyote, fox, and the rarely seen mountain lion.

Idaho has large herds of elk and both mule and white-tailed deer. Moose populations are growing, while bighorn sheep, pronghorn antelope, and mountain goats have stable numbers in most of their range.

Unfortunately the salmon and the steelhead trout runs have been decimated by the dams on the lower Snake River in Washington State. Sturgeon, too, have been damaged by dams. The fish could make a comeback with continued efforts from environmental protection agencies.

Land ownership: Perhaps the best thing about Idaho geography is that the American people own 62 percent of it, more than any state except Utah and Nevada. The national forests and Bureau of Land Management (BLM) lands in Idaho are part of America's heritage. They belong to all of us, and with eternal vigilance, monitoring, and fighting off threats, the politicians and special interests will not take them.

Forest Fires

In August 1910 forest fires swept over three million acres of northern Idaho and northwestern Montana. On August 20 and 21 alone, in the "Big Blowup," several million acres burned, along with dozens of towns, and eighty-seven people died. Rain and snow on August 23 halted the firestorm, but this event left an impact on the forest and on forest policy that lasted for at least seventy-five years.

Even today, in some parts of the remote Idaho mountains, there are vast meadows but few large trees. The great fire also launched the forest service on an extensive crusade to stamp out all forest fires.

As firefighting technology improved, the annual acreage of forest fires declined precipitously, but most of Idaho's forestland is forest that has been subject to natural burns every twenty to thirty years, depending on the type of trees. As years pass with no fires, small trees grow up under the big trees, forming a fuel ladder in which the forest giants are more likely to ignite in a fire.

In some parts of Idaho, the problem of too much fire suppression was complicated by bad logging practices, especially in ponderosa pine country, which originally consisted of scattered large ponderosa (yellow) pine with an understory of grass and small bushes beneath the fire-resistant boles of the pines. "Park-like" is how early timbers described the area, but the yellow pine was a prize for timber interests. The biggest—and hence most fire-resistant—trees were cut, and the gentle ground fires were suppressed. The result was not harmless natural ground fires every twenty to thirty years, but hot fires in the dense coniferous forest that grew where the ponderosa had been cut.

Beginning in the late 1970s, the forest service began to experiment with allowing some naturally ignited fires to burn in remote areas. Fires were also deliberately set in a few places during the spring, when fires burn light and tend not to spread. This may have been too little and too late, however.

In 1980 giant fires burned in the Frank Church–River of No Return Wilderness, and also the Italian Peaks, and in the dry years since, many large fires have burned both inside and outside Idaho wilderness areas. In particular the years 1988, 1989, 1992, and 1994 saw many large forest fires; but the summer of 2000 almost became another 1910. Including range fires, almost 1.3 million acres of land inside Idaho burned in the summer of 2000.

Major fires in 2000 burned in every part of the state except the Selkirk Mountains rain forest of the extreme northwestern part of the panhandle. The largest fires were in central Idaho. Hundreds of thousands of acres burned in the Frank Church–River of No Return Wilderness and the roaded forest to its east and west. The largest single blaze was the 217,000-acre Clear Creek Fire, which included the lower portion of the Big Horn Crags in the wilderness area but mostly burned developed forestland to the east.

Other large fires included the Burgdorf Fire northeast of McCall, the Trail Creek Fire just southwest of the Sawtooth Wilderness, and scores of others in the range of 1,000 to 20,000 acres. In 2012 the Mustang Complex Fire burned more than 350,000 acres north of Salmon.

These fires burned hot enough in some places to sterilize the soil. Such areas take a long time to recover. However, most fire areas saw a medium to light burn, with many patches of unburned area inside the perimeters of the fires. Left alone, burned areas that were not disturbed with heavy firefighting machinery will recover. There is little concern about recovery from the burns inside the Frank Church and the Selway–Bitterroot Wildernesses, which were by default at least not aggressively fought.

For the fires in which heavy machinery was used to build fire lines, or which were salvage-logged, recovery is more problematic. Machinery disturbs the blackened, but intact, ground. This accelerates runoff and, worse, grinds in the seeds of exotic weeds, such as spotted knapweed, that have invaded central Idaho. The legacy of the fires of 2000 may be not meadows and a slow return to forest, but rather, in disturbed lands, permanent gigantic patches of weeds that are not native to Idaho and are useless to wildlife.

Over the years the terrain covered by many of the hikes described in this guide has burned, including some since 2000. We have rehiked most of these trails to bring the descriptions up to date.

Hiking in burns has previously been an unusual experience, but it is becoming more common. Depending on the time of day, the light, and your mood, burns can be either beautiful or ugly and depressing. Fortunately, total burns do not usually extend over great distances, so you will find many unburned patches of trees. Meadows respond very nicely after burns. Fires often produce brilliant floral displays of lupine, fireweed, and aster for a few years. Morel mushrooms are also abundant for a year or two after a burn. Patchy burns can benefit wildlife.

You should be very cautious camping or hiking inside a burn because the dead trees—the snags—tend to fall, especially in windy conditions when the ground is wet, such as in a windy May or June. Burned lodgepole pine forests are the most dangerous because these trees have shallow roots. While three-quarters of a burned forest of subalpine fir may be standing fifty years after the fire, within a decade 50 to 75 percent of burned lodgepole will have fallen.

Pine Beetles

Pine beetles infect forests by eating the wood beneath the bark and killing the tree. This is also reason for cautious hiking in predominantly pine forests. The pine beetle is currently in decline and has infected less than 750,000 acres of Idaho forests.

Leave No Trace

Leave No Trace Principles

- Leave with everything you brought in.
- Leave no sign of your visit.
- Leave the landscape as you found it.

Most of us know better than to litter—in or out of the backcountry. Be sure you leave nothing, regardless of how small it is, along the trail or at your campsite. This means you should pack out everything, including orange peels, flip tops, cigarette butts, and gum wrappers. Also, pick up any trash that others leave behind.

Follow the main trail. Avoid cutting switchbacks and walking on vegetation beside the trail. Don't pick up "souvenirs," such as rocks, antlers, and wildflowers. The next person wants to see them, too, and collecting such souvenirs violates many regulations.

Avoid making loud noises on the trail (unless you are in bear country) or in camp. Be courteous. Remember, sound travels easily in the backcountry, especially across water.

Carry a lightweight trowel to bury human waste 6 to 8 inches deep at least 200 feet from any water source. Pack out used toilet paper.

Go without a campfire. Carry a stove for cooking and a flashlight, candle lantern, or headlamp for light. For emergencies, learn how to build a no-trace fire.

Camp in obviously used sites when they are available. Otherwise, camp and cook on durable surfaces, such as bedrock, sand, gravel bars, and bare ground.

Leave no trace—and put your ear to the ground and listen carefully. Thousands of people coming behind you are thanking you for your courtesy and good sense.

Make It a Safe Trip

The Boy Scouts of America have been guided for decades by what is perhaps the single best piece of safety advice—be prepared! For starters, this means carrying survival and first-aid materials, proper clothing, a compass, and a topographic map—and knowing how to use them. Perhaps the second-best piece of safety advice is to tell somebody where you're going and when you plan to return. Pilots must file flight plans before every trip, and anybody venturing into a blank spot on the map should do the same. File your "flight plan" with a friend or relative before taking off.

Close behind your flight plan and being prepared with proper equipment is physical conditioning. Not only does being fit make wilderness travel more fun, it makes it safer. Don't underestimate the strain that multiple days carrying a heavy backpack will put on your body. Get in shape before your backpacking trip by loading the pack you will be using with increasingly heavier loads and going on hikes or long walks with it. This will help get your hip muscles into condition so that they are prepared to carry the weight needed for overnight trips. Here are a few more tips:

- Check the weather forecast. Be careful not to get caught at high altitude during a bad storm or along a stream in a flash flood. Watch cloud formations closely so you don't get stranded on a ridgeline during a lightning storm. Avoid traveling during prolonged periods of cold weather. Knowing the weather outlook is especially important when taking a multiday backpacking trip. But always remember that, regardless of the forecast, localized thunderstorms can happen most afternoons in the mountains, so be prepared, especially when hiking up high in exposed areas.

- Avoid traveling alone in the wilderness; keep your party together.

- Don't exhaust yourself or other members of your party by traveling too far or too fast. Let the slowest person set the pace.

- Study basic survival and first aid before leaving home.

- Before you leave for the trailhead, find out as much as you can about the route, especially its potential hazards.

- Don't wait until you're confused to look at your maps. Follow them as you go along, so you have a continual fix on your location. Identify prominent landmarks, and take care to notice how their images change as you progress along the trail.

- If you get lost, don't panic. Sit down and relax for a few minutes while you carefully check your topo map and take a compass reading. Then plan your next move. It's often smart to retrace your steps until you find familiar ground, even if you think it might lengthen your trip. Lots of people get temporarily lost in the wilderness and survive—usually by calmly and rationally dealing with the situation.

- Stay clear of all wild animals.

- Take a first-aid kit that includes, at a minimum, a sewing needle, a snakebite kit, aspirin (or other painkiller), antibacterial ointment, antiseptic swabs, butterfly bandages, adhesive tape, adhesive strips, gauze pads, two triangular bandages, two inflatable splints, moleskin or Second Skin for blisters, 3-inch gauze, a CPR shield, rubber gloves, and lightweight first-aid instructions.

- Take a survival kit that includes, at a minimum, a compass, a whistle, matches in a waterproof container, a cigarette lighter, a candle, a signal mirror, a flashlight, fire starter, aluminum foil, water purification tablets, a space blanket or large trash bag, and a flare.

- Don't forget that knowledge is the best defense against unexpected hazards.

- Purchase good quality backpacking equipment. These days they make good gear much lighter than in old days, when the backpack itself could weigh almost ten pounds. You'd be amazed at the difference shedding ten pounds off your equipment can make (think having two twelve-packs tied to your waist—that's about ten pounds). Also, warm, waterproof clothing and sturdy waterproof boots are a

BACKPACKING WITH CHILDREN

Backpacking with children is all about seeing and experiencing nature through their eyes. Kids like to explore and have fun. They like to stop and point out bugs and plants, look under rocks, jump in puddles, and throw sticks. If you're taking a toddler or young child on a hike, start with a trail that you're familiar with. Trails that have interesting things for kids, like piles of leaves to play in or a small stream to wade through during the summer, will make the hike much more enjoyable for them and will keep them from getting bored.

You can keep your child's attention if you have a strategy before starting on the trail. Using games is not only an effective way to keep a child's attention, it's also a great way to teach him or her about nature. Quiz children on the names of plants and animals. If your children are old enough, let them carry their own day packs filled with treats and a favorite (small) toy. So that you are sure to go at their pace and not yours, let them lead the way. Playing follow the leader works particularly well when you have a group of children. Have each child take a turn at being the leader.

Kids shouldn't have to carry much weight, if any. A little day pack with a security blanket and stuffed animal is probably enough for a five- or six-year-old. Once kids get to be eight or ten, they can carry more—maybe a sleeping bag and a bottle of water and snacks. But as the parent, it's going to be your job to carry "the load," so be prepared with a sturdy, large backpack. It's also a good idea to invest in relatively lightweight and stuffable gear for kids. As kids get older, you can buy them a decent little backpack with a compact suspension system so they can carry more of their own gear. But again, don't overdo it. That extra weight on their little bodies makes a big difference.

Make sure kids have good hiking shoes with sturdy soles. Sneakers don't cut it on a rocky trail in the backcountry.

Carry bear spray, of course, but don't talk about bears or otherwise make it a big deal beyond making sure they understand how important it is to keep a clean camp and not drop food scraps and crumbs on the ground. If kids think the adults are frightened of bears, then they are going to be as well, so keep that kind of talk among adults. Also, talking and playing word games with kids while hiking is a great way to make some "noise" to alert bears that you are coming—so don't feel like you have to hush up the kids!

Another good idea is to bring along a few special candy treats that can help head off a full-on meltdown. One adult can hike a short ways ahead of the kids on the trail and "hide" wrapped candies on rocks or low branches (in plain sight, of course). Nothing makes a kid hustle up the trail like the prospect of finding a treat.

Setting up a base camp, where you can fish, watch wildlife, and go on short day hikes, is a great way to introduce young children to backpacking. If they have to pack up and move every day, it gets arduous, so if you're on a multiday trip try to plan at least two nights in a row at the same campsite, especially for kids six and younger. And be flexible. If it appears the kids are getting exhausted, don't push them; just revise your hiking plans as best you can to accommodate their needs. If you can give kids a positive impression of backpacking when they are youngsters, they will be more likely to keep backpacking into their teen and adult years.

necessity, especially in the high country where snow can happen just about any time of year. Cotton clothes like jeans, in addition to being heavy and bulky, absorb water and lose insulation value when wet, so stick with the wide range of synthetic materials available. Down sleeping bags are nice because they compress easily and are lightweight, but remember that down loses insulation value when wet, whereas synthetic insulation will still keep you warm. If you like down bags, take extra precautions to keep them dry, and if you're backpacking into a wet area or the forecast is for rain, consider taking a sleeping bag with synthetic insulation.

Should I Drink the Water?

There are few backpacking pleasures that can top a cool drink from a high-country lake or stream. Unfortunately, that cool sip from a cold mountain stream may be hazardous to your health.

The most common problem is wild strains of the intestinal bacteria *E. coli*, which teems in areas heavily used by humans or grazing animals. The most serious problem is the protozoan *Giardia lamblia*. The best measure to avoid both is the purchase of a water filter. These are available from mountaineering supply companies and many sporting goods stores. They range in cost from $40 to $100 per unit and are worth the investment if you like to hike. The second-best option is to purchase water purification tablets, in which the active ingredient is iodine, from a pharmacy or outdoor equipment store. Make sure to check the expiration date on the bottle. If you bring a filter, it's never a bad idea to bring some purification tablets too, as backup. More than one water filter has conked out in the backcountry.

E. coli will manifest in a few hours and is characterized by stomach pain and diarrhea. Giardiasis is caused by ingestion of the dormant cyst form of a protozoan. These cysts can survive, even in cold streams (40 degrees Fahrenheit), for up to three months and can be spread by domestic livestock, wild animals, and humans. Onset of symptoms can occur from within several days to six weeks. Professional medical treatment is required.

Since it is beyond the scope of this book to advise on how to treat these various medical problems, we strongly suggest you purchase a good backcountry first-aid manual.

A final note—some backcountry water is drinkable without treatment. Use caution. Is the area very remote? Freely flowing springs that lack seepage areas above or around their margins are the best bet for a safe backcountry drink. If you decide to try it, you do so at your own risk.

Be Mountain Lion Alert

Most of Idaho's backcountry is mountain lion territory. These big cats are found even along trails abutting cities like Boise or Pocatello.

Though many people consider themselves lucky indeed to see a mountain lion in the wild, the big cats—nature's perfect predator—are potentially dangerous. Attacks on humans are extremely rare, but it's wise to educate yourself before heading into mountain lion habitat.

Safety Guidelines for Traveling in Mountain Lion Country

To stay as safe as possible when hiking in mountain lion country, follow this advice.

1. Travel with a friend or group and stay together.
2. Don't let small children wander away by themselves.
3. Don't let pets run unleashed.
4. Avoid hiking at dawn and dusk—the times mountain lions are most active.
5. Know how to behave if you encounter a mountain lion.

What to Do If You Encounter a Mountain Lion

In the vast majority of mountain lion encounters, these animals exhibit avoidance, indifference, or curiosity that doesn't result in human injury. They see you much more often than you see them. It is natural to be alarmed if you have an encounter of any kind. However, try to keep your cool and consider the following:

- Recognize threatening mountain lion behavior. A few cues may help you gauge the risk of attack. If a mountain lion is more than 50 yards away and directs its attention to you, it may be only curious. This situation presents only a slight risk for adults but a more serious risk for unaccompanied children. At this point, you should move away, while keeping the animal in your peripheral vision. Also, look for rocks, sticks, or something to use as a weapon, just in case.

- If a mountain lion is crouched and staring at you less than 50 yards away, it may be assessing the chances of a successful attack. If this behavior continues, the risk of attack may be high.

- Do not approach a mountain lion. Give the animal the opportunity to move on. Slowly back away, but maintain eye contact if close. Mountain lions are not known to attack humans to defend their young or a kill, but they have been reported to "charge" in rare instances and may want to stay in the area. It's best to choose another route or time to hike through the area.

- Do not run from a mountain lion. Running may stimulate the mountain lion's predatory response.
- Make noise. If you encounter a mountain lion, be vocal; talk or yell loudly and regularly. Try not to panic. Shout to make others in the area aware of the situation.
- Maintain eye contact. Eye contact presents a challenge to the mountain lion, showing you are aware of its presence. Eye contact also helps you know where it is. However, if the behavior of the mountain lion is not threatening (if the animal is, for example, grooming itself or periodically looking away), maintain visual contact through your peripheral vision and move away.
- Appear larger than you are. Raise your arms above your head and make steady waving motions. Raise your jacket or another object above your head. Do not bend over, since this will make you appear smaller and more preylike.
- If you are with small children, pick them up. Bring children close to you, maintain eye contact with the mountain lion, and pull the children up without bending over. If you are with other children or adults, band together.
- Defend yourself and others. If attacked, fight back. Try to remain standing. Do not feign death. Pick up a branch or rock; pull out a knife, pepper spray, or other deterrent. Individuals have fended off mountain lions with rocks, tree limbs, and even cameras. Keep in mind this is a last effort, and defending pets is not recommended.
- Respect any warning signs posted by agencies.
- Teach others in your group how to behave in case of a mountain lion encounter.
- Report encounters. Record your location and the details of any encounter, and notify the nearest landowner or land management agency. The land management agency (federal, state, or county) may want to visit the site and, if appropriate, post education or warning signs. Fish and wildlife agencies should also be notified because they record and track such encounters.
- If physical injury occurs, it is important to leave the area and not disturb the site of attack. Mountain lions that have attacked people must be killed, and an undisturbed site is critical for effectively locating the dangerous mountain lion.

Be Bear Aware

Bears inhabit most of Idaho's mountains and some of the lower country as well. While the vast majority of Idaho bears are black bears, a few grizzly bears wander the panhandle near the Washington–British Columbia border. A significant number of grizzlies also live in a small area near Yellowstone National Park.

The first step of any hike in bear country is an attitude adjustment. Being prepared for bears means not only having the right equipment, such as pepper spray, but also having the right information. Bears rarely attack humans, but they don't like to be surprised, and a female can be very defensive when she has cubs.

*Hanging food and garbage
between two trees*

*Hanging food and garbage
over a tree branch*

*Hanging food and garbage
over a leaning tree*

The greatest danger from bears occurs if you handle your food improperly. If a bear eats your food, and destroys your equipment in doing so, your trip is ruined. If you are deep in the wilderness, your life may be at risk as a result. Moreover, letting a bear get human food rapidly conditions it to seek human food in the future. The slogan "A fed bear is a dead bear" is often true. Think of following proper bear etiquette as protecting the bears as much as protecting yourself.

Camping in Bear Country

The presence of food, cooking, and garbage can attract a bear into camp. Plus, you are in bear country at night, when bears are usually most active.

A few basic practices greatly minimize the chance of a bad encounter. To be as safe as possible, store everything that has any food smell. Ziplock bags are perfect for reducing food smell, and they help keep food from spilling on your pack, clothing, or other gear. Before going to bed change into other clothes for sleeping and hang clothes with food smells with the food and garbage. If you take soiled clothes into the tent, you aren't separating your sleeping area from food smells. Try to keep food odors off your pack, but if you fail, put the food bag inside and hang the pack.

Finalize your food storage plans before it gets dark. Not only is it difficult to store food after darkness falls, but it's easier to forget some juicy morsel on the ground. Store food in airtight, sturdy, waterproof bags to prevent odors from circulating throughout the forest. You can purchase dry bags at most outdoor specialty stores, but you can get by with a trash compactor bag. Don't use regular garbage bags—they can break too easily.

See the diagrams for ways to hang a bear bag. If you have two bags to hang, divide your food into two equal sacks. Use a stone to toss the end of a piece of nylon cord over the limb well out from the trunk, then tie half your food to the end. Pull the food up to the limb, then tie your remaining food sack onto the cord as high as you can reach. Stuff the excess cord into the food sack and use a stick to push the second sack several feet higher than your head. The first sack will act as a counterweight and descend a few feet, but it should remain at least as high as the second sack. In the morning, use a stick to pull down one of the sacks.

Avoid smelly foods and consciously reduce the number of dishes you use. Pack out all food scraps. By consuming everything on your plate as well as paying careful attention to storage, you will make your backpacking culinary experience not only more enjoyable and hassle-free but also more bearproof.

Read Globe Pequot Press's *Bear Aware* by Bill Schneider for complete information on camping in bear country.

Remember Rattlesnakes

Rattlesnakes are present in much of the lower country in Idaho. This is especially true of the rugged, low-elevation canyons in the central part of the state.

Rattlesnakes strike humans only out of self-defense, when they're startled or otherwise afraid. The solution, of course, is to avoid scaring them. Look where you place your feet and hands when hiking in rattlesnake country, and carry a walking stick.

If you do encounter a rattlesnake, slowly back away and give it a chance to move away. Almost invariably, it will seize the opportunity and slither off. If it doesn't, simply give the snake a wide berth and leave well enough alone. Do not throw rocks or sticks at it.

If you're bitten by a rattlesnake, don't panic. Rattlesnake bites are rarely fatal to healthy adults. Use a snakebite kit immediately to extract as much of the venom as possible. (It may actually be a "dry bite," in which no venom is delivered; the snake intended only to frighten you.) Do not run or otherwise speed up your circulation, since that increases the spread of the venom in your bloodstream. Keep the bite site lower than your heart to decrease the spread of venom. Seek medical attention as soon as possible.

	One-night trips	Two-plus-night trips	Loop or partial loop hikes	Wilderness	Peak climbing	Scenery	Lakes	Wildflowers	Wildlife
1. Long Canyon		●	●			●		●	●
2. Salmo–Priest Divide Loop		●	●	●				●	●
3. Two Mouths Lake	●						●	●	●
4. Lower Selway River	●	●		●					
5. Selway Crags via Big Fog and Legend Lakes		●		●	●	●	●	●	
6. Seven Lakes Loop		●	●	●		●	●	●	●
7. White Cap Creek		●	●	●		●	●	●	●
8. Larkins Lake	●	●				●	●	●	●
9. Pete Ott Lake and Vicinity	●	●				●	●	●	
10. Goat Lake	●	●				●	●	●	●
11. Steep Lakes Loop		●	●			●	●	●	
12. Meadow Creek	●	●				●		●	
13. Oregon Butte Area	●			●	●	●	●	●	
14. Bighorn Crags: Reflection Lake		●		●		●	●		
15. Bighorn Crags: Ship Island Lake		●		●	●	●	●		●
16. Sheep Hill Area		●		●	●				

	One-night trips	Two-plus-night trips	Loop or partial loop hikes	Wilderness	Peak Climbing	Scenery	Lakes	Wildflowers	Wildlife
17. Sleeping Deer Mountain	●				●	●	●		
18. Soldier Lakes–Patrol Ridge Loop		●	●	●		●	●		
19. Stoddard Lake		●		●		●	●		
20. West Yankee Fork–Crimson Lake		●		●		●	●		●
21. Box Lake	●					●	●		
22. Lava Butte Lakes	●	●				●	●	●	
23. Jennie Lake	●						●	●	
24. Rainbow Lakes	●	●				●	●	●	●
25. Seven Devils Loop		●	●	●	●	●	●		●
26. Bench Lakes	●			●		●	●		
27. Toxaway–Pettit Loop		●	●	●		●	●		
28. Boulder Chain Lakes		●				●	●	●	
29. Fourth of July Creek to Born Lakes	●	●				●	●		●
30. Fall Creek	●	●			●	●	●		
31. Left Fork of Fall Creek	●	●				●	●		●
32. Right Fork of Fall Creek	●	●			●	●	●		
33. Iron Bog Lake	●	●				●	●		

	One-night trips	Two-plus-night trips	Loop or partial loop hikes	Wilderness	Peak Climbing	Scenery	Lakes	Wildflowers	Wildlife
34. Bear Creek Lake	●				●	●	●		
35. Merriam Lake	●					●	●		
36. Big Creek–Big Timber Creek Loop		●	●			●	●	●	
37. Buck and Bear Valley Lakes	●	●					●	●	●
38. Mill Creek Lake and Firebox Summit	●	●					●		
39. Nez Perce Lake	●						●		
40. Salamander Lake Loop	●	●	●			●	●	●	
41. Webber Creek	●	●	●			●	●	●	●
42. Palisades Creek–Upper Palisades Lake–Waterfall Canyon	●	●				●	●		●
43. South Fork of Tin Cup Creek to Lau Creek	●								●
44. Worm Creek	●							●	●
45. Independence Lakes	●				●	●	●		
46. Third Fork Rock Creek–Wahlstrom Hollow Loop	●		●					●	

Map Legend

85	Interstate Highway	)⁻(	Bridge
76	US Highway	■	Building/Point of Interest
28	State Highway	▲	Campground
2658	County/Forest Road	⌒	Cave
	Local Road		Cliff
	Unpaved Road	—	Dam
	Featured Trail	▲	Mountain/Peak
	Trail	P	Parking
	Paved Trail/Bike Path	)(	Pass/Gap
	State Line	×	Peak/Summit
	Ditch/Scarp	⊼	Picnic Area
	Small River or Creek		Ranger Station
	Intermittent Stream	//	Rapids
	Marsh/Swamp	※	Rocks
	Body of Water		Scenic View/Viewpoint
	Dunes	⚲	Spring
		○	Town
	National Forest/Park	①	Trailhead
	National Wilderness Area	❓	Visitor/Information Center
	State/County Park	≈	Waterfall

Selkirk Mountains and Salmo-Priest Wilderness

I n the far northwest corner of Idaho and northeast Washington rises one of the major mountain ranges of the Northern Rockies—the Selkirks. They are largely the product of the huge Kaniksu Batholith, emplaced, then uplifted and eroded into a rugged, glaciated, 250-mile-long range stretching northward deep into British Columbia. Here they differentiate into many subranges, and then they finally merge with the Monashee Range to become the Cariboo Mountains.

This "big tree" country is nurtured by heavy annual rain and snowfall. The result is a mix of huge western red cedar, Douglas fir, white pine, and spruce, usually covered by a healthy growth of moss and lichen. This is rain forest, both in Idaho and in interior British Columbia, and although the forest has been heavily logged, some very special places remain intact. Even in the logged areas, the glaciated crest of the range provides cirques with undeveloped mountain lakes, horns and pyramidal peaks of hard granite, and some big trees in places too rough to have been timbered.

The lichen of the lower-elevation, unlogged rain forest provides a major source of food for the only band of woodland caribou remaining in the United States. Not to be confused with the barren ground caribou, the rare woodland caribou struggles to hang on, with about thirty-five animals roaming the international border. Another rare inhabitant of the Selkirks is the grizzly bear. About thirty of the great bears wander the southern section of the Selkirks, the area between northwest Idaho and Nelson, British Columbia. The great bear is rarely seen, but the smaller black bear is abundant. Many of the walks in these mountains are along trails where most of the trailside forest understory consists of August bear food—berries, including currant, snowberry, serviceberry, gooseberry, thimbleberry, elderberry, and especially huckleberry.

The bulk of the lower-elevation rain forest in the American Selkirks is concentrated around the South Salmo River of northeast Washington and the Upper Priest River nearby in Idaho, and in Long Canyon just northwest of Bonners Ferry, Idaho.

The 39,976-acre Salmo–Priest Wilderness was created by the Washington Wilderness Act of 1984 after a long battle. The Upper Priest River in Idaho was supposed to follow the Salmo into wilderness classification in separate legislation, but Idaho's political establishment became intensely anti-environment, and the Upper Priest

Beautiful high country of the Selkirks. PHOTO BY JOHN KRATZ

was never added. So, ironically, the Salmo–Priest Wilderness contains no Priest. The Upper Priest area is, however, managed by the USDA Forest Service just as though it were designated wilderness; but lacking congressional protection, its administrative protection could blow away with shifting political winds.

Idaho conservationists have also labored to protect as wilderness the crest of the Selkirks and Long Canyon, the only major mountain canyon in the Idaho Selkirks that has not been logged at all. Both the crest zone and Long Canyon are presently being protected by the administrative power of the forest service. This protection, too, is subject to change if politics so dictate.

—Ralph Maughan

1 Long Canyon

Long Canyon is a splendid example of a northern climax rain forest. Opportunities arise for wildlife viewing, mushroom hunting, and fishing. It is a magnificent ridge walk.

Start: Approximately 10 miles northwest of Bonners Ferry
Type of hike: Near loop
Distance: 30 miles
Approximate hiking time: 5–6 days
Difficulty: Strenuous due to sometimes tough stream crossings, a ridge walk, and a steep descent with faint spots and long gaps between water sources
Best season: July–October (depending on snow)
Trail surface: Dirt and rocks
Land status: Idaho Panhandle National Forests
Canine compatibility: On leash
Fees and permits: None
Maps: USGS Smith Peak, Pyramid Peak, Smith Falls, and Shorty Peak ID; Kaniksu National Forest-Idaho Panhandle National Forests map

Trail contact: Bonners Ferry Ranger District; (208) 267-5561; www.fs.usda.gov/ipnf
Special considerations: Since this area is popular, exceptional, and fragile, please keep parties small, select entry days of light use, and use backpacking stoves instead of fires. The three crossings of Long Canyon Creek are difficult during high water. Conditions in the rain forest portion are often very wet, but there is no reliable water on the steep climb (the first 5 miles) and no water on the last 5 miles down Parker Ridge. You will need a shuttle if you exit at Parker Creek.
Parking and trailhead facilities: Parker Creek has no trailhead, just room for about two vehicles on the side of the road. The Long Canyon Trailhead has parking for about eight vehicles and includes a horse-loading ramp. Both Parker Creek and Long Canyon Creek Trailheads are in partial shade.

Finding the trailhead: From Bonners Ferry, drive north on US 95. You soon come to the junction with ID 1, which leads north to Canada. Take ID 1. Travel 1 mile down ID 1, then turn left onto the paved side road. This road leads downhill to the floor of the Kootenai Valley and a road junction. Turn left and cross over the Kootenai River; then continue west directly toward the Selkirk Mountain front. The canyon you are looking into is Fisher Creek. At the base of the mountains is the paved Westside Road. You reach it at a T intersection. Turn right onto Westside Road. At about 3.7 miles the road crosses Parker Creek (which is the return route for the loop); just north of the creek is Parker Creek Trail (Trail 14). About 2.8 miles farther north is Long Canyon Creek, and 0.5 mile past the creek crossing is a sign and a side road that leads to the Long Canyon Trailhead. GPS: N48 57.34' / W116 32.72'

The Hike

Long Canyon is one of the last two unlogged drainages of the American Selkirk Mountains. Parker Canyon, which lies next to it, is the other. The other drainages still have high recreation values, especially near the crest of the range, but they have been

The trailhead at Long Canyon. PHOTO BY CATHY KRATZ

partially or completely logged. This prime area consists mainly of hemlock, western red cedar, white pine, and larch in the middle third. The upper third and ridges are covered with Engelmann spruce and subalpine fir. Wildlife abounds. A few grizzlies and woodland caribou still live in the area. The Selkirk Mountains are the only place that the woodland caribou, an endangered species, still exists in the United States. Mushroom hunting in this rain forest, particularly in September, is good. Two of the three highest mountains in northern Idaho flank Long Canyon: Smith Peak at 7,653 feet and Parker Peak at 7,670 feet. The drainage holds four large lakes.

Long Canyon proper covers about 20,000 acres. Whether or not to log this virgin old-growth timber was debated for years. Many have sought to protect Long Canyon and designate it part of the Selkirk Crest Wilderness. The proposal takes in not only Long and Parker Canyons but also the rugged crest area of glacier-polished granite peaks, subalpine lakes, and ridges. Long Canyon supplies irreplaceable old-growth forest for wildlife, the only such forest in northern Idaho for primitive recreation, and a natural forest by which to gauge success in managing other forests. For the present, the attitude of the forest service has changed toward managing this area for primitive backcountry recreation with no thought of timber. But because the area hasn't been designated wilderness by Congress, all this could change with a bad president or bad Congress.

The good, reconstructed Trail 16 runs most of the length of the narrow Long Canyon of Canyon Creek. It entails a 2,800-foot elevation gain to the junction with Smith Lake Fork and a 5,200-foot elevation gain total to Pyramid Pass. The steepness of this entry is the very reason this canyon hasn't been logged, although Myrtle and Smith Creeks also have steep entrances and roads were blasted up into them. Long Canyon Creek itself is difficult to reach until some 5 miles in. As a result water sources require bushwhacks.

From the trailhead, the path winds through the timber. Then it switchbacks 600 feet to the ridge between Smith Creek to the north and Long Canyon Creek to the south. After a gentle 0.5 mile, the trail approaches Long Canyon Creek and makes a 90-degree turn up into that canyon but does not descend into it for a long way. The first 3 miles are through forest, with the trail staying a good 400 to 600 feet above the creek and climbing up the canyon. Next, the trail continues above the creek and goes through a mostly rocky section of slate, still climbing.

The lower section's slate eventually yields to granite, signaling a gentler grade, and eventually the trail and the creek meet. The ponderosa pine, aspen, and cottonwood will have disappeared when you reach the first crossing of Long Canyon Creek just past the 6-mile mark, where you enter the rain forest. This magnificent forest, about 0.5 mile wide, continues for 7 miles. Apparently forest fires have always stopped here due to the wetness. Experience has shown that clothing can't be dried, no matter how warm the weather. But then, that's why the mushrooms are so abundant. Despite major rehabilitation efforts by various volunteer groups, this lowest creek crossing can be tricky even late in the season, and the water is always cold.

In 1.5 miles the trail crosses the creek again. This, too, can be difficult. There is one more crossing at about 9 miles. At about mile 11, reach a very large, open area near Smith Lake Creek. The creek tumbles down numerous small waterfalls and flows into Long Canyon Creek at the only real flat in the valley bottom.

Slightly more than 1.5 miles upstream, the hemlock-cedar forest begins to play out in the higher altitude (over 4,000 feet), and gives way to spruce and fir. In late summer huckleberries, present on most of the trail, often bear abundant fruit. Here,

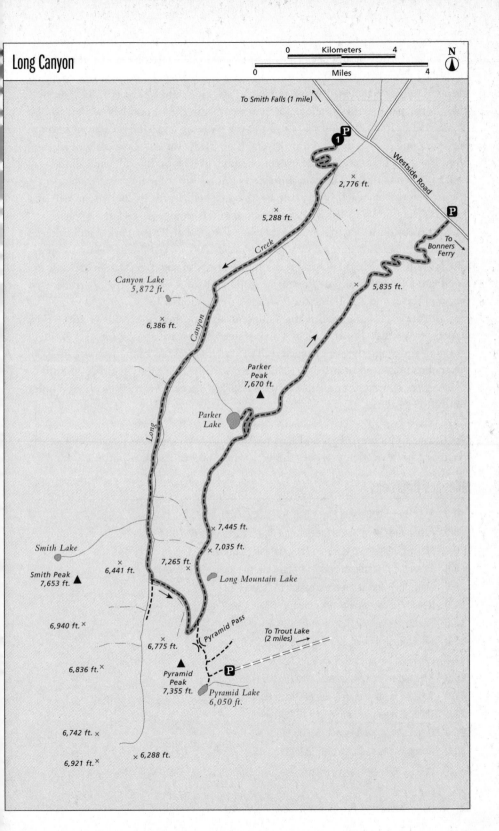

Long Canyon

0   Kilometers   4

0   Miles   4

N

To Smith Falls (1 mile)

P
1

Westside Road

× 2,776 ft.

× 5,288 ft.

Creek

Canyon Lake
5,872 ft.

P

To
Bonners
Ferry

× 5,835 ft.

× 6,386 ft.

Canyon

Parker
Peak
7,670 ft. ▲

Parker
Lake

Long

× 7,445 ft.

× 7,035 ft.

Smith Lake

× 7,265 ft.

Smith Peak
7,653 ft. ▲

× 6,441 ft.

Long Mountain Lake

6,940 ft. ×

Pyramid Pass

To Trout Lake
(2 miles)

× 6,775 ft.

P

6,836 ft. ×

Pyramid
Peak
7,355 ft. ▲

Pyramid Lake
6,050 ft.

6,742 ft. ×

× 6,288 ft.

6,921 ft. ×

Trail 16 fades out. The upper third of Long Canyon no longer has a maintained trail.

Where Trail 16 fades, Trail 7 fords the creek and leaves Long Canyon to climb steeply (especially at first) toward Pyramid Pass. From the ford it is 2,400 feet in 4 miles to the pass—but 0.5 mile below the pass, begin the second half of the loop by taking Trail 221, which climbs northeast to the ridgetop and soon breaks out into the open on Long Mountain. There are several lakes below the ridge on Long Mountain. From Long Mountain, with one exception, the trail stays on the ridgeline all the way back to Westside Road. There are fine views but no water for the last 5 miles.

Just before you reach big Parker Peak, a side trail leaves to the left (north) and drops 500 feet down to Parker Lake, where the trail ends.

An exception to staying on the ridgeline is found at Parker Peak. Here the trail keeps to the east and drops down, passing about 600 to 1,100 feet below the peak, which is 7,670 feet high, making it the highest peak in the American Selkirks. It has a tremendous north wall, but there is no good view of it from the trail. Fortunately a spur trail leaves and climbs Parker Peak for a tremendous view.

Past Parker Peak, the trail is fairly uneventful, with the big exception of the final descent to Westside Road, which is a very steep, knee-jarring descent of 3,200 feet on top of and along the very rugged wall of Parker Creek! As of the summer of 2000, this trail had received maintenance, and the descent was in pretty good condition.

Be aware that the last available water is a spring just off a switchback about 5 miles from Westside Road.

Options: Continue to Pyramid Pass (7,080 feet) and over it to reach Ball Lake or Pyramid Lake. A road approaches this area where you can park a shuttle.

Miles and Directions

0.0 Start on Long Canyon Creek Trail 16 (1,820 feet).

0.5 Reach the top of Smith Creek–Long Canyon Creek toe (2,700 feet).

0.8 Make a right-angle turn into Long Canyon (2,600 feet).

6.0 Make the first stream crossing; enter the rain forest (3,800 feet).

7.5 Make the second stream crossing (4,000 feet).

11.0 Reach the meadow at the mouth of Smith Lake Creek (4,400 feet).

14.5 Reach the Trail 221 junction (6,400 feet).

16.0 Pass the high point on Long Mountain (7,200 feet).

17.5 Pass just below Peak 7,445 (7,390 feet).

20.0 Reach the Parker Lake side trail (6,850 feet).

21.5 The trail is immediately below Parker Peak (6,400 feet).

22.5 The trail regains the ridgeline (6,600 feet).

25.0 Begin the major descent (5,700 feet).

30.0 Reach Westside Road (1,805 feet).

2 Salmo-Priest Divide Loop

Along the northern Washington and Idaho border there are still mountains with vast old-growth rain forests. This is the wild homeland of the endangered mountain caribou, the Canada lynx, and the grizzly bear.

Start: Extreme northeastern Washington and northwestern Idaho; 90 miles north-by-northeast of Spokane, Washington
Type of hike: Loop
Distance: 16.1 miles
Approximate hiking time: 3-4 days
Difficulty: Moderately strenuous
Best season: Mid-July-late September
Trail surface: Dirt and rocks
Land status: Salmo-Priest Wilderness Area; Colville National Forest (in Washington State); Idaho Panhandle National Forests
Canine compatibility: On leash. Not allowed in wilderness.
Fees and permits: None

Maps: USGS Continental Mountain and Salmo Mountain. The forest service's Salmo-Priest Wilderness map is the most accurate.
Trail contact: Sullivan Lake Ranger District; (509) 446-7500
Special considerations: Early-season hikers face a difficult ford of the South Salmo River. Late-season hikers face difficulty finding water beyond the headwaters of the South Salmo River. Watch for black bears and a possible grizzly during berry season (August).
Parking and trailhead facilities: The trailhead has room for about ten vehicles. The two ends of the trail loop leave from the trailhead about 50 yards from each other. The pleasant trailhead has an outhouse, a small spring, a loading ramp, and partial shade.

Finding the trailhead: Drive north on WA 31 to Metaline Falls, Washington. Then take WA 6 toward the Canadian border, but after just 1.5 miles turn right onto Pend Oreille CR 9345. This road is paved to scenic Sullivan Lake, but just before Sullivan Lake, 5.5 miles from WA 6, turn left onto FR 22. This road is paved for about 0.5 mile, then becomes a good gravel road up Sullivan Creek. The trailhead is now about 18 miles away. Continue on FR 22 until you reach FR 2220. (FR 22 turns right here and climbs out of the canyon at this plainly evident junction. It leads to the upper Priest River area and also to Granite Creek.) Continue on FR 2220 to the end of the gentle part of Sullivan Creek. The road makes a sweeping turn of about 90 degrees, just beyond Gypsy Meadows, and climbs steeply up Deemer Creek to Salmo Pass. Turn right at the pass and continue a short distance to the trailhead. While the road is steep in places, it is good gravel all the way. GPS: N48 57.33' / W117 4.85'

The Hike

Going clockwise, take well-marked Trail 506 down toward the South Salmo River. You drop immediately and follow well-constructed switchbacks down through an increasingly beautiful old-growth forest to the river. There are plenty of springs and small creeks. You wind down among huge Douglas fir, white pine, and western red cedar. Some are more than 1,000 years old. The understory consists of many kinds of

Photo by Ralph Maughan

berries, devil's claw, ferns, carpets of moss, and many more species. The high-elevation beginning of this trail may cross deep snow under the trees into early to mid-July.

The drop to the river is 3.5 miles and a descent of almost 2,000 feet. The stream is clear, beautiful, and fairly large. There once was a bridge, but it washed out, and there are no immediate plans to build a new one. Fords in July can be difficult, although you may find a fallen giant nearby that can serve as a bridge. Be mindful that these big logs are treacherous in wet weather or when kept wet by spray from the river.

Across the river, the trail heads upstream. After 1.2 miles you cross Crutch Creek, and the trail begins to climb above the river. Late in the season or during a dry season, Crutch Creek is the only reliable water source until you reach the very head of the river.

Cross into Idaho and leave the Salmo–Priest Wilderness 0.8 mile past Crutch Creek. Maybe someday Idaho will have an environmentally friendly congressional delegation that will add the upper Priest River drainage of this roadless area to the Salmo–Priest Wilderness so that it actually includes the Priest.

The climb up the river gradually steepens as you reach its headwaters under 7,572-foot Snowy Top Mountain. Finally the trail switchbacks to a beautiful saddle—Snowy Top Pass—between Snowy Top just to the north and Little Snowy Top to the south. Lots of folks climb Snowy Top. On top you get a view of the Selkirk Mountains in Idaho, Washington, and British Columbia, the latter just 0.25 mile to the north. You can see the international border clearing. It will take you two or three extra hours to climb the peak and then return to the trail.

At the pass, the trail (now numbered 512) turns south. You are on the Salmo–Priest River Divide, also called the Shedroof Divide, as you move farther south. Views are into the old-growth forest of the upper Priest River and the Selkirk Crest to the east. Distant clear-cuts are almost always visible where there's a view, bringing the realization that this country was saved in just the nick of time. The Idaho portion remains not permanently protected.

Once over the Snowy Top Pass saddle, the trail traverses a steep slope under Little Snowy Top Mountain. Just 0.4 mile past Little Snowy Top, Trail 349 exits to the left, taking a tremendous plunge of 70 switchbacks, 4.5 miles, and 3,400 feet to the upper Priest River. I did not check out this trail, although I did meet the founder of the Pacific Northwest Trail, of which this trail is a part, who said it is well constructed.

The Salmo–Priest loop trail continues its scenic course just on the Priest River side of the divide until it drops to a saddle at the head of Hughes Creek. If there are snowdrifts, you will probably find some water to drink along the divide, and occasionally there are seeps and small springs for a while after snowmelt.

As you descend the 600 feet to Hughes Creek Saddle, you get some good views of Shedroof Mountain and understand why it has that name. Hughes Creek was partially logged—that is obvious—but the forest service has since followed a much more environmentally friendly management course for the lengthy drainage.

The trail climbs from the saddle until it crosses under steep, unnamed Peak 6,682. During this section you cross back into Washington and into the designated wilderness. Here, under the steepest mountain slope, you are likely to find a spring or two that runs most of the year. If snow patches remain, this stretch may be somewhat difficult due to steepness.

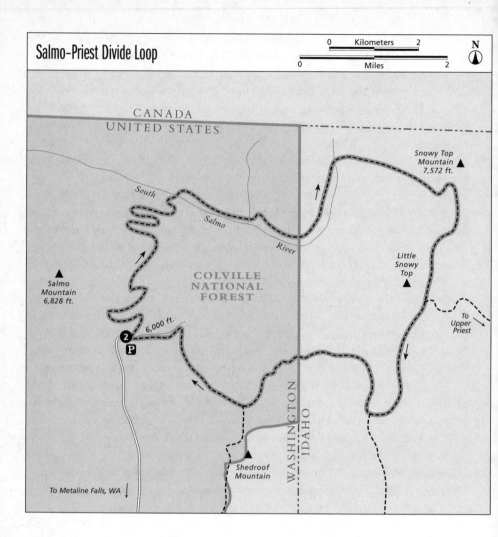

0   Kilometers   2

0   Miles   2

N

CANADA
UNITED STATES

Snowy Top
Mountain
7,572 ft.

South

Salmo

River

Salmo
Mountain
6,828 ft.

COLVILLE
NATIONAL
FOREST

Little
Snowy
Top

To
Upper
Priest

6,000 ft.

2

P

WASHINGTON
IDAHO

Shedroof
Mountain

To Metaline Falls, WA

About 2.5 miles from the saddle is the top of the Shedroof Divide and a trail junction. Take Trail 535 back to the trailhead. Trail numbers are no longer marked in the wilderness area, but the direction sign is clear. The trail climbs about 200 feet and reaches some of the highest elevations of the trip. The first part of the last leg is just outside the wilderness area. There are good views of the head of Sullivan Creek and the mountains beyond to the south, and there is a clear-cut right at the base of Shedroof Mountain. It has filled in well, but the origin of the young trees is obvious. Perhaps in twenty years it will look like a regenerated burn. The trail passes through some pleasant meadows just below the ridgetop, then goes into an unremarkable forest and crosses the ridge back into the wilderness area. Once you are into the wilderness area, you drop 120 feet in 0.3 mile and again leave the wilderness, soon coming to a closed road that is reverting to the wild. There are good views from this road of the scenic peaks forming the north side of the South Salmo River canyon. The tops of these mountains, since the international boundary runs horizontally across them, are in Canada.

After 0.5 mile, you reach the last part of the hike, an old road that has been mechanically obliterated by the forest service to prevent motor vehicle use and has been replaced by a good trail stabilized by boulders on both sides. It is another 0.3 mile to the trailhead.

Options: Trail 512 continues southward down the Shedroof Divide past Shedroof Mountain. This is a pleasant down-and-back, although water is scarce after the snowmelt.

—Ralph Maughan

Miles and Directions

0.0   Start at the trailhead (5,910 feet).

3.5   Reach the South Salmo River (4,040 feet).

4.7   Cross Crutch Creek (4,310 feet).

9.7   Reach Snowy Top Pass (6,410 feet).

12.3   Reach the Hughes Creek Saddle (5,590 feet).

13.5   Pass possible springs (6,200 feet).

13.8   Reach the trail junction on Shedroof Divide (6,300 feet).

14.8   Pass the high point on return leg of loop (6,400 feet).

15.2   The trail leaves the wilderness area (6,120 feet).

15.3   Reach the closed old road (6,080 feet).

16.1   Arrive back at the trailhead (5,910 feet).

3 Two Mouths Lakes

These two beautiful lakes are set in granite, right on top of the Selkirk Crest.

Start: 15 miles west of Bonners Ferry
Type of hike: Out-and-back
Distance: 8 miles
Approximate hiking time: 2 days
Difficulty: Moderate
Best season: July–September
Trail surface: Dirt and rocks
Land status: Idaho Panhandle National Forests
Canine compatibility: On leash
Fees and permits: None

Maps: USGS Roman Nose and The Wigwams ID; Idaho Panhandle National Forests–Kaniksu National Forest map
Trail contact: Bonners Ferry Ranger District; (208) 267-5561; www.fs.usda.gov/ipnf
Special considerations: Huckleberries line the trail. They ripen in August, so watch for bears.
Parking and trailhead facilities: The undeveloped trailhead has room for about eight vehicles by the roadside. There is no shade, but there is a good view of a hulking granite dome just to the south.

Finding the trailhead: Begin from downtown Bonners Ferry, which is just off US 95. Drive toward the Kootenai River to Riverside Street. Follow Riverside Street west, out of town, to the Kootenai Wildlife Refuge. Pass the refuge headquarters, which sits near the mouth of Myrtle Creek, at about 5 miles. Continue past the headquarters 1.5 miles on the paved road until you reach the gravel road up Myrtle Creek. The Myrtle Creek road, FR 663, is at an oblique angle to the paved road, and the sign is hard to see.

Drive up and into big and deep Myrtle Creek Canyon on FR 663. Watch for logging trucks. The road is narrow in places, and the drop into Myrtle Creek is a long way down. Stay on this main road as it approaches the head of the canyon. After about 10.5 miles, you pass the side road to Myrtle Lake; the main road is renumbered FR 633A. From here it is 2 miles to the Two Mouths Trailhead. GPS: N48 43.21' / W116 37.51'

The Hike

The trail is well marked, and you are likely to find a cluster of vehicles at the trailhead, underscoring that you are at the right place.

The trail (Trail 268) is a rapidly overgrowing logging road for about the first 1.5 miles. You begin hiking gradually uphill to the north, but you soon enter Peak Creek. The trail makes a right angle and starts up Peak Creek. Soon the trail splits, and a decaying, closed logging road goes to the right and crosses Peak Creek. Stay on the trail to the left.

The trail contours back and forth up the mountainside until it drops into the next drainage to the south, Slide Creek. Just before dropping into Slide Creek, the old road ends. The trail climbs slowly in this increasingly damp canyon. Soon Slide Creek is

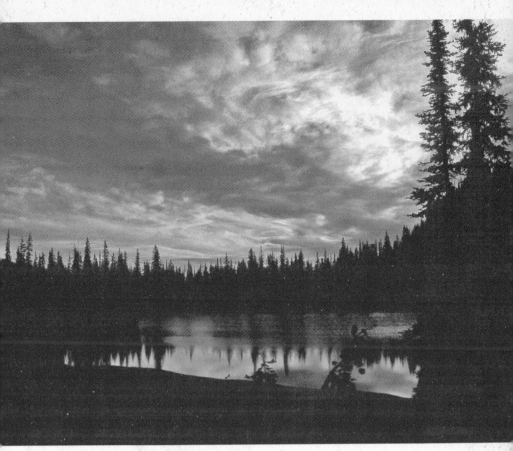

Two Mouth Lakes at dawn. PHOTO BY RALPH MAUGHAN

not far below the trail. The forest is damp, and there are some very big conifers, even including a few giant white pines.

The damp upper part of Slide Creek is very well maintained. Perhaps 0.5 mile of corduroy plank has been built to protect the vast areas of seeps the trail crosses.

There is a large granite dome to the south. Its top is Point 6,168. The Wigwams topo map shows the trail crossing Slide Creek and passing across the steepest part of the dome. Were this so, it would be one of the most amazing trails in the world. Of course, the map is wrong. The trail climbs to near the very top of Slide Creek and then makes a half circle to climb steeply up the much gentler back side of the dome to a pass above Two Mouths Lakes. If you have difficulty on this trail, it will be in early season.

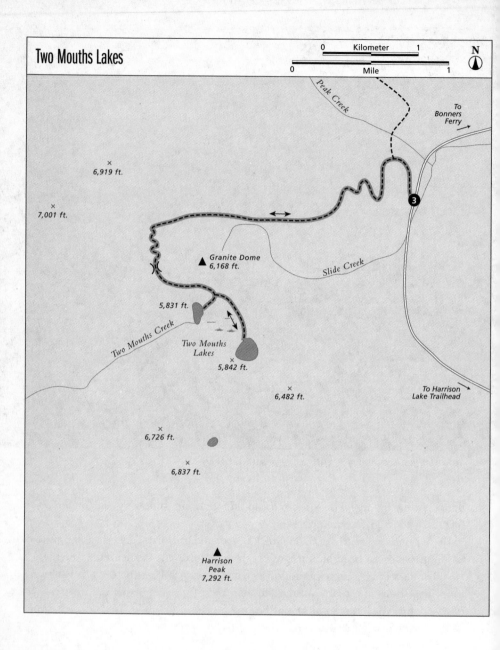

Two Mouths Lakes

0 Kilometer 1
0 Mile 1

N

× 6,919 ft.

× 7,001 ft.

Peak Creek

To Bonners Ferry

3

▲ Granite Dome 6,168 ft.

Slide Creek

5,831 ft.

Two Mouths Creek

Two Mouths Lakes

× 5,842 ft.

To Harrison Lake Trailhead

× 6,482 ft.

× 6,726 ft.

× 6,837 ft.

▲ Harrison Peak 7,292 ft.

It is a north-facing slope in a very wet and snowy mountain range. Before July, take an ice ax.

At the pass, which is the Selkirk Crest, you have a fine view north and northwest to the unnamed glaciated peaks around the head of Slide Creek. The highest is Peak 7,001.

From the pass the trail drops down toward Two Mouths Lakes. It soon splits, with the left fork leading to the east lake and the right fork to the west lake. The lakes are about 0.3 mile apart. The east lake is 5 feet higher in elevation than the west. Springs emerge below the granite wall that encases the east lake, and a gentle spring-fed creek meanders lazily through meadow, bog, and granite outcrops to the west lake. The area is relentlessly granite slickrock except for the meadows. It seems as if every peak were chiseled by a giant sculptor.

Options: The trail ends at the lakes. The options are to climb around on peaks and take photos, unless you are fishing. I found the granite slabs fascinating (at least for one day).

—Ralph Maughan

Miles and Directions

0.0 Start at the trailhead (4,440 feet).

0.5 An old logging road leaves to the right and crosses Peak Creek; keep left (4,600 feet).

1.5 The trail crosses into Slide Creek drainage (5,350 feet).

2.5 Reach upper, boggy Slide Creek (5,600 feet).

3.2 Reach the pass on the crest (6,160 feet).

4.0 Reach the lakes (about 5,840 feet).

8.0 Arrive back at the trailhead.

Salmon River and Clearwater Mountains

I f you can imagine a continuous mass of mountain ridges and canyons 300 miles long and more than 100 miles wide, you can picture the Salmon River and the Clearwater Mountains. This mass makes up most of central and north-central Idaho and the bulk of what is considered the Northern Rocky Mountains in Idaho.

Here, three great wilderness areas have been designated: the Frank Church–River of No Return, the Selway–Bitterroot, and the Gospel–Hump. More wilderness still should be designated.

This rugged stretch of ridges has largely precluded human habitation and development and has cut northern Idaho off from southern Idaho, both economically and socially. Historically, mining and, later, timbering, mostly fueled by taxpayer subsidies, have led to some human habitation in the Salmon River–Clearwater Mountains.

The mountain front that rises immediately north of Boise to where the main stem of the Salmon River cuts directly through the central Idaho mountains from east to west is generally called the Salmon River Mountains. The western boundary is the North Fork of the Payette River; the eastern boundary is the Salmon River as it courses between Challis and Salmon City.

North of the Salmon River Canyon across central Idaho, these mountains are called the Clearwater Mountains, although there is no clear geological distinction. This huge mountain fastness is primarily made of granitelike igneous rocks formed out of one of the largest batholiths in the world—the Idaho Batholith. A batholith is an enormous intrusion of molten rock that pushes toward the earth's surface but cools and crystallizes before it reaches the surface as lava. It is then gradually exposed by uplifting, weather, and water.

Geologists subdivide the Idaho Batholith into a southern and a northern section. The southern is the Atlanta Batholith; the northern, the Bitterroot Batholith. Most people think batholithic rock is all granite. In fact, only some of it is. Whether an igneous crystalline rock is granite depends on its percentage composition of various minerals. Many of these rocks lack the composition of granite. We use the term *granitelike* for these abundant crystalline rocks, such as quartz monzonite and granodiorite.

Finally, much of the eastern part of the Salmon River Mountains consists of huge

Mountains of the wild Salmo-Priest area. PHOTO BY LUKE KRATZ

piles of volcanic rock from ancient tremendous eruptions. These rocks, the Challis Volcanics, are often very colorful. They consist of rhyolite and andesite, but no basalt. These eruptions buried part of the Atlanta lobe of the Idaho Batholith and injected thousands of dikes into the batholith. We find that the color and variety of rock forms in east-central Idaho make some of the most picturesque mountains of the state.

Portions of the Salmon River and Clearwater Mountain masses are broken into subranges and have earned their own names due to their distinctive elevation, scenery, or historic factors. We use some of these distinctions and organize many Salmon River Mountain hikes by subrange. Examples of these subranges include the Boise Mountains, Trinity Mountains, the Lick Creek Mountains, the Gospels, the Bighorn Crags, and the Selway Crags.

The lower elevations of the Salmon River and Clearwater Mountains are accessible as early as April, since the canyon bottoms are as low as 1,500 feet. The peaks reach to 10,000 feet. Strangely, the highest portions of these mountains surround the deep canyons of the Middle, South Fork, and main Salmon River. This is due to isostasy, wherein the removal by erosion of the mountain mass that once filled these enormous, 5,000-foot-deep canyons actually caused the adjacent land to rise.

The number of hiking and backpacking trails in this 30,000-square-mile region is immense. This book includes only a portion of these trails.

While the geology of the Salmon River and Clearwater Mountains is very similar, the climate is not. It becomes increasingly damp as you move from the Boise Front to the heart of the Frank Church–River of No Return Wilderness, and wetter still as you climb north into the Clearwater River drainage. These mountains are, as a result, not one big mass of very similar scenery.

All of the major wildlife species of the Northern Rockies inhabit these mountains, except the grizzly bear. This includes rare mammals such as lynx and wolverine. Plans are afoot to restore the grizzly to its rightful place in central Idaho, but there is much resistance. The newly restored wolf population is doing well here and spreading in all directions. Hopefully, the salmon and steelhead runs that have become little more than museum tokens will be restored to resemble the time when central Idaho streams ran red with spawning salmon.

—Ralph Maughan

Selway-Bitterroot Wilderness

The northern third of the great wild country of central Idaho is largely contained within the 1.4-million-acre Selway–Bitterroot Wilderness.

Geologically similar to much of the River of No Return Wilderness country to the south, the Selway–Bitterroot sits atop the huge granitic bulge of the Idaho Batholith. This northern portion is often referred to as the Bitterroot Batholith. Its rocky bones jut to the surface in the form of the Selway Crags in the wilderness's northwest corner and the towering Bitterroot Range to the east, on the Idaho–Montana border, as well as all of the lesser ridges.

Essentially all of the Selway–Bitterroot is steep country of ridges and canyons. The canyons center on the Selway River (a unit of the National Wild and Scenic Rivers System) and its many tributaries, such as Moose Creek. Much of the wilderness is

Selway River. PHOTO BY JOHN KRATZ

heavily forested, and most of the area is natural fire country. It was partly burned by the great fires of 1910 and 2000.

Efforts by the timber industry and the forest service to dismember the old Selway–Bitterroot Primitive Area when it was administratively reclassified as a wilderness area in the early 1960s gave impetus to the efforts of conservationists nationwide to establish the National Wilderness Preservation System. These efforts were successful in 1964 when Congress passed the Wilderness Act, providing for permanent protection of designated wildernesses by US statute instead of by bureaucratic discretion.

The success of the Wilderness Act and of the classification of the Frank Church–River of No Return Wilderness in 1980, which restored wilderness protection to much of the area ripped out of the Selway–Bitterroot Primitive Area by the forest service in 1963, means that the Selway River today runs clear and clean. The sandy soils derived from the granitic batholith, which run like sugar when logging and road building strip them of their protective cover of vegetation, are secure in this wilderness area. Chief among the areas restored is the north side of Magruder Corridor, on the Selway–Bitterroot's south side.

The same protection was not obtained for the Lochsa Face on the north side of the wilderness. The Lochsa River, another famed stream in the National Wild and Scenic Rivers System, is today threatened by logging on surrounding steep slopes, much of it carried out by means of subsidies that make it artificially attractive to cut timber but end up costing more than the trees are worth—a process that some people call "welfare logging."

It will be interesting to watch the regeneration of those portions of the wilderness burned by the wildfires of 2000. Because fire is natural and normal in the area, full regeneration should be expected, but noxious weeds have invaded the lower canyons over the last twenty years, especially spotted knapweed, the tall, many-headed pink flower that blooms in August. This weed from across the oceans could forestall recovery of this great wilderness as it chokes out everything else. The specter of global warming portends that future fires may not be natural.

—Ralph Maughan

4 Lower Selway River

This is a beautiful wilderness river in a deep forested canyon. There is early- and late-season access as well as routes to many loop backpacking trips.

Start: 132 road miles east of Lewiston in the Selway-Bitterroot Wilderness
Type of hike: Out-and-back featured route with loop options.
Distance: 12 miles round-trip, although many loops of great distance can be started from this trail. Plan an adventure that suits your taste.
Approximate hiking time: 2 or more days
Difficulty: Moderately easy. Most of the options are strenuous.
Best season: July–September
Trail surface: Rocks and dirt
Land status: Selway-Bitterroot Wilderness; Nez Perce National Forest

Canine compatibility: On leash; not allowed in wilderness
Fees and permits: None
Maps: USGS Fog Mountain and Selway Falls ID; Selway-Bitterroot Wilderness map; Nez Perce National Forest map
Trail contact: Moose Creek Ranger District; (208) 926-4258; www.fs.usda.gov/nezperceclearwater
Parking and trailhead facilities: Parking for twenty to thirty vehicles. Three developed sites, pit toilets, but no running water. (For information about other Selway River campgrounds, see Hike 12, Meadow Creek.)

Finding the trailhead: From Lewiston, drive east on US 12 for 114 miles, up the Clearwater River to Lowell, Idaho. Here, the Lochsa and Selway Rivers meld their waters to form the Middle Fork of the Clearwater River. All three rivers are units in the National Wild and Scenic Rivers System.

From Lowell, cross the river and continue right (east) onto Selway River Road (FR 223). It is about 18 miles to the trailhead. This road is paved for 7 miles to O'Hara Creek and then turns to gravel. It is usually passable throughout the hiking season, except occasionally during the peak of spring snowmelt (late May to mid-June), when the river may flood its banks and the road in places. Stay on the main road, always with the river on your right. You'll pass scenic Selway Falls and continue along the river for a mile or so to the road's end at Race Creek Campground. GPS: N46 2.65' / W115 17.01'

The Hike

Due to its low elevation, this is one of the earliest accessible trails in northern Idaho. It begins at 1,780 feet elevation, at the upstream end of the lower parking area, where you will see the trail register. The trail (Trail 4) heads upstream (east) along the north side of the Selway. It sparkles with mica on sunny days as it winds along the river through a canyon cutting through decomposing Idaho Batholith granite. The first, level 1.5 miles is outside the wilderness area, but the forest service has banned trail bikes in this area so it is wilderness in fact, even if not by law.

You'll see the sign marking the wilderness boundary shortly after you cross Packer Creek at about mile 1.5. This and other creeks flow steeply down from Fog Mountain (6,538 feet) to the Selway (1,785 feet). They roar with icy clear snowmelt during May and June, but they can be easily crossed on appropriately placed logs. Although the Selway also runs bank-full in spring, it nevertheless runs clear because it drains more than a million acres of pristine Selway–Bitterroot Wilderness. Alas, the fishing doesn't get really good until the water begins to recede (in some years, late July). All along the trail are nice rest stops under big cedars or on the numerous sand beaches. This trail is perfect for leisurely weekend family hikes, but watch small children closely since the trail traverses ledges and cliffs that drop abruptly to the river.

About 2.5 miles in, you cross Teepee Creek; 0.5 mile farther you meet Otter Butte–Highline Lakes Trail. Continue on the main river trail through mixed ponderosa pine, western red cedar, and Douglas fir to reach Renshaw Creek at 3.5 miles. The forest here is young and vigorous, especially on the north-facing slopes across the river. Young conifers have replaced a forest scorched by the tremendous fire of 1910, which swept over three million acres of northern Idaho in a matter of days. Numerous picturesque snags still stand as reminders of the great fire.

There are several nice, heavily used campsites at Renshaw Creek, and this is where you will lose most day hikers. From here the trail climbs about 100 feet in a mile and then stays high for a while. There are great views up and down the canyon, with occasional upstream glimpses of snowcapped mountain ridges. At about 6 miles, you'll reach Cupboard Creek, a beach, and roaring rapids with a big drop. Cupboard Creek is a good goal for hikers out for a weekend trip.

The Selway River itself is a very important stream for fish. Chinook salmon and steelhead trout spawn in the river and its tributaries. It also has abundant rainbow, brook, cutthroat, and bull trout (the latter is on the threatened species list, as is this run of salmon). Wildlife in the area include deer, elk, moose, black bear, beaver, river otter, and an occasional wolf.

Options: Otter Butte–Highline Lakes Trail: If you wish to take this trail, you must make a difficult (impossible in spring) ford of the river. Once across, climb a steep 3.3 miles and 4,300 feet from the river level to Otter Butte (6,088 feet). Then the trail climbs Highline Ridge to the crest of Mink Mountain (7,260 feet) and drops down into the cirque basin of the two Highline Lakes. It is a strenuous hike but rewarding for those interested in panoramic views and mountain lakes less crowded than those of the Selway Crags farther north. The Highline Lakes can also be reached, without such an extreme climb, from a trailhead at Indian Hill (6,810 feet).

Big Fog Saddle Trail: From Cupboard Creek, an unsigned side

Lower Selway River

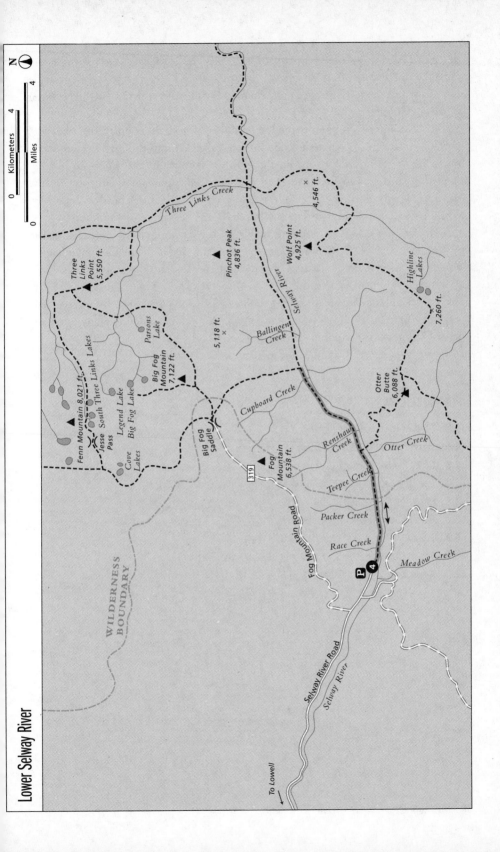

trail (Trail 710, not on the topographic quadrangle) takes off from the river trail and climbs about 4,100 feet from river level (approximately 1,800 feet) to Big Fog Saddle (5,900 feet) and the terminus of Fog Mountain Road, from which many hikers enter the Selway Crags.

For hikers interested in an extended trip into the Selway country, the river trail continues upstream, and there are side trails to take you into the high country. Your choices are limited only by your imagination (or stamina, if you choose to hike up out of the canyon). On the river trail, you can walk upstream all the way to the Magruder Road's crossing of the Selway, and then into the river's headwaters, which are inside the 2.4-million-acre Frank Church–River of No Return Wilderness.

A challenging one-way loop trip involving the Lower Selway trail starts at Big Fog Saddle (see Hike 5, Selway Crags via Big Fog and Legend Lakes) and loops through the Selway Crags via the Cove Lakes, Jesse Pass, and the South Three Links Lakes. It then drops down to the Selway River via Three Links Creek Trail. From here it is 15 miles downstream to the trailhead at Race Creek. The total distance is more than 30 miles, with lots of ups and downs. A week is needed to really enjoy the country. Logistics will require two vehicles, one to get you to Big Fog Saddle and one waiting at Race Creek Campground when you finish the hike.

—Don L. Crawford

Miles and Directions

0.0 Start at the Race Creek trailhead (1,780 feet).

1.5 Reach the wilderness boundary (1,800 feet).

2.5 Cross Teepee Creek (1,800 feet).

3.0 Pass the Otter Butte-Highline Lakes Trail (requires ford; 1,800 feet).

3.5 Pass Renshaw Creek (1,800 feet).

5.0 Pass Maiden Creek (1,830 feet).

5.5 Reach the top of a short climb (1,934 feet).

6.0 Reach Cupboard Creek (1,830 feet). Retrace your steps.

12.0 Arrive back at the trailhead.

5 Selway Crags via Big Fog and Legend Lakes

The Crags entrance up Big Fog Mountain provides access to ridgeline hiking in the Selway–Bitterroot Wilderness to lightly used alpine lakes. Much of the trail traverses old burns with picturesque snags and panoramic views.

Start: 146 road miles east of Lewiston
Type of hike: Out and back with options for loops
Distance: 8.6 miles
Approximate hiking time: 2–3 days
Difficulty: Strenuous due to elevation gain and loss and cross-country navigation
Best season: July–mid-October
Trail surface: Dirt and rocks
Land status: Selway–Bitterroot Wilderness; Nez Perce National Forest
Maps: USGS Fog Mountain and Fenn Mountain ID; Selway–Bitterroot Wilderness map; Nez Perce National Forest map

Canine compatibility: Not allowed
Fees and permits: None
Trail contact: Moose Creek Ranger District; (208) 926-4258
Special considerations: Snow keeps Fog Mountain Road closed before July and after October. Access to Legend and Big Fog Lakes is cross-country and requires navigational skills.
Parking and trailhead facilities: At Big Fog Saddle you'll find ample parking but few good campsites. This undeveloped site is heavily used despite the difficult access.

Finding the trailhead: From Lewiston drive east on US 12 for 114 miles to Lowell. From Lowell, continue right (east) onto Selway River Road (FR 223). Follow Selway River Road upstream for about 17 miles. Just short of Selway Falls and directly after the Gedney Creek crossing, you will come to Fog Mountain Road (FR 319), which meets Selway River Road from the left (north). Take Fog Mountain Road. If you miss this turn, you'll come to the end of the river road after another mile, at Race Creek Campground.

Fog Mountain Road ends at Big Fog Saddle after a drive of about 14 miles with a steep climb of 4,100 feet! A sign at the bottom warns that it's steep, narrow, and winding. Indeed, Fog Mountain Road is extremely steep and loaded with rocks that can kiss an oil pan or burn out an automatic transmission. GPS: N46 6.83' / W115 12.24'

The Hike

The Selway Crags are large in area, containing numerous alpine lakes hidden within deep cirques and surrounded by jagged peaks. The hiker who takes the trail described here avoids the crowds, which tend to congregate at just a few of the lakes, and finds real solitude among the crags. Big Fog Lake and Legend Lake lie in a beautiful basin to the south of the main peaks. They are reached by a strenuous hike across the top of Big Fog Mountain (7,122 feet). From this trail, the panorama of the Selway–Bitterroot Wilderness unfolds to the north, south, and east as far as the eye can see.

Three trailheads are located at Big Fog Saddle. The far left trail drops down to the northwest to cross Canteen Creek. It then climbs 6 miles to the Cove Lakes. This is one of the most popular trails in the entire wilderness. The far right trail heads east and contours the south side of Big Fog Mountain, passes Parsons Lake, and then joins the Three Links Lakes. These lakes lie directly below Fenn Mountain (8,021 feet) in the heart of the crags.

The center trail (Trail 343) heads northeast up and over Big Fog Mountain, and then follows a high ridge north into the south side of the crags. This is the trail to take. Reconnoiter the trailhead choices carefully before starting out. The first time I hiked in the crags, I headed for the Cove Lakes (like almost everyone else), took the wrong trail by mistake, and ended up at Legend Lake (with no regrets).

Fog Mountain Trail is the only one that starts out with a stiff climb. It initially switchbacks from the 5,920-foot level to 6,880 feet in a distance of 1 mile. Most of this area was once burned, and there are many snags. Once atop the ridge, you'll have an easier time as the trail climbs more gently to a high point at 6,920 feet. This is a good spot to rest and have lunch as you look northward across the glacier-carved canyon of Canteen Creek to its sheer white-and-gray rock headwall rising abruptly more than 1,500 feet to peaks as high as 7,623 feet.

The trail continues northeast along the ridgeline and skirts the south side of Big Fog Mountain (7,122 feet). This is wide-open country, where cross-country travel is easy and trails tend to disappear. From Big Fog Mountain, you're mostly on your own. Don't continue eastward on the main trail, for it will drop down in a distance of 2 miles to a point (6,312 feet) above Parsons Lake. Instead, now 1.5 miles into the journey, turn to your left at Big Fog Mountain and onto Trail 363 to follow the sharp ridgeline north. The trail is generally good, but from this point on you may find yourself on animal trails that abruptly fade away to nothing. These "goat" trails are numerous and easy to take by mistake. You cannot go wrong, however, since the ridge drops off sharply on both the east and west. The ridgelines are beautiful in early September when the abundant buckwheat turns a golden brown.

This narrow ridgeline separates the Canteen Creek drainage (west) from that of Three Links Creek (east). Big Fog Lake and Legend Lake lie in cirques that form the headwaters of the West Fork of Three Links Creek. You'll drop from the 7,000-foot level to a windy saddle (6,795 feet) about 0.8 mile north of Big Fog Mountain. From here you look directly down on a small, unnamed lake to your right (east). Continue to contour northward along the 6,800-foot line (refer to your topo), and after passing through a rocky, marshy area with crags above you to the left, you'll see Big Fog Lake well below you to the east. The entire lake is visible from above. It is frequented by moose. Indeed, I have had the luck of seeing moose every time I've hiked in the crags.

Access to Big Fog Lake is easiest by continuing on to Legend Lake, and then approaching Big Fog from the north. Still on the trail, continue north. The Selway Crags are visible to the northeast, especially the sharp ridge separating the cirque of Legend Lake on the south from that of the South Three Links Lakes on the north. As

Selway Crags via Big Fog and Legend Lakes

East Peak
7,852 ft.

Chimney
Peak
7,650 ft.

THE CRAGS

THE CRAGS

To Louse
Lake

Florence
Lake

Rainbow
Lake

Fenn Mountain 8,021 ft.

5,550 ft.

Three Links Creek

SELWAY–
BITTERROOT
WILDERNESS
BOUNDARY

South Three Links Lakes

Jesse
Pass

Legend Lake

Big Fog
Lake

West Fork

× 7,596 ft.

Parsons Lake

Big Fog
Mountain
7,122 ft.

Big Fog
Saddle

5
P

5,118 ft.
×

4,836 ft.
×

FR319

Fog
Mountain
6,538 ft.

Fog Mountain Road

To Selway
River

Selway River

you continue northward and approach this massive wall of sheer rock and talus, there is but faint sign of any trail. At mile 3.5 you'll reach Point 7,315 and the end of the trail shown on maps. Drop down from the east side of Point 7,315 for 500 feet and 0.3 mile cross-country to reach the deep, blue waters of Legend Lake (6,800 feet). There is a small, but nice, campsite at the west end of the lake.

No trail leads from Legend Lake to Big Fog Lake, so start downhill from the east side of Legend, then turn south to skirt above the cliffs, and then aim for Point 6,464 (shown on the topo) to drop easily down to the north side of Big Fog. No campsites are evident, but there is a flat spot above the lake on the northeast side (near Point 6,464). This is a fragile site; make it a fireless camp if you choose to stay the night. Photographers will like this spot, especially in the early-morning hours on clear days.

Options: There is no simple loop through the crags via Big Fog and Legend Lakes that does not require some backtracking. From Big Fog Mountain, you can continue east and connect with South Three Links Lakes Trail via forest service Trail 693. From the upper of these three lakes (6,780 feet), you can climb by trail over Jesse Pass (7,200 feet), and then drop down to the Cove Lakes (6,320 feet). Cove Lakes Trail then provides a route back to Big Fog Saddle. This is a strenuous loop with many ups and downs. But in reality, there are no hikes in the rugged Selway Crags that can be considered easy. All, however, can be considered infinitely worthwhile.

—Don L. Crawford

Miles and Directions

0.0 Start at the Big Fog Saddle trailhead (5,920 feet).

1.0 Reach the Big Fog Mountain ridge (6,880 feet).

1.5 Take Trail 363 at the junction below Big Fog Mountain (7,000 feet),

2.3 Reach a saddle (6,795 feet).

3.5 Reach Point 7,315.

3.8 Arrive at Legend Lake (6,800 feet).

4.3 Reach Big Fog Lake (6,464 feet).

8.6 Arrive back at the trailhead.

6 Seven Lakes Loop

The Seven Lakes Loop is an extensive adventure to several lush and rocky lake basins in the rarely visited northern portion of the Selway Crags, with a stopover at Stanley Hot Springs on the way.

Start: Trailhead parking area at Wilderness Gateway, milepost 122 on US 12; 120 miles east of Lewiston, Idaho, and 100 miles west of Missoula, Montana
Type of hike: Lollipop loop
Distance: 22.9 miles
Approximate hiking time: 3–4 days
Difficulty: Strenuous due to length
Best season: July–October; after high-water season due to ford crossing at Boulder Creek
Trail surface: Dirt and rock
Land status: Selway-Bitterroot Wilderness; Clearwater National Forest
Canine compatibility: Not allowed

Fees and permits: None
Maps: USGS Huckleberry Butte and Greenside Butte ID
Trail contact: Lochsa Ranger District; (208) 926-4275; www.fs.usda.gov/nezperceclearwater
Special considerations: Due to the ford crossing of Boulder Creek at mile 4.5, this hike is not possible during high water (May and June). However, you can take Lochsa Peak Trail (Trail 220), which leaves from the southern end of the same wilderness gateway. This alternative route is a 23-mile out-and-back hike and does not pass Stanley Hot Springs.

Finding the trailhead: From Lewiston, travel up the Clearwater River on US 12 drive approximately 120 miles until you reach the Wilderness Gateway Campground at milepost 122. From Missoula, Montana, take US 12 100 miles to cross the bridge over Boulder Creek, and access the Boulder Creek Trail (Trail 211) on the east side of the stream. GPS: N45 20.16' / W115 18.76'

The Hike

The Selway Crags are a small group of rugged mountains between the Lochsa River to the north and the Selway River to the south, in the western portion of the Selway–Bitterroot Wilderness. Most backpackers visit the more popular lakes in the central Selway Crags area farther south; the trails there are accessed from steep and rough roads leaving the Selway River. This hike is a strenuous yet rewarding alternative if you'd like to experience the crags' ruggedness and isolation but don't want to drive for hours on unmaintained four-by-four forest roads to get to the trailhead. This hike's trailhead is easily reached from US 12.

The abrupt elevation gains in the Selway Crags create varying life zones ranging from wet cedar forests to high, subalpine forests and peaks; plant and wildlife diversity here is high. The Seven Lakes area of the crags is composed of several small lake basins in subalpine forest and meadows surrounded by rocky buttes. This route provides opportunities for exploring ten or more lakes and the ridges surrounding their basins, including summiting 7,362-foot Stanley Butte. Backpackers also have a good chance to observe wildlife and catch fish in the lakes and streams. As an even greater incentive for completing the difficult route, you can reward yourself with a relaxing soak at Stanley Hot Springs on the way in and out of the Seven Lakes area.

The hike begins near the mouth of Boulder Creek at a low 2,019 feet in elevation. The Lochsa River Canyon here is dominated by moist forests of cedar, white pine, and ponderosa pine with a fern understory. The trail starts to climb immediately and skirts the hillside above the south side of the creek. After the first 0.5 mile the trail begins to pass through open forests of birch, maple, scattered conifers, and dense ferns. For the next couple of miles, the trail gives scenic vistas of the Lochsa River and Lochsa Peak behind you, along with thickly forested peaks ahead.

After 2.7 miles pass a sign marking the entrance to the Selway–Bitterroot Wilderness. At just over 4 miles, you reach an open hillside with gorgeous views and a marked junction with the Rock Lake Creek Trail (Trail 2210). You want to veer right on this trail and start heading down the hill toward the rushing sound of Boulder Creek. *Do not attempt to ford the creek during high water.* The Seven Lakes can be accessed from an alternative route (Lochsa Peak Trail, or Trail 220, from Wilderness Gateway) during dangerous spring runoff. While this is a fairly easy ford to make during low-water season, always exercise extreme caution. I prefer the help of a walking stick collected from the forest; I also take along a pair of sandals or old tennis shoes so I can keep my hiking boots dry.

After fording Boulder Creek, you reach a nice campsite that might be a good option for the first night. Half a mile up the trail you encounter the magical Stanley Hot Springs, situated in an open glade in dense cedar forest. This is the last point on the route where you might find other hikers. Most backpackers prefer to spend the first night at one of the many campsites in the vicinity and save the remaining 5 miles of climbing to the lake basins for the second day. This also gives you more time to relax in the hot springs and fish the Huckleberry and Boulder Creeks. When I arrived at about 2 p.m. in early July, the pools were just beginning to get shaded by trees. Since Stanley Hot Springs sees relatively high use, be sure to practice low-impact techniques while camping in the area.

From Stanley Hot Springs, Rock Lake Trail continues south through thick forests—it's possible to lose the trail here due to the many spur trails leading to campsites. To avoid this, veer left shortly after you leave the springs area, following the trail south and up the hillside. After 0.5 mile the trail reaches the junction with Greenside Butte Trail (Trail 222). I met three trail maintenance workers here who were clearing the trails and were very surprised and glad to see another hiker. They told me they rarely encounter hikers in the area, and horse parties only once every ten days or so.

At this junction, bear left and follow the Greenside Butte Trail for a couple of miles of steep climbing. Here the elevation changes abruptly from 4,000 to nearly 6,000 feet, and you can observe the forest transform from lower cedar forest to Douglas fir forest, and finally to lodgepole pine forest at the ridgeline of Greenside Butte.

A mile and a half past the junction, the trail crosses a tributary of Rock Lake Creek in a gorgeous meadow; this is a good spot to take a break and get water. Three

Looking north toward Greenside Butte. PHOTO BY JOHN KRATZ

miles after the junction, you reach the ridge south of Greenside Butte, and the trail now follows a gentler grade. Gorgeous views of the Surprise Creek drainage to the east and the Central Crags area to the south begin to open up. For the next mile you are treated to an easy ridge walk. There is spectacular scenery to enjoy, including a view of Rock Lake through the trees, 500 feet below you.

The trail now begins a gradual descent into the Seven Lakes basin. Four miles after the junction with Greenside Butte Trail, you reach a signed junction with Lochsa Peak Trail (Trail 220). Veer left at the junction and hike 0.5 mile east to reach campsites at the Seven Lakes. This a great place to camp on the first or second night of the trek. For a quick survey of the vicinity, climb the enormous granite boulder between the two main Seven Lakes. From here you can see the Seven Lakes on both sides of you, the ridge west of Stanley Butte to the southeast, and Surprise Creek drainage to the south.

Before traveling west to the next lake basin, I highly recommend making the 3-mile round-trip day hike to the top of Stanley Butte. Trail 220 provides access to the peak itself. Just follow this trail southeast out of camp, climbing along open ridges with patches of spruce, whitebark pine, and lodgepole pine forest. From the top of Stanley Butte, you can see a full panorama of the Selway–Bitterroot Wilderness. The Bitterroot Mountains form a crest in the eastern horizon while the giants of the central crags—Fenn Mountain, East Peak, and Chimney Peak—all loom above lake basins and canyons a few miles to the south.

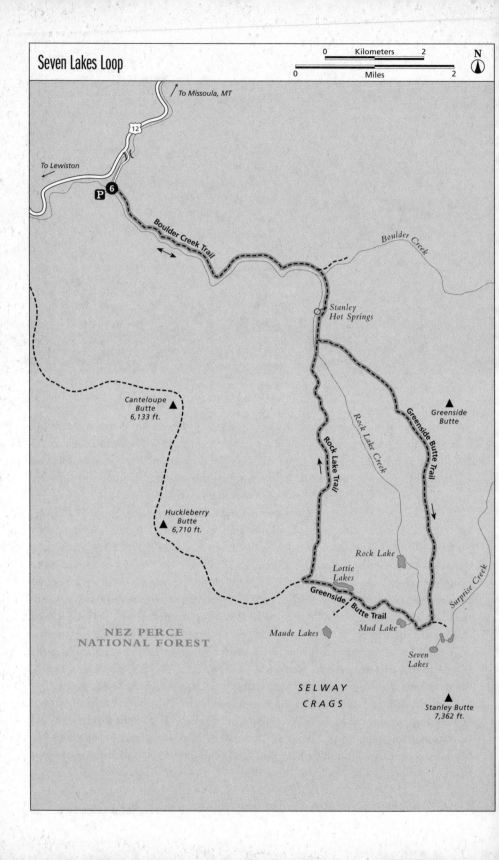

On the next day, retrace your steps 0.5 mile to the junction with Greenside Butte Trail 222. This time, continue west on Trail 220 to reach other lakes in the vicinity. You have your choice of making camp at a number of lakes along this trail. First you will reach Mud Lake, about a mile past the Seven Lakes. At 1.5 miles you reach a rocky opening in the forest with incredible views of the Lottie Lakes in the green valley below. Continue downhill another mile from this ridge to the Lottie Lakes, passing close by East Maude Lake on the way. You will find a good campsite between Upper and Lower Lottie Lake. The scenery is beautiful in this area; while somewhat less rocky than Seven Lakes, the vegetation is more lush. If you choose to explore or fish the nearby Maude Lakes, there is a trail heading south from the campsite between the Lottie Lakes.

The final portion of the route returns to Stanley Hot Springs via Rock Creek Trail (Trail 2210). Head west on Trail 220 for less than a mile to reach the junction with Rock Creek Trail. Bear right on this trail and climb for 0.5 mile or so before descending for 4 miles into Huckleberry Creek and the familiar Stanley Hot Springs. Follow the trail past the hot springs, ford Boulder Creek again, and return to the trailhead on the same Boulder Creek Trail (Trail 211) that you came in on.

Miles and Directions

0.0   Start at the trailhead parking area for the Wilderness Gateway.

0.3   Reach the inception of the trail at the Boulder Creek Trailhead.

2.7   The trail enters the Selway–Bitterroot Wilderness.

4.3   At the junction with Trail 2210, bear right.

4.5   Ford Boulder Creek.

4.6   Pass a good campsite at Boulder Creek.

5.0   Reach Stanley Hot Springs.

5.5   At the junction with Trail 222, bear left.

8.2   Reach an overlook near the top of Greenside Butte.

9.5   Meet Trail 220.

10.0   Cross a bridge over Surprise Creek.

10.5   Backtrack to the junction with Trail 220; bear left.

11.0   Reach Rock Lake Creek.

11.4   Reach an overlook with views of the Lottie Lakes below.

11.9   Pass East Maude Lake.

12.5   Reach the campsite between Upper and Lower Lottie Lakes.

13.3   At the junction with Trail 2210, bear right.

17.3   At the junction with Trail 222, continue forward on Trail 2210.

17.9   Arrive back at Stanley Hot Springs.

18.4   Ford Boulder Creek.

22.6   Reach the Wilderness Gateway.

22.9   Arrive back at the trailhead parking area.

7 White Cap Creek

If you really want to get away from it all, this is the hike for you. It is quite a long hike into deep, deep wilderness with lakes and amazing scenery.

Start: 65 miles west of Darby, Montana. White Cap Creek drains from the west slope of the Bitterroot Mountains in the Selway–Bitterroot Wilderness.
Type of hike: Out-and-back, although loops of more than a week can be done using this trail as part of the loop
Distance: 45 miles
Approximate hiking time: 6–7 days or more
Difficulty: Moderately strenuous once the snowmelt has receded
Best season: August
Trail surface: Dirt and rock
Land status: Selway–Bitterroot Wilderness; Bitterroot National Forest

Canine compatibility: Not allowed
Fees and permits: None
Maps: USGS Burnt Strip Mountain, Mt. George, Mt. Paloma, and Tin Cup Lake ID
Trail contact: Bitterroot National Forest; (406) 363-7100
Special considerations: Bring wading shoes. Rattlesnakes are present in the lower part of White Cap Creek. Black bears are common. Make sure you hang your food: You don't want a bear to eat your rations when you are 25 miles from the trailhead.
Parking and trailhead facilities: There is ample parking, a 12-unit campground, loading ramps, and a latrine.

Finding the trailhead: To reach the trailhead you must access the Magruder Corridor Road, which meanders more than 100 miles from Conner, Montana, on the east to Red River Ranger Station near Elk City. The Montana access leaves US 93 at Conner, where you turn west up the West Fork of the Bitterroot River on paved Road 473. After 13 miles on Road 473, you come to a junction on the right, leading 18 paved miles to Nez Perce Pass across the Bitterroot Divide. A high-standard gravel road leads 15 miles from the pass to the Magruder Crossing bridge over the Selway River, a popular boat-launch site. From here the road becomes one lane, although with a good rock base. It climbs 3,000 feet and 12 miles to skirt Salmon Mountain.

From the west side out of Grangeville, take ID 13 west 9 miles to ID 14 on the right (south). From here, it is 31 miles to Elk City. Before Elk City, turn right onto paved FR 222, and continue 13 miles to Red River Ranger Station. Half a mile south of the station is a large sign warning of the hazards of driving the Montana Road (FR 468). Turn left. This trailhead starts at the Paradise Ranger Station, set in the mouth of White Cap Creek, which is a 12-mile drive down the Selway River after you turn north off the Magruder Corridor Road.

Much of the area near the road corridor (FR 468) in Montana burned in the big fires of 2000. The fire only burned in a few places right along the roadside. GPS: N45 52.05' / W114 43.8'

The Hike

Depending on the number of days you've allotted, your destination can be Cooper Flat, Patzy Ann Falls, the Triple Lakes, or White Cap Lakes, the farthest being White Cap Lakes, about 27 miles from the trailhead.

A major forest fire burned the south side of White Cap Creek some years ago, and its impact is still quite evident. An area 3 to 4 miles up White Cap Creek, near and on Mt. Paloma Trail, burned in the fires of 2000.

The entire Selway–Bitterroot Wilderness is under a natural fire plan that allows naturally caused fires to burn themselves out when conditions are not extreme. In years like 2000, when conditions are extreme and there are multitudes of fires everywhere, fighting fires inside the wilderness area is the last priority regardless of what a fire management plan says. Aside from these burns, this country is heavily forested.

The trail (Trail 24) begins just past the ranger station near an outfitter's camp, following the river up what is at first a fairly narrow canyon and staying on the north side of the creek. You don't have to ford White Cap Creek, but you need wading shoes for some of the tributaries. This is a big creek. It could be named the White Cap River.

The trail is well maintained to Patzy Ann Falls, but in the early season you can expect to cross winter deadfall. In the lower elevations you might see rattlesnakes on the trail. Black bears are common; keep a clean camp and hang your food bag.

Cooper Flat, about 7 miles from the trailhead, takes a day to reach. There is an old forest service cabin, but it isn't open to public use. Here White Cap Creek is joined by a major tributary, Canyon Creek. A major trail crosses White Cap Creek on a bridge, providing access to Cooper Flat. The trail heads up the narrow, timbered mouth of Canyon Creek. This narrow mouth is deceptive, however, because Canyon Creek widens considerably after 1.5 miles. This is a potential side hike.

The second day you may want to hike to Cliff Creek, 7 miles farther. The White Cap canyon has a nice broad bottom for about a mile near the confluence of Cliff Creek. In June, however, both Paloma Creek (2.5 miles past Canyon Creek) and Cliff Creek are high with runoff, and crossing may be dangerous. It is not unusual during spring melt for White Cap Creek to rise more than a foot by midafternoon. The trail to Cliff Creek is good except for early-season deadfall and avalanche debris in bad

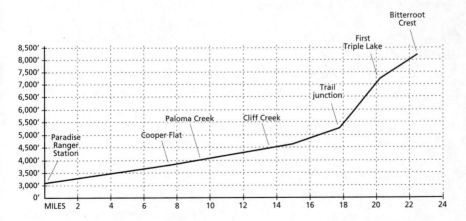

avalanche years: Broken timber, rocks, and mud may form a short, miserable jungle over the trail.

On day three your options double, for after 4 miles you reach a trail junction near fabulous Patzy Ann Falls. You can either climb 3.5 miles and 2,000 feet to Triple Lakes, or continue up White Cap Creek on the fainter Trail 701 to end at the White Cap Lakes. (It's 4 miles from the beginning of Trail 701 to the largest of these lakes, at 6,910 feet.) This trail is not shown on the 1991 Tin Cup Lake USGS quadrangle.

Triple Lakes have excellent fishing. The trail leads to the middle lake (the lower one, to the west, is well off the trail). The highest lake requires about 0.25 mile of easy off-trail hiking. You'll find much alpine larch, which grows in Idaho only along the Bitterroot Divide. From the lakes, the trail snakes over the Bitterroot Divide into Montana and down to large (and popular) Tin Cup Lake.

To get to White Cap Creek Lakes, at the head of White Cap Creek, follow the lower route across Triple Lakes Creek below Patzy Ann Falls. The trail might have much deadfall and many detours made by animals and hunters. Keep your eye on the aged tree blazes. Do not cross White Cap Creek. Stay on the east side for 4.5 miles, passing through huge trees in a subalpine environment. The ground cover consists largely of huckleberries, which means bears in August.

At the 4.5-mile point, ford White Cap Creek. You are 0.5 mile from, and several hundred feet below, the lakes. The broad ford is shallow and easy even early in the season. After a bit more forest, the trail slants steeply upward through a meadow below a rock outcrop, leading to the outlet stream. A short walk upstream takes you to White Cap Lakes. There are a couple of lightly used campsites on the northeast side of the largest lake. Once you've reached your destination, take pride in your accomplishment. Very few make it to this area.

Fishing in the large, relatively low-elevation lake is outstanding and worth the 27 miles. California golden trout were first stocked here in 1973. You should plan on at least three days to reach the lake from the trailhead, and three days to hike out. Of course, you'll probably want a few extra days to explore the area.

Options: The major option is consists of hiking to the head of White Cap Creek and the White Cap Lakes, as described. From the lakes you can cross the Bitterroot Crest and hike out Tin Cup Creek just above Darby, Montana. This is a very long shuttle.

Trail 46/45, not ground-checked, appears to provide a side loop of about 9 miles, going over Vance Point (6,823 feet) and coming down Fall Creek to White Cap Creek. Another side trail goes up the ridge between Lookout Creek and Cedar Creek to Cedar Saddle, and down the ridge between Cedar Creek and Barefoot Creek to White Cap Creek. From Cedar Saddle, you can also follow the trail to Mount Paloma before returning to White Cap Creek.

Longer loops are possible. The stretch of wilderness seems to be endless.

—Philip Blomquist with Erik Fisher

White Cap Creek

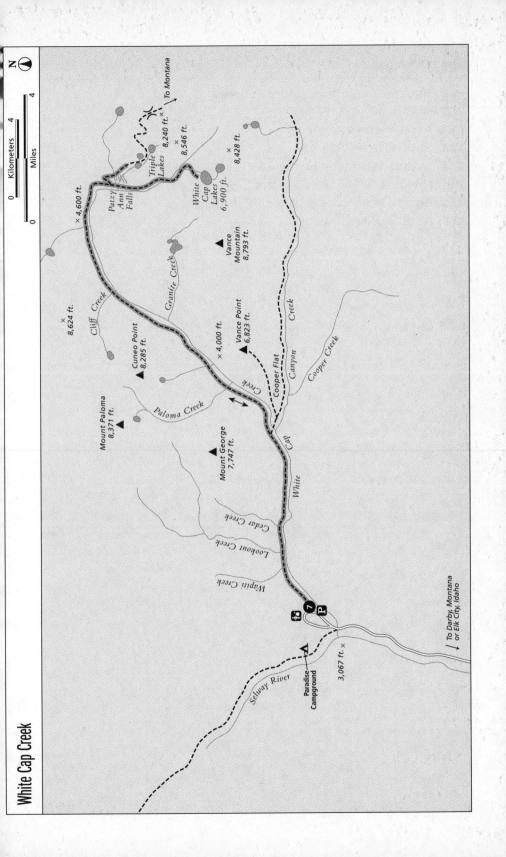

Miles and Directions

0.0 Start at the Paradise Ranger Station (3,070 feet).

7.3 Reach Cooper Flat (3,750 feet).

9.3 Pass Paloma Creek (3,950 feet).

13.8 Reach Cliff Creek (4,550 feet).

17.7 Reach the trail junction (Trails 24 and 701) near Patzy Ann Falls (5,300 feet).

20.4 Arrive at the first Triple Lake (7,240 feet).

22.5 Reach the Bitterroot Crest (8,190 feet). Retrace your steps.

45.0 Arrive back at the trailhead.

Mallard-Larkins Proposed Wilderness

The large Mallard–Larkins Roadless Area, consisting of more than 300,000 acres, lies astride the long ridge dividing the St. Joe and Clearwater River valleys. Crossing the low-grade Fly Hill Road, the area extends eastward to the Montana border.

The idea of protecting this area as designated wilderness originated with Lewiston forester and sawmill designer Morton Brigham, who began visiting the region as early as 1938. In a 1973 article in *Living Wilderness*, Brigham shared his vision with a broader public, and the magnificent area has been included in every serious Idaho wilderness debate since then.

Idaho conservation and hunting and fishing groups now propose the establishment of a 265,000-acre wilderness. It would include the high lakes near Mallard Peak (see Hike 8, Larkins Lake), the deep valleys of Buck and Foehl Creeks, and the valley of the Little North Fork of the Clearwater River. On the south, the Elizabeth Lakes would be included, as would the stunning subalpine scenery around Five Lakes Butte.

The wildest part of the wilderness lies to the east, in Chamberlain and Vanderbilt Creeks. Here, in a huge valley with the Bitterroot Range as an eastern border, you can find deer, elk, moose, certainly wolves, and perhaps even an occasional grizzly bear. Few trails enter this eastern section.

Fly Hill, Smith Ridge, and Surveyor Ridge Roads all provide good access to the Mallard–Larkins, even into the higher elevations. Several outfitters make their livings in the area, and they, along with hunters and fishers, have been among its best friends.

Wilderness boundaries for Mallard–Larkins, as proposed by both the forest service and various Idaho politicians, have been uniformly poor, often running on straight lines across cliffs. The boundary proposed by both Idaho and national conservation groups follows roads and valleys in an attempt to be both identifiable and ecologically sound. Strenuous legal efforts have—so far, anyway—fended off the numerous logging road intrusions planned by the forest service and private companies.

In the 1983 congressional examination of Idaho wilderness, the Mallard–Larkins received more public support for wilderness classification than any other area. Despite that, government agencies and many Idaho politicians still wage an unrelenting war against the designation.

The Mallard–Larkins Pioneer Area is a scenic, but small, bit of country, and the only portion of the Mallard–Larkins with any official protection. It comprises about 20,000 acres and was actually created to forestall wilderness designation. The forest service instead used its administrative authority to create the pioneer area.

The pioneer area was aptly described as "a castle, a fortress surrounded by a sea of bad policy," by Charles Pezeshki in his 1998 book *Wild to the Last: Environmental Conflict in the Clearwater Country*. Pezeshki is among many who have complained about the overharvesting of timber from the Clearwater National Forest and the adjacent state trust lands in the Floodwood State Forest. Then there is the industrial deforestation practiced on private "checkerboard" lands, entire sections of forest given to the railroad company in 1864 and now mostly owned by Plum Creek, a company spun off from the Burlington Northern Railroad. For more information, see *Railroads and Clearcuts: Legacy of Congress's 1864 Northern Railroad Grant*, by Derrick Jensen and George Draffan. For information about how to help protect the rest of the Mallard–Larkins and not just the high country in the pioneer area, contact The Lands Council.

—Ralph and Jackie Maughan and Dennis Baird

8 Larkins Lake

Late-summer hiking is available to this high mountain lake country, with cutthroat trout fishing and a chance to see mountain goats, moose, elk, deer, and an occasional black bear.

Start: About 80 miles northeast of Lewiston and 30 miles northeast of Pierce
Type of hike: Out-and-back, with options for making a base camp and taking day hikes
Distance: 13.6 miles
Approximate hiking time: 2–4 days
Difficulty: Moderately strenuous due to elevation gain
Best season: Mid-July–mid-October
Trail surface: Dirt and rock
Land status: Clearwater National Forest
Canine compatibility: On leash
Fees and permits: None
Maps: USGS Buzzard Roost and Mallard Peak ID; Clearwater National Forest map

Trail contact: North Fork Ranger District; (208) 476-3775
Special considerations: No water is available along the trail. Mosquitoes can be voracious at Larkins Lake. Wildlife, including mountain goats, deer, and elk, but especially the goats, are reported to have become so tame at this popular spot that they can be a hazard. Food should be hung high enough that an elk perched on its hind feet cannot reach it.
Parking and trailhead facilities: The trailhead includes a hitching post on the left and latrines and forest service trail mileage signs on the right.

Finding the trailhead: From Lewiston, drive 48 miles east on US 12 to Greer. Turn left onto ID 11, where the Greer grade travels 9 steep and winding miles out of the canyon to emerge on the Weippe Prairie. You'll pass through Weippe at mile 57, then Pierce at mile 66, and finally Headquarters at mile 86. This is where ID 11 and the pavement end. Just north of Headquarters, take a right and drive 4 miles down the good, dirt FR 246. You'll come to a fork where you'll go left onto FR 251. This road continues for 10 miles as it drops into the East Fork of Beaver Creek to meet FR 247. Continue on Forest 247 for 7 miles as it follows Beaver Creek to the North Fork of the Clearwater. From Headquarters, you will have traveled 21 miles, and although this drive is long, it's quite scenic.

Cross the river and turn left. (A right turn leads 0.25 mile to the Aquarius Campground.) In 1 mile you'll come to Isabella Creek, where you turn right (north) onto dirt FR 700. Stay left on steep and winding FR 700 (Smith Ridge) for 9 miles, where you'll reach the trailhead and Trail 240. GPS: N46 54.41' / W115 40.71'

The Hike

The good Trail 240 climbs almost 1,200 feet in 2 miles as it winds through white pine, Douglas fir, and grand fir forest to cross into the Mallard–Larkins Pioneer Area. Ferns line the lower levels, giving way to colorful wildflowers, huckleberry bushes, and at higher altitudes bear grass. One mile in, you'll pass a trail on the right (south),

Big cedar groves at the trailhead up Isabelle Creek. PHOTO BY LUKE KRATZ

but continue east as you near Grassy Point. Here the trail swings north to climb onto Goat Ridge. On top is a side trail leading right (south) to Grassy Point.

Continue north for another 0.5 mile to the Goat Ridge Benchmark, where you'll stay right and continue on Trail 240. In another 0.5 mile you'll pass the cutoff (Trail 96) to Elmer Creek on the right (east). Here's a good place to view Mallard Peak to the east.

The trail continues up and down along Goat Ridge to skirt the south reach of Larkins Peak at Benchmark 6,391. Here a side trail to the left (north) climbs Larkins Peak (6,661 feet). Larkins Peak, in its upper reaches, hosts subalpine fir, Douglas fir, and thickets of alder. From the top, 3,000 feet below and to the north, is the Little

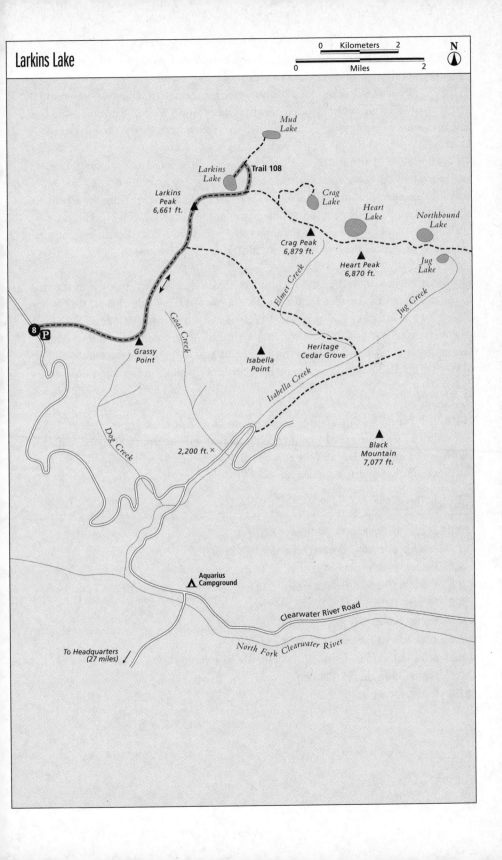

Larkins Lake

0 — Kilometers — 2
0 — Miles — 2

N

Mud Lake

Larkins Lake

Trail 108

Crag Lake

Larkins Peak
6,661 ft.

Heart Lake

Northbound Lake

Crag Peak
6,879 ft.

Heart Peak
6,870 ft.

Jug Lake

Elmer Creek

8 P

Jug Creek

Goat Creek

Grassy Point

Isabella Point

Heritage Cedar Grove

Dog Creek

Isabella Creek

2,200 ft. ×

Black Mountain
7,077 ft.

Aquarius Campground

Clearwater River Road

North Fork Clearwater River

To Headquarters
(27 miles)

North Fork of the Clearwater. Back at the junction and on the trail again, you can peer 700 feet down to Larkins Lake, a clear, cold, inviting gem.

Now comes the descent. Going north-northeast, in 1 mile and 100 feet you'll come to another junction; turn left (north) and drop on Trail 108 another 400 feet and 0.75 mile to a four-way junction. Take the extreme left (south) trail to arrive at Larkins Lake, in less than 0.5 mile with a descent of 200 feet.

Oval in shape, Larkins Lake is 12 acres in size and has four large camping areas. It's also home base for moose, cutthroat trout (which greedily grab at a dry fly), and goats, which graze near the top of the steep face of Larkins Peak, visible from the lakeshore. It's a popular hike, so expect to see others on the trail, especially on weekends.

The lake is not noted for large fish; it's too popular for that. But the fish that are here have a short feeding season and are hungry most of the time.

Options: Nearby, up out of the Larkins Lake basin and about a mile down the trail to the north, lies the smaller Mud Lake. To the east sits Crag Lake, below 6,879-foot Crag Peak, and farther still is 40-acre Heart Lake, known for its occasional larger cutthroat trout. These lakes dot the subalpine high country, nestled in glacial cirques. Other lakes stocked with fish on either side of Smith Ridge are Northbound and Skyland. The stocked trout species include cutthroat, brook, brown, and rainbow.

—Bill Francis

Note: Bill Francis, newspaper reporter and outdoorsman, died in a truck rollover on his way to receive an award for his environmental writing. In 1999, along with his best friends Gene and Jennie Winter, we took his ashes to fly with the goshawks over the North Fork country he so loved.

Miles and Directions

0.0 Start at the Smith Ridge Trailhead (4,920 feet).

1.0 Reach the Salmon Ridge Trail junction (5,388 feet).

2.0 Pass the Grassy Point Trail junction.

2.5 Reach the Goat Ridge Benchmark (6,372 feet).

3.0 Pass the Elmer Creek junction (6,160 feet).

4.5 Pas the Larkins Peak junction (6,391 feet).

5.5 At the Trail 108 junction (6,120 feet), go left.

6.3 At the Larkins Lake junction (5,720 feet), take an extreme left.

6.8 Reach Larkins Lake (5,600 feet).

13.6 Arrive back at the trailhead.

9 Pete Ott Lake and Vicinity

Scenic lakes dot the southeast corner of the Mallard–Larkins Proposed Wilderness with some distant views of the vast "ocean" of the Clearwater Mountains.

Start: About 85 miles east of Lewiston deep in the Clearwater Mountains
Type of hike: Out-and-back, with day hike options
Distance: 5 miles
Approximate hiking time: 2–3 days
Difficulty: Moderately easy
Best season: Late July–mid-September
Trail surface: Dirt and rock
Land status: Clearwater National Forest
Canine compatibility: On leash
Fees and permits: None
Map: USGS Elizabeth Mountain ID

Trail contact: North Fork Ranger District; (208) 476-4541
Special considerations: The access road requires a four-wheel-drive vehicle.
Parking and trailhead facilities: There is room to park about six vehicles at the undeveloped trailhead, which has partial shade. An old road continues to the right toward Flat Mountain, but it is abandoned, soon becoming a trail and then just a game track. Take the obvious trail, Trail 176, that goes to the left (approximately north).

Finding the trailhead: It's a long drive to the trailhead, so it is best to do this hike if you are already way up the North Fork of the Clearwater, or if you want to do some exploration beyond Pete Ott Lake itself.

From Lewiston, drive 48 miles east on US 12 to Greer. Turn left onto ID 11, where the Greer grade travels 9 steep and winding miles out of the canyon to emerge on the Weippe Prairie. You'll pass through Weippe at mile 57. At mile 68, you reach a junction with ID 11 and French Mountain Road (FR 250). This is just south of the small town of Pierce. Turn onto French Mountain Road. This road climbs through low mountains and then descends Orogrande Creek to the North Fork of the Clearwater River. This is 29 miles from the ID 11 turnoff. Cross the North Fork bridge, turn right (still on FR 250), and drive upstream along the North Fork. Go about 15 miles to Cold Springs Road (FR 711), then turn left onto gravel FR 711. If you arrive at Kelly Forks, you have gone 3 miles too far up the North Fork.

When you are 1.7 miles up FR 711, turn right onto FR 5295, which begins a steep and long climb up to a high saddle between Flat Mountain and Cold Springs Peak. There is a maze of old logging roads, but most are gated. Stay on FR 5295 until you reach FR 5297. Follow FR 5297 until you reach FR 5297A, which makes the final climb to the ridgetop. Signs should help if these road numbers change. This is 7.4 miles and 3,000 feet above the turnoff from FR 711. GPS: N46 45.75' / W115 18.15'

The Hike

Trail 176 is a fairly gentle trail for ATVs that leads toward Cold Springs Peak, a high point on Pot Mountain Ridge in the Mallard–Larkins roadless area.

Views near the trailhead of to Pete Ott Lake. PHOTO BY LUKE KRATZ

The trail passes above Ring Lake, which is barely visible below. Then it passes behind Point 6,310. Just beyond this point the trail to Pete Ott Lake, Ice Lake, and the Elizabeth Lakes (Trail 445) leaves to the right and heads steeply downslope to the northeast. When we visited in 1999, we found Trail 176 blocked by a large blowdown just before the junction of Trail 445. The side trail was easy to miss. Trail 445 is closed to ATVs but not motorcycles. Contact the North Fork Ranger District if you see marauding ATVs on the trail.

After traveling 0.3 mile from the junction and making a descent of 300 feet, an unmarked trail descends to Ice Lake, a small lake in a small cirque set against a big northeast-facing cliff. Due to its location, Ice Lake has ice well into June.

Another 0.3 mile brings you to the unmarked trail to Pete Ott Lake. It leaves to the right and heads downhill 200 feet to the lake. If you find yourself climbing up a forested mountainside, you have missed the trail. Turn back.

Pete Ott is about three times as large as Ice Lake. It, too, sits with its back toward a steep cirque wall. The lakeshore is heavily forested, but has a number of somewhat overused campsites. You have good

Pete Ott Lake and Vicinity

× 6,388 ft.

Trail 169

6,250 ft. ×

6,661 ft. ×

Cold Springs Peak 6,371 ft.

6,771 ft. ×

Trail 445

6,310 ft. ×

FR5297A

To Cold Springs Creek Road (FR711)

Trail 176

P
9

Flat Mountain

views across the lake to the cliffs, to which cling brush and pyramid-shaped conifers. In September this foliage turns bright red and gold.

Options: Trail 169 continues past Cold Springs Peak along Pot Mountain Ridge all the way to Fly Hill.

Past the Pete Ott Lake trail turn, Trail 445 continues to climb, and then contours high above Pete Ott Creek, giving cross-country access to the Elizabeth Lakes. When it reaches Elizabeth Mountain, it descends steeply to the North Fork.

There is a faint trail down Elizabeth Creek from Ice Lake. The lower portion of Elizabeth Creek burned in a major forest fire in the summer of 2000. Fire rehabilitation often results in old trails being recut. Fires can also make trails impassable if not recut. Check with the forest service.

—Ralph Maughan

Miles and Directions

0.0 Begin on Trail 176 (6,260 feet).

1.5 Turn off onto Trail 455 (6,240 feet)

2.1 Take the side trail to Pete Ott Lake (5,960 feet).

2.5 Reach Pete Ott Lake (5,680 feet). Retrace your steps.

5.0 Arrive back at the trailhead.

Proposed Great Burn Wilderness

The Great Burn was the result of the intense fires of 1910 on the Idaho–Montana border. Now, a century or so later, much of the Bitterroot Divide still lacks good commercial stands of timber. The Great Burn Wilderness would protect the area permanently. It is stunningly beautiful country, with many meadows brimming with wildlife, including two or three wolf packs and a possible reinhabitation area for grizzly bears, not to mention the huge elk herds.

Geologically, the Bitterroot Divide may be considered a prominent subrange of the vast Clearwater Mountains. It reaches its greatest height in the Selway–Bitterroot Wilderness just to the south of the Great Burn and south of US 12.

Fortunately, the forest service has recommended much of the Great Burn area for wilderness designation. Unfortunately, however, it hasn't recommended enough. The Kelly Creek drainage to the north and northeast has mostly been left out of the wilderness proposal, along with Cayuse Creek, a major tributary of Kelly Creek. The trees have grown back in these drainages to a greater extent, and both of these nationally famous trout streams are threatened by logging and road-building plans.

—Ralph Maughan

The Great Burn area at the Goat Lake trailhead. PHOTO BY JOHN KRATZ

10 Goat Lake

Goat Lake is a cirque mountain lake in the proposed Great Burn Wilderness of Idaho and Montana, set amid 7,000–8,000-foot peaks and with numerous trail connections to other lakes and the Bitterroot Divide. There are good views into the 100,000-acre proposed Weitas Creek Wilderness.

Start: 55 miles southwest of Missoula, Montana, and 165 miles northeast of Lewiston, Idaho

Type of hike: Out-and-back

Distance: 11 miles

Approximate hiking time: 2–3 days

Difficulty: Moderate

Best season: Mid-July–mid-September

Trail surface: Dirt and rock

Land status: Clearwater National Forest

Canine compatibility: On leash

Fees and permits: None

Maps: USGS Rhodes Peak ID; Clearwater National Forest map

Trail contact: North Fork Ranger District; (208) 476-4541

Special considerations: The 28-mile dirt road to the Goat Lake Trailhead is passable in passenger cars with good tires but, depending upon snowpack and weather, may have snow at higher elevations. The last 0.5 mile after the turnoff to the trailhead requires four-wheel-drive and high-clearance vehicles. Traveling on this scenic but long gravel-and-dirt road takes about four or five hours.

Parking and trailhead facilities: This is an undeveloped site in the sun.

Finding the trailhead: From Missoula, drive south to Lolo, Montana, and turn right (west) onto US 12. Travel 45 miles west to Parachute Hill Road (FR 569), just before the turnoff to Lochsa Lodge and the Powell Ranger Station.

From Lewiston, drive east on US 12 for 164 miles to Parachute Hill Road, just after the turnoff to Lochsa Lodge and the Powell Ranger Station.

Parachute Hill Road is to the north, and a sign at the beginning gives distances to Rock Point (7 miles), Papoose Saddle (8 miles), and Cayuse Junction (19 miles). The road climbs for more than 3,500 feet to Papoose Saddle, drops into Cayuse Creek Canyon, and then climbs again to Blacklead Mountain.

Drive north up Parachute Hill Road for 2.7 miles to a three-way fork. Take the middle fork (FR 569) and continue 1.7 miles to another fork. Keep left. Another 1.6 miles farther is the signed Powell Junction. This is the end of FR 569. Proceed on FR 500 (the Lewis and Clark Trail) for another mile to Papoose Saddle. Continue straight ahead, and after 11.5 miles arrive at Cayuse Junction.

At Cayuse Junction, turn right onto FR 581. A sign here states it is 8.2 miles to the unsigned turnoff (right) to Blacklead Mountain. It is another rocky, rutted, narrow, and steep 0.5 mile to the first of two trailheads.

If you have a two-wheel-drive vehicle, park about 0.25 mile before the summit of Blacklead Mountain and walk the jeep road to the final trailhead. This walk of about 0.75 mile crosses over Blacklead Mountain. You will enjoy beautiful views all the way.

If you have a four-wheel-drive vehicle, drive over Blacklead Mountain to the small trailhead 240 feet down and about 0.5 mile north. It is located on a saddle where the Deer Creek Trail (Trail 513) takes off to the north. GPS: N46 38.39' / W114 51.08'

The Hike

The trail to Goat Lake starts from the parking area at the end of a jeep track that leads over Blacklead Mountain. The summit offers an outstanding view of the proposed Great Burn Wilderness of the Bitterroot Divide. To the northeast is the divide, the heart of the wilderness. To the north and northwest is the Kelly Creek drainage. To the south is Cayuse Creek, and due west is the Bighorn–Weitas Creek Roadless Area.

From the end of the jeep trail, the Deer Creek Trail (Trail 513) takes off to the north. Look instead for the unsigned Trail 508 on the right (east), which drops 280 feet in several switchbacks to pass an old mine digging and a grave (a pile of stones with a worn wooden marker). This side ridge is untimbered, and the valley below is pocketed with fir, pine, and small meadows.

After dropping about 0.5 mile, you'll come to a small, cold, clear spring that flows right out of the mountain to form Billy Rhodes Creek. After the spring, the trail drops less steeply. The next 0.25 mile is easy to follow but can't be seen from the ridge above as it passes through a bear grass meadow and patches of lodgepole pine and alpine fir.

Shortly after the trail levels out at about 6,650 feet, it splits. Go left. The right fork goes to Silver Creek and ultimately Cayuse Creek. The trail levels as it contours around the ridge for about 2 miles to cross the two small streams. These flow out of two impressive cirques (which the topo shows as lakeless). Numerous rock outcroppings begin to appear on the ridge above.

Come out onto a wide open stretch of ridge. To the southeast is a view across Silver Creek to Williams Peak (7,501 feet), a gray slab dominating the skyline. On the eastern horizon is Rhodes Peak (7,930 feet). Goat Lake still can't be seen because it is hidden by its own cirque wall, which juts in front of the trail.

The lake comes into view as you round the southern end of the cirque wall. Surrounded by the 180-degree wall that rises abruptly to 1,000 feet above, this beautiful lake makes you automatically reach for your fishing rod. However, the outlet side of the lake on the northeast, although marshy, makes for an especially nice view of the lake and its wall.

An extra attraction for hikers is the number of trail connections to other lakes, to Cayuse Creek, and to the Bitterroot Divide. A good extension from Goat Lake is the trail over Williams Peak and down to Williams Lake (7,005 feet). This trail ultimately reaches the divide via Rhodes Peak.

The return to the trailhead from Goat Lake is leisurely and mostly level,

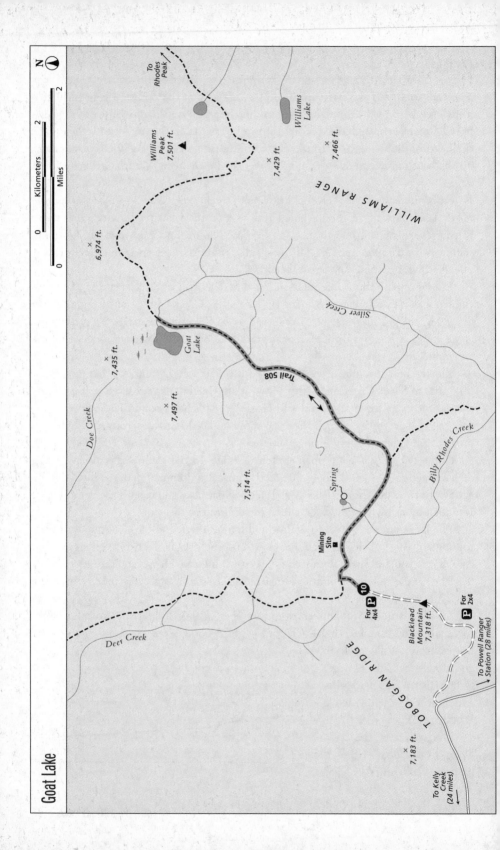

Goat Lake

N

Kilometers
0   2
Miles
0   2

To
Rhodes
Peak

Williams Peak
7,501 ft. ▲

Williams
Lake

7,429 ft. ×

7,466 ft. ×

WILLIAMS RANGE

6,974 ft. ×

7,435 ft. ×

Doe Creek

Goat
Lake

Silver Creek

7,497 ft. ×

Trail 508

7,514 ft. ×

Spring

Mining
Site

Billy Rhodes Creek

Deer Creek

For
4x4 P 10

Blacklead
Mountain
7,318 ft.

For
2x4 P

To Powell Ranger
Station (28 miles)

TOBOGGAN RIDGE

7,183 ft. ×

To Kelly
Creek
(24 miles)

except for the last steep climb back to the top of Blacklead Mountain. From the top, you can look northeastward back across the proposed Great Burn Wilderness as you plan your next hike into this remote and magnificent region.

—Don L. Crawford

Miles and Directions

0.0 Start at the two-wheel-drive vehicle parking area (7,100 feet).

0.3 Summit Blacklead Mountain (7,318 feet).

0.8 Reach the four-wheel-drive vehicle parking area and the trail to Goat Lake (7,060 feet).

1.2 Pass the spring (6,780 feet).

1.5 Pass the trail junction to Silver Creek (6,780 feet).

3.5 Cross a second perennial stream.

5.5 Reach Goat Lake (6,492 feet). Retrace your steps.

11.0 Arrive back at the trailhead.

11 Steep Lakes Loop

This beautiful ridgeline hike lies along the Idaho–Montana border.

Start: Approximately 150 miles east of Lewiston, Idaho, or 60 miles west of Missoula, Montana, in the Clearwater National Forest northeast of Kelly Creek
Type of hike: Requires a short shuttle unless you are willing to walk roads for 4 miles to make a loop
Distance: 18 miles (not counting the 4 miles of road for the loop option)
Approximate hiking time: 4–5 days
Difficulty: Moderately strenuous
Best season: August
Trail surface: Dirt and rock
Land status: Clearwater National Forest

Canine compatibility: On leash
Fees and permits: None
Maps: USGS Bruin Hill and Straight Peak ID
Trail contact: North Fork Ranger District, (208) 476-4541
Special considerations: The greatest difficulty on this trip is that each night you have to climb down off the Bitterroot Divide to camp. In many places, that requires a steep descent. There are some campsites on or near the ridgeline. Lightning danger exists on the divide.
Parking and trailhead facilities: There is a small parking area. The trailhead is undeveloped.

Finding the trailhead: Access to the trailhead is possible in a number of ways. The best route is from Superior, Montana, traveling west over Hoodoo Pass (paved FR 250), then downstream along Long Creek to its junction with Lake Creek. Both streams are tributaries of the North Fork of the Clearwater River. Proceed up Lake Creek on FR 295 about 7 miles to a barrier. The barrier and trailhead are near the mouth of Siam Creek.

Much longer back-road access is available from Idaho. Due to the distance and complexity, it is not described here. GPS: N46 50.77' / W114 59.18'

The Hike

The proposed Great Burn Wilderness is located in the northern part of the Bitterroot Mountain system. This large expanse of backcountry encompasses land in both Idaho and Montana.

The present-day environment of the region was shaped by the Great Idaho Fire of 1910 (hence the name Great Burn). This catastrophic event burned three million acres in northern Idaho in just a few days and destroyed a number of early towns. Major fires continued to burn in the area until 1919. As a result, a century after the fires much of the area proposed for wilderness is still quite open. The lack of big trees has kept the timber companies at bay.

The Steep Lakes cirque is nestled at the headwaters of the North Fork of the Clearwater River. This lake basin, aptly named for its precipitous position below the ridge separating Idaho and Montana, is seldom visited. The only way to reach these lakes is on foot or by horse via the Boundary Trail. The best month is probably August, although thunderstorms are most common then, and this hike is on an exposed ridge. Early July finds snowdrifts. In September the foliage on the ridge turns a beautiful red and gold, but by mid-September the air is getting cold.

This 18-mile near-loop begins by following the closed logging road at the barrier just below Lake Creek's tributary, Siam Creek. From the trailhead, it is 5 miles to large Fish Lake. The old road track has turned into a broad trail (Trail 419). Unfortunately, at present, dirt bikes and ATVs are allowed to travel to the lake. This is the source of numerous complaints, but wilderness designation would prevent this situation.

The hike begins in a narrow canyon, which broadens as you ascend. Two miles below Fish Lake, you meet Trail 478 coming from the south. At this junction the trail becomes Trail 478, and you also begin a moderately steep climb of 600 feet in 2 miles to Fish Lake.

Special fishing regulations delay the opening day for Fish Lake and Steep Lakes until August 1 to protect the spawning of west slope cutthroat in Fish Lake and the California golden trout in Steep Lakes. Because of the regulations, the fishing is quite good. However, if you prize solitude and quiet, do not walk to Fish Lake on August 1!

You reach Stateline Trail (Trail 738) just beyond Fish Lake, which is barely inside Idaho. Motorized travel is prohibited on this trail, which follows the Bitterroot Divide closely. This trail actually begins quite a way to the south—a few miles north of Lolo Pass where US 12 crosses into Idaho—and it follows the state line for more than 45 miles to Hoodoo Pass.

The view from the trail is excellent into both states. Some twenty lakes are scattered along it on both sides of the divide. Elk, moose, and deer abound in the area, making it a popular hunting destination in the fall. The area has been claimed by several wolf packs in recent years. It is possible to see a pack of as many as fifteen wolves in the area.

The section of Stateline Trail from Fish Lake northward to Goose Lake is not busy. The route is moderately difficult in places as the trail disappears on some of the more rocky and open parts of the ridgeline. Finding the route is no great problem, however, because the ridgeline is the only logical route of travel. Most of the lakes below on either side of the ridge are reached only with off-trail hiking. There is no water on top of the Bitterroot Divide, except for temporary snowmelt.

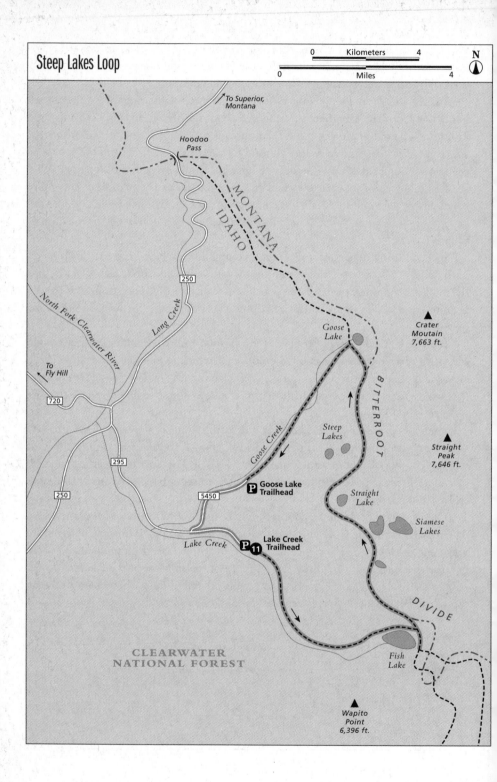

Steep Lakes Loop

Before you reach the Steep Lakes, you pass the Siamese Lakes and Straight Lake, which are in Montana. The upper Siamese Lake is an excellent overnight camping choice after a first night at Fish Lake. Fishing for cutthroat trout is excellent here.

The country near Steep Lakes is appropriately named and has probably the best view of the hike. Straight Peak, on the Montana side, is a sight to behold from Boundary Trail, and the Steep Lakes cirque has to be one of the most sublime locations in Idaho. The Steep Lakes are deep and dark blue, set among rugged cliffs. The lower Steep Lake supports a naturally reproducing population of California golden trout. The limit here for this rare fish is two. Carefully release all others so that once again the flash of crimson and gold may strike your dry fly.

From Steep Lakes, Stateline Trail continues 4 miles to the Goose Lake basin. The trail leaves the Bitterroot Divide and follows a ridge down 1.2 miles from Goose Lake. This small, shallow, fishless lake is a watering hole for moose and elk. It is marshy around the lake. A sign at the trail junction here should steer you down Goose Creek Trail (Trail 414). It's about 4 miles down this well-maintained and easy-to-follow trail to the Goose Creek Trailhead. The first 2 miles descend gently through open country. Just before you cross Steep Creek, the grade increases considerably. Goose Creek Trail is closed to motor vehicles. From the trailhead, it is a road walk of about 4 miles back to your vehicle in Lake Creek. You may be able to thumb a ride.

—Phil Blomquist; revised by Ralph Maughan

Miles and Directions

0.0 Start at the Lake Creek Trailhead (4,600 feet).

3.0 Reach the junction with Trail 478; begin the steep climb to Fish Lake (5,258 feet).

5.0 Reach Fish Lake (5,890 feet).

5.2 Reach the beginning of the Stateline Trail (5,940 feet).

5.4 Mount the Bitterroot Divide into Montana (6,108 feet).

6.5 Reach a point above a cirque lake (6,985).

7.3 Reach a point above a second cirque lake (7,021 feet).

8.1 Pass through the saddle above the Siamese Lakes (6,870 feet).

9.1 Reach the high point above Straight Lake (7,322 feet).

10.2 Reach the highest point of hike (7,350 feet).

11.2 The lowest of the Steep Lakes is due west and below (6,920 feet).

11.8 Reach a point above an unnamed Montana lake (7,000 feet).

12.9 The trail passes just below Point 6,746 (6,710 feet).

14.2 Arrive at Goose Lake (5,763 feet).

15.2 Goose Lake Trail crosses Steep Creek (5,100 feet).

18.0 Arrive at the Goose Lake Trailhead (4,450 feet).

Meadow Creek

The Meadow Creek Roadless Area abuts the western side of the Selway–Bitterroot Wilderness but is not part of the designated wilderness. Conservationists lobbied hard to have the Meadow Creek Roadless Area, particularly its east side, added to the Selway–Bitterroot Wilderness in 1980, when Idaho senator Frank Church was guiding the River of No Return Wilderness bill through Congress. While Senator Church ultimately did agree to make some significant additions along the southern edge of the Selway–Bitterroot (along the Magruder Corridor), he was never convinced to add Meadow Creek. For political reasons, most likely timber interests in nearby Elk City, Idaho, Senator Church ignored the pleadings of conservationists, even though he understood the need to preserve this pristine, but fragile, area.

The Burnt Backbone logging project was planned for the early 1990s in the Horse Creek drainage of lower Meadow Creek. It was shelved and has not resurfaced, but these things tend to never go away. In general, timber interests have always coveted the upper reaches of the drainage, in particular the west side where there is more timber. Nevertheless, the Meadow Creek drainage is still largely roadless, and the Nez Perce National Forest plan for the area is to leave it mostly as is, at least for a while.

A new threat to solitude and wilderness qualities comes from increased use by off-road vehicles, including ATVs. A motorized route to accommodate ATVs and motorcycles is proposed in upper Meadow Creek. The first 3 miles in the lower portion are presently open to motorcycles and bicycles.

We encourage the forest service, rather than go ahead with plans for motorized development, to instead recognize the beauty and importance of Meadow Creek as de facto wilderness. Better yet, perhaps someday we will see this magnificent area added to the Selway–Bitterroot Wilderness.

—Don L. Crawford and Jackie Jackson Maughan

12 Meadow Creek

This is the second most heavily used trail in this vicinity of the Selway River—and for good reason. It's a shady hike along fern-covered, stone wall formations beside sizable Meadow Creek.

Start: 130 miles east of Lewiston
Type of hike: Out-and-back. The first portion makes a good family backpack.
Distance: 28 miles for featured route, although shorter trips are possible.
Approximate hiking time: 2–4 days
Difficulty: Easy for first 3 miles, difficult for 1.5 miles, then moderate
Best season: Early April–November
Trail surface: Dirt and rock
Land status: Nez Perce National Forest
Canine compatibility: On leash
Fees and permits: The Meadow Creek Guard Station, available by reservation from May 1 to Sept 15, is 15 miles up the trail. Also available for reserved rental is the Lookout Butte fire tower, 20 miles downriver from the Meadow Creek Trailhead.

Maps: USGS Selway Falls, Anderson Butte, Vermilion Peak, and Sable Hill ID; Nez Perce National Forest map
Trail contact: Moose Creek Ranger District; (208) 926-4258
Special considerations: Rainbow and cutthroat trout inhabit these waters, but be aware that protected chinook salmon and steelhead birth and spawn along the Selway tributaries; check Idaho Fish and Game regulations. The first 3 miles are open to motorcycles and bicycles.
Parking and trailhead facilities: There are eleven campgrounds strung along the Selway River, but only the large O'Hara (thirty-two sites) has water. Slims and Selway Falls are closest to the trailhead. Both have outhouses and sites for two and seven parties, respectively. Park at Slims Campground, and find the trailhead at the south (upstream) end of the area.

Finding the trailhead: From Lewiston, drive east on US 12 for 114 miles to Lowell, where the Lochsa and Selway Rivers join to form the Clearwater (Three Forks). Cross the bridge and continue east on Selway River Road (FR 223) for 19 miles to Slims Campground and the trailhead.

The road is paved for the first 6 miles to O'Hara Creek Bridge. From there it is gravel for 11 miles to Selway Falls, a magnificent sight, especially in the spring. At dusk, ospreys fish here and all along the river. Cross the Selway on the one-lane bridge just above the Selway Falls Guard Station, and begin following Meadow Creek for 2 miles along a narrow, but good, dirt road. Just before Slims Campground, side roads take off to Elk City and the active Indian Hill fire lookout. GPS: N46 01.72' / W115 17.37'

The Hike

The trail begins at 1,800 feet and continues with virtually no change in elevation for the first 3 miles. The canyon of Meadow Creek is narrower than that of the Selway and has a tree canopy, which provides a welcome retreat from the heat in these low-elevation canyons. Fern- and lichen-covered rock walls add to the coolness. Mica glitters in the mostly dirt surface of the trail.

Rapid waters of Meadow Creek. PHOTO BY LINDSEY TUCKER

Meadow Creek quietly rushes over boulders and logjams or pools in the shade of old-growth cedars. While the bank is mostly rocky, there are some pockets of sand. The trail offers opportunities to slip over to the creek's edge to rest or fish. My experience is that in the lower 3 miles you can catch a rainbow or cutthroat about every other cast, but most are small (3 to 6 inches). Still, occasionally you catch a bigger one (10 to 12 inches) here.

A little over a mile up the trail, you will encounter bridged Squirrel Creek, the first of many streams that empty into Meadow Creek. Rabbit Creek follows 0.5 mile later and is narrow enough to step over.

Little Creek marks the end of the easy part of the trail. The forest map shows a trail to Horse Point on the west side of Meadow Creek here, but it doesn't really exist

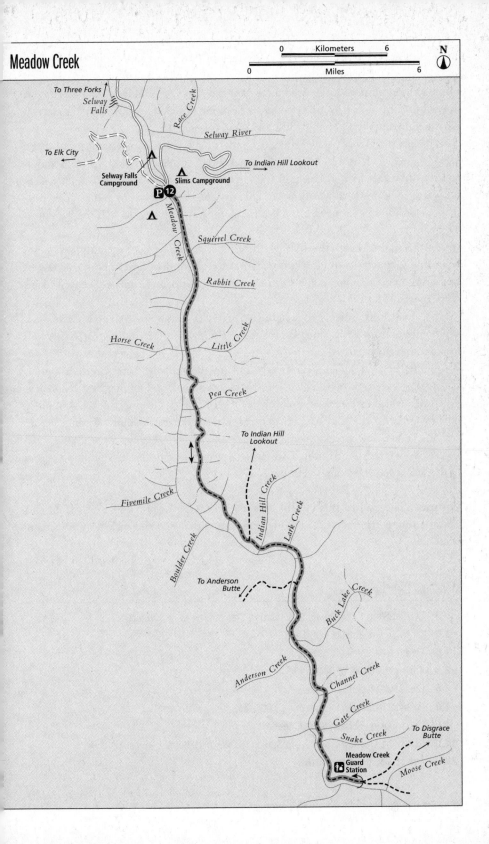

0   Kilometers   6

0   Miles   6

N

To Three Forks

Selway
Falls

Race Creek

Selway River

To Elk City

Selway Falls
Campground

Slims Campground

To Indian Hill Lookout

P 12

Meadow Creek

Squirrel Creek

Rabbit Creek

Horse Creek

Little Creek

Pea Creek

To Indian Hill
Lookout

Fivemile Creek

Indian Hill Creek

Lark Creek

Boulder Creek

To Anderson
Butte

Buck Lake Creek

Anderson Creek

Channel Creek

Gate Creek

Snake Creek

To Disgrace
Butte

Meadow Creek
Guard
Station

Moose Creek

anymore. Just on the other side of Little Creek bridge, a ramble through the brush to Meadow Creek's edge is worthwhile. Horse Creek tumbles out of the steep west wall of the canyon into beautiful, deep pools. You can stand on boulders and look straight down into clear water 10 to 20 feet deep. Looking upstream, you will see the canyon narrow into a trailless gorge of cliffs and whitewater.

The next stretch of trail brings 0.5 mile of switchbacks, not indicated on the USGS map, which ascend from Little Creek along the steep hillside to an elevation almost 1,000 feet higher. The trail then stays at this level for about 3 miles before dropping back down to Meadow Creek. Pea Creek, the only one indicated as permanent on the USGS maps, is a mere trickle in July. This trickle veils the mouth of a cave.

As the trail traverses the hillside, the timber opens up on this fairly dry, west-facing ridge to expose the vast timber stands to the south and west. This is a view of one of the most remote, fragile sections of this de facto, undesignated, central Idaho wilderness.

The trail drops quickly to where Indian Hill Creek joins Meadow Creek. Just before the bottom is the junction on the left with Trail 603 leading to Indian Hill lookout at 6,810 feet.

A mile beyond Indian Hill Creek, and just beyond the Lark Creek bridge, is a junction with Trail 608, which fords Meadow Creek and climbs west to Anderson Butte. Meadow Creek Trail continues 6 more miles, crossing Buck Lake Creek, Channel Creek, Gate Creek, and Snake Creek, none of which requires fording, before arriving at Meadow Creek Guard Station.

Meadow Creek Recreation Trail can be a peaceful excursion until hunting season in the fall, when it becomes very busy.

Options: The trail to Indian Hill lookout (6,810 feet) is a 3,000-foot climb. This 13-mile round-trip requires a shuttle vehicle at either end and makes an interesting possibility.

—Don L. Crawford

Miles and Directions

0.0 Start at Slims Campground and Meadow Creek trailhead (1,800 feet).

1.0 Cross Squirrel Creek (1,880 feet).

1.5 Ford Rabbit Creek (1,960 feet).

2.5 Cross Little Creek (2,040 feet).

4.5 Cross Pea Creek (3,000 feet).

7.8 Pass the Indian Hill lookout trail (3,000 feet).

8.0 Cross Indian Hill Creek (2,600 feet).

14.0 Reach the Meadow Creek Guard Station (3,000 feet). Retrace your steps.

28.0 Arrive back at the trailhead.

Gospel-Hump Wilderness

Born of controversy and compromise, the 206,053-acre Gospel–Hump Wilderness is one of Idaho's most wild and least visited places. It was established by Congress in 1978 after several years of legal and political battles. Lengthy negotiations between conservation and development interests preceded introduction of legislation. The final settlement, enacted by Congress as part of the Endangered American Wilderness Act (PL 95-237), not only established the wilderness but also allocated roadless land along the South Fork of the Clearwater River to timber development. Still other roadless land was the subject of wildlife and fishery studies completed in 1982, and the 1983 Nez Perce Forest Plan made final decisions on the uses of the "study" lands. Neither the final wilderness boundary nor the final allocation of lands for development pleased all the interested parties, and for years environmental protesters have tried to stop the Cove-Mallard timber sale to the area's east. Nevertheless, creation of a Gospel–Hump Wilderness by Congress had been most unlikely, and when the unexpected opportunity appeared, environmentalists at the time made the necessary compromises. Had this not been so, there would be no Gospel–Hump Wilderness today and the Cove-Mallard sale would have been cut anyway (and probably much more).

Elevations within the wilderness range from 1,970 feet, at the Wind River Pack Bridge on the Salmon River, to 8,940 feet at the summit of Buffalo Hump, a lovely and quite dramatic mountain. Vegetation types along the Salmon River breaks (southern) portion of the wilderness consist chiefly of grass and large-diameter ponderosa pine. The old wagon road (now a trail) leading east from the Gospels toward Buffalo Hump serves as a hydrologic divide for the wilderness. To the north, streams flow into the South Fork of the Clearwater in deep, but often wide, valleys. Lovely meadows predominate here, with fir species and lodgepole pine the most common type of trees found. Brush is thicker on this side as well, due to higher rainfall. Precipitation on the Salmon River side is as low as 18 inches a year, but reaches 60 inches farther north.

This climatic variation also affects visitor use. The Wind River (southwest) side and the trails associated with it are often snow-free by March, yet trails on the north side, leading into the Ten and Twenty Mile Creeks country off the Sourdough Road, don't open up until late June or July. The high country around Wildhorse Lake on the east edge of the wilderness is the last to open, although increased mining activity in the Buffalo Hump mining district, which was excluded from the wilderness, could mean earlier plowing some years.

The wilderness is rich in fish and wildlife. Both resident and anadromous fish can be found in some streams, and most of the numerous lakes in the wilderness have fish as well. Several of the north-side drainages are especially popular with moose, and there is evidence of elk migration back and forth across the wilderness, with large wintering populations found on the Salmon River side. Both goats and sheep are fairly common on the canyon breaks, especially in Crooked Creek. Cougars are

A clearing on the bumpy road to Jumbo Camp. PHOTO BY LUKE KRATZ

common, black bears uncommon, and there is occasional wolf use on the east side of the wilderness. The large deer and elk populations make hunter camps a common autumn sight.

The road system leading to Gospel–Hump trailheads is generally well kept and well marked. On the southwest side of the wilderness, the Salmon River road to Wind River is a charming drive in itself. On the northeast side, equally charming is the road from Crooked Creek up to Wildhorse Lake, where the trail to North Pole Mountain begins. On the west side, the Gospels Road is by far the most lovely vehicle access route to the wilderness, offering dramatic views south into Wind River and across the Salmon River into the adjacent Frank Church–River of No Return Wilderness. On the north side, ID 14 follows the South Fork of the Clearwater River on what is known both as Sourdough Road and the Southern Nez Perce Trail and is the key route accessing this edge of the wilderness.

Trails within the wilderness range from well kept to not maintained at all. As a result, the Gospel–Hump Wilderness offers a superb chance to escape crowds and yet still enjoy fine stream or lakeside camping, hunting, and fishing. The rough country southwest of Buffalo Hump is by far the least visited part of the wilderness, but spring hikers in the Wind River and Crooked Creek country can also expect no crowds.

A 1983 management plan and subsequent documents offer guidance to the forest service on how to manage the wilderness and would make interesting reading for visitors as well. The plan also outlines several threats to the wilderness, including mineral exploration and development (chiefly for gold) among those parts of the wilderness that border the mining district exclusion, and development of a major resort on private land within the wilderness at lovely, historic Shepp Ranch.

—Dennis Baird

13 Oregon Butte Area

The classic Gospel–Hump hike is known for profuse wildflowers, solitude, fishing, and a spectacular vista of Salmon River Canyon. It is also a historic mining district and has glory holes.

Start: 50 linear miles southeast of Grangeville in the Gospel–Hump Wilderness
Type of hike: Out-and-back
Distance: 7 miles
Approximate hiking time: 2 days
Difficulty: Moderate
Best season: Mid-July–August
Trail surface: Dirt and rock
Land status: Gospel–Hump Wilderness; Nez Perce National Forest
Canine compatibility: Not allowed
Fees and permits: None
Maps: USGS Buffalo Hump ID; Gospel–Hump Wilderness map
Trail contact: Red River Ranger District; (208) 842-2245

Special considerations: Past Orogrande Summit, this is one of the worst roads in Idaho and requires patience, high clearance, four-wheel drive, and a rig that can take a beating. Two hikes in the vicinity that don't require four-wheel drive are Fish Lake and Wild Horse Lake to North Pole Mountain. (See Options at the end of this hike.)
Parking and trailhead facilities: Large, undeveloped site. No potable water or improvements. Orogrande Summit Campground (five sites) is the closest campground. Wild Horse Lake Campground (four sites) is just past Orogrande Summit and is a 2-mile side trip. Both have pit toilets but no potable water.

Finding the trailhead: From Grangeville, take paved ID 14 for 42 miles east up the winding, scenic South Fork of the Clearwater River to Crooked River Road. On this well-marked gravel road, cross the South Fork and proceed 13 miles toward Orogrande, a turn-of-the-century mining town that is now just a cluster of summer homes. Watch for moose along the Crooked River in the overgrown mine tailings ponds.

One mile past Orogrande, turn right onto Orogrande Summit Road (FR 233). This is where the gravel ends, but the road is good. It climbs steadily through dense conifer woods to Orogrande Summit, the watershed divide between the Salmon and Clearwater Rivers. On top, the right fork leads 2 miles into Wild Horse Lake. The left goes to your destination, Jumbo Canyon.

Just past this intersection, the road deteriorates as it descends into Lake Creek. The next 3 miles are negotiable by truck but tough for a sedan because of large rocks. Don't try to get past the summit in a car unless you are an experienced mountain driver and don't mind beating up your vehicle.

Half a mile past Lake Creek Campground, the road is passable to four-wheel-drive vehicles only. This 3-mile section is badly washed out; water flows over it even in the summer. In several places it climbs steep ledges of bedrock that are challenging even with four-wheel drive. The road tops out near Hump Lake (7,850 feet) at a spectacular view of the Buffalo Hump, plus a much-improved road. A right turn here is a 0.5-mile side trip to the lake at the base of the Buffalo Hump.

Continuing another 2.5 miles brings you to a private airstrip on the old Calendar Mine property. Past the turnoff to the airstrip, the road drops gradually into the headwaters of Jumbo Creek and, in about 1.8 miles, the trailhead at the end of the road near Jumbo Mine. GPS: N45 33.55' / W115 41.25'

The Hike

The Gospel–Hump area, just north of where the Salmon River runs through the maze of the Salmon River Mountains, is characterized by pronounced glacial features on the north and east side of the ridges and by fairly gentle south and west slopes.

The trails typically wander along the more gentle slopes through subalpine fir, whitebark pine, and Engelmann spruce combined with numerous open parks and meadows. The meadows are wet most of the year and display many kinds of wildflowers, such as alpine heather, shooting star, pinks, and lupine.

Mountain goats and a few bighorn sheep inhabit the heights, while mule deer and elk are common on the lower slopes. Moose migrate from lake to lake and are particularly common in Jumbo Canyon. The eastern part of the Gospel–Hump is the country most likely to be visited by the wolves reintroduced into central Idaho in 1995–1996.

Oregon Butte lies about 7 miles southeast of one of the most unusual features of the Gospel–Hump Wilderness, the Buffalo Hump. This granite exfoliated dome is named for its east–west profile, which resembles a buffalo.

The trail to Oregon Butte lookout and Oregon Butte Lake begins in a wet meadow in the headwaters of Jumbo Creek. After a boggy creek crossing, it switchbacks steeply for 0.25 mile to a low saddle between Jumbo Creek and the East Fork of Sheep Creek. Here you'll find a seemingly confusing system of trails and shortcuts. The trail to the right (Trail 201) leads into the East Fork of Sheep Creek. Stay left; this will put you on Trail 202.

About 0.25 mile past the junction, on the right, is a trail into the Brandon Lakes. The Brandon Lakes lie in two adjacent east-facing cirques on Quartzite Ridge. Both of the lakes' basins were burned over in 1969 in the Elk Creek Fire, which caused evacuation of Oregon Butte lookout. Quartzite Ridge is very rugged and supports a small population of mountain goats.

The trail now climbs slowly, staying on the ridge between Sheep Creek and Jumbo Canyon, and in another 0.25 mile, on the left, an easy-to-follow fisher's trail leads down from a broad saddle into Deer Lake.

From this junction the trail climbs moderately for 1 mile to the Teepee Flats Saddle. Keeping to the right at the intersection will put you on the trail that switchbacks to Oregon Butte lookout for a superb view of Salmon River Canyon and the Wallowa Mountains in Oregon. This lookout is one of the few wilderness lookouts still staffed every season. First established as a tent camp in the 1920s, it is on the National Historic Lookout Register.

This part of the Gospel–Hump Wilderness remains little used. The summer

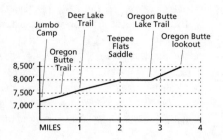

MaryAnn, coauthor of this hike, did fire watch on Oregon Butte lookout, she learned the meaning of solitude and loved it.

Options: Teepee Flats is a possible base for hikes into Round, Oregon Butte, and Fawn Lakes. About 200 yards before the trail levels off above Teepee Flats, a rather indistinct fisher's trail goes to Round Lake. It follows a small perennial stream down into a cirque, crosses the stream to avoid a bog, then drops through dense old-growth spruce to Round Lake. The lake is hard to find if you lose the trail but has excellent angling for big fish.

A bit more than half a mile past Teepee Flats, a trail on the left side drops fairly rapidly into the West Fork of Crooked Creek. Another 0.5 mile or so down the West Fork Trail, a distinct fisher's route leaves the main trail and continues to Oregon Butte Lake. This lake is rarely fished and even less frequently stocked. It has a few large fish, which are hard to catch. However, the lake is highly scenic, and the hike is well worth it.

Another trail follows Drumlumen Ridge out to Fawn Lake. The first 0.5 mile crosses a meadow and is indistinct. However, the trail is easy to find once it leaves the meadow if you stay on top of Drumlumen Ridge. The fishing at Fawn Lake is not as productive as at other lakes in the vicinity, but the area often has moose.

If you have a little extra time and are interested in old mines, the Jumbo Mine is a half-hour hike from the trailhead at Jumbo Canyon. To find the mine, follow Jumbo Canyon Trail (Trail 230) down a steep granite slope to where it reaches the valley floor. On the way down this hill, you can see the mine buildings on your left and to the north. Cross Jumbo Creek on the trail, and shortly thereafter you will see old mine tailings near the trail. Follow them uphill less than 0.25 mile from the trail, and you will come upon the old mine and mill buildings. Heavy machinery for processing is still evident at the mill site. How could such equipment possibly have been brought in with no road the last 0.5 mile? One old-timer in Grangeville explained that the machinery was skidded in from Grangeville in the middle of the winter over an old trail that followed the Clearwater–Salmon River divide. An elaborate winch-and-pulley system was devised to get the machinery down the cliffs in Jumbo Creek.

If you are interested in a short day hike into Shining Lake, which offers slow fishing for big fish, follow these directions. The junction for the trail into Shining Lake (Trail 228) is about 0.5 mile past the junction for Oregon Butte Trail. The trail is hard to find, but if you lose it, remember that the lake is about the same elevation as the saddle. It lies in an indistinct glacial cirque 1 mile due north of the saddle. It has a perennial outlet stream, and if all else fails you can follow the outlet up to the lake.

Other options in the area include Fish Lake (USGS Orogrande ID): Just after topping Orogrande Summit, descend 1.75 miles to the Fish Lake Trailhead. If you find the descent too rough, you can park at the summit. From the trailhead it's 2 miles to the lake, a excellent place to look for moose.

Oregon Butte Area

To Orogrande
(16 miles)

Jumbo
■ Mine

To Shining Lake
Butte Trail

13
P

Jumbo Creek

East Fork Sheep Creek

GOSPEL-HUMP WILDERNESS AREA

To Brandon
Lakes

Deer
Lake

Quartzite Ridge

Round
Lake

Teepee
Flats
Saddle

To Fawn Lake
(2.3 miles)

West Fork Crooked Creek

Bull Creek

Oregon
Butte
Lake

Oregon
Butte
8,464 ft.

NEZ
PERCE
NATIONAL
FOREST

Wild Horse Lake to North Pole Mountain (USGS North Pole ID): This trail climbs 1,500 feet in 2 miles along the eastern spur to the summit of this dramatic peak.

—Dan and MaryAnn Green

Miles and Directions

0.0 Start at the Jumbo Camp trailhead (7,200 feet).

0.5 Pick up the Oregon Butte Trail (7,440 feet).

0.8 On Quartzite Ridge, pass the Brandon Lakes Trail.

1.0 Pass the Deer Lake Trail (7,680 feet).

2.0 Reach Teepee Flats Saddle (8,000 feet).

2.8 Reach the junction of the West Fork Crooked Creek and Oregon Butte Lake Trails (8,000 feet). **Option:** Follow the West Fork Crooked Creek Trail 0.5 mile to where a fisher's trail cuts off right, up to Oregon Butte Lake.

3.5 Reach the Oregon Butte lookout (8,464 feet). Retrace your steps.

7.0 Arrive back at the trailhead.

GETTING INTO SHAPE

Unless you want to be sore—and possibly have to shorten your trip or vacation—be sure to get in shape before a big hike. If you're terribly out of shape, start a walking program early, preferably eight weeks in advance. Start with a fifteen-minute walk during your lunch hour or after work, and gradually increase your walking time to an hour. You should also increase your elevation gain. Walking briskly up hills really strengthens your leg muscles and gets your heart rate up. If you work in a storied office building, take the stairs instead of the elevator. If you prefer going to a gym, walk the treadmill or use a stair machine. You can further increase your strength and endurance by walking with a loaded backpack. Stationary exercises you might consider are squats, leg lifts, sit-ups, and push-ups. Other good ways to get in shape include biking, running, aerobics, and, of course, short hikes. Stretching before and after a hike keeps muscles flexible and helps avoid injuries.

Frank Church-River of No Return Wilderness

The story of how the River of No Return Wilderness came to be is not quite as romantic as its name. But it's sure to arouse passion and nostalgia in the hearts of the many who put their minds, mouths, and money into this labor of love. Although many concessions were made, this was a victory to which every major environmental group contributed. It was the last wilderness area established by Congress in Idaho. Since then, brown Idaho politicians have created a generation of wilderness drought.

At 2.4 million acres this is the largest wilderness area in the lower forty-eight states. Its birth as official wilderness in 1980 was breathtaking in that several decades of effort could have been lost. The Central Idaho Wilderness Act was passed in August 1980. In November 1980 the act's most important sponsor, Senator Frank Church, lost his bid for reelection. A scant three months' delay in passage could have sunk the whole ship.

Several years later, after Church's death, the name "River of No Return Wilderness" was modified by Congress with Church's name added. The name of Frank Church, a man of great achievement in American history, on the wilderness area may be remembered when other deeds have been forgotten.

The River of No Return is the Salmon River, declared unnavigable by explorers Lewis and Clark back in about 1804. It remains that way except for recreational navigation: It provides some of the best whitewater boating in the world.

The wilderness itself comprises the former Idaho and Salmon River Breaks Primitive Areas and adjacent wildlands previously unprotected. The need to protect the wildlands of central Idaho was recognized way back in 1931 when, on its own initiative, the forest service established the Idaho Primitive Area. This administratively protected area included a million acres of rugged Salmon River Mountains out of an area of wild country four times that size existing in one vast mountain fastness.

A "primitive area" was a temporary classification, however, and in the late 1930s the forest service began to study and reclassify the various primitive areas around the nation with the permanent status of wilderness. Unfortunately, rather than keeping a bit of America wild forever, the reclassification often turned out to be a method of stripping an area of all potential merchantable timber and "protecting" the rest—the rocks. "We will allow no logging above timberline," assured one regional forester.

Conservationists began to seek a more reliable form of protecting the wild country than the old method of administrative decree. Although many forest service leaders were strong proponents of wilderness, conservationists realized that something stronger was needed—something that would be difficult to rescind. The answer was to pass a law guaranteeing some lands by US statute permanently as wilderness.

For many years, the battle to create a national wilderness system was fought in Congress. Progress was slow, but in 1964 a federal bill creating the National Wilderness Preservation System was signed into law. Senator Church was a cosponsor and a leading supporter of the Wilderness Act.

In 1963, the year just before the Wilderness Act, the forest service had, by administrative fiat, reclassified much of the 1.8-million Selway–Bitterroot Primitive Area, just north of Idaho Primitive Area. While the resulting 1.2-million-acre Selway–Bitterroot Wilderness was the largest in the nation at the time, hundreds of thousands of acres of forest, canyon, and mountain meadow had first been torn out of the primitive area, including Elk Summit, the Magruder Corridor, and Meadow Creek. Twenty years later Congress made the Magruder Corridor part of the Selway–Bitterroot Wilderness, and conservationists still battle to keep Elk Summit and Meadow Creek (see Hike 12, Meadow Creek) off the chopping block.

Conservationists redoubled their efforts after passage of the Wilderness Act. The National Wilderness Preservation System at first included only those areas already classified as "wilderness" by the forest service. However, additions could be made. The remaining unreclassified primitive areas were to be studied for wilderness classification over a ten-year period. Recommendations for their futures were to be made to Congress. Among the areas in Idaho, this review included the Idaho and Salmon River Breaks Primitive Areas.

In 1972 the 200,000-acre Sawtooth Primitive Area was successfully reclassified as the Sawtooth Wilderness, but the great Idaho Primitive Area and its neighbor, the Salmon River Breaks Primitive Area, totaling 1.4 million acres, were saved for last.

In 1974 the forest service began to solicit public opinion to determine the future of these areas. Options ranged from protecting the entire 1.4 million acres of the two primitive areas down to protecting nothing at all. Losing any part of the official primitive areas seemed, in the words of one Idaho conservationist, like choosing which of your children would live and which would die.

But the future of the paper primitive areas wasn't the only worry. These areas were surrounded by another million acres of orphan wildland that had been protected only by their inhospitality to development. Environmentalists had a brainstorm, one that would save both. All the existing wildlands in central Idaho, those with pedigree and those without, should be protected.

This idea was embodied in the 2.4-million-acre River of No Return Wilderness bill. The bill was drawn up and presented in public meetings. From one end of the state to the other, in public hearing halls packed to the rafters and hot with debate and histrionics, the contenders made their cases—the 500,000-acre "roadless recreation area" proposed by the Boise-Cascade Corporation versus the 2.4-million-acre bill for a River of No Return Wilderness, along with the middle-of-the-road forest service option of 1.4 million acres. Environmentalists turned the tide. When the results were in, the 2.4-million-acre option was overwhelmingly endorsed by the citizens of Idaho. Finally then, in 1980, this public support convinced enough politicians that almost all of the 2.4 million acres (more than 3,500 square miles) became formally protected wilderness.

The individual victories in the bill's passage were many. Among lands now protected, in addition to the former primitive areas, were the headwaters of Camas Creek

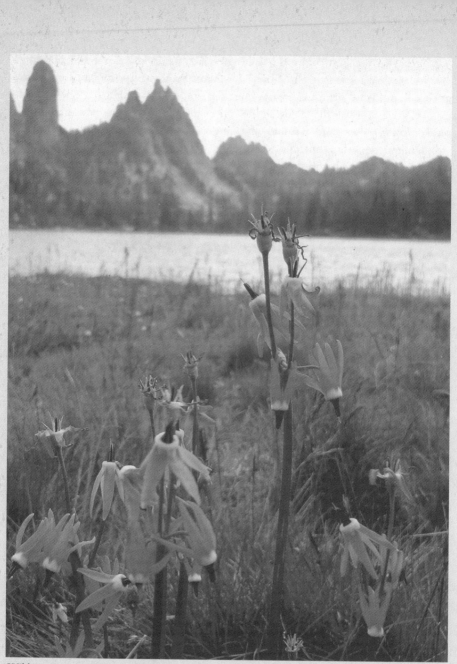

Wild gentions. PHOTO BY JOSH KEELEY

and Warm Springs Creek. The airy upper reaches of Loon Creek were included as a detached portion of the wilderness. Sulphur Creek and Elk Creek, important spawning streams for salmon and nurseries for elk, were saved from below-cost logging. Marsh Creek and lower Bear Valley Creek were included, making the headwaters of the Middle Fork of the Salmon sacrosanct from off-road vehicles and other internal combustion intrusions. Poker and Ayer Meadows, slated for noisy auto campground futures, were instead kept for the elk and sandhill crane. The entire watershed of the Middle Fork, both inside the wilderness and out, was withdrawn from dredge mining.

Bitter compromises were made, too. The lower portion of the Bighorn Crags and the Panther Creek breaks were made part of the wilderness, but cobalt mining was declared the dominant use. This came after a Canadian mining company, in a fit of altruism no doubt, mounted a public relations campaign highlighting the risk that the United States would run out of this "strategic" mineral. Subsequent to this concession, the foreign firm lobbied for a government subsidy to make cobalt mining profitable. To date, no mining has taken place.

Small miners were allowed to continue working low-value diggings in Big Creek, the Middle Fork's main tributary. Mining was allowed on Thunder Mountain, adjacent to the west boundary of the wilderness. Since that time, several bad spills of mining waste have found their way into adjacent wilderness streams.

With the exception of the subdued topography of Elk Creek on the south end of the wilderness and the vast plateau called Chamberlain Basin, the Frank Church–River of No Return Wilderness is a sea with waves of one steep mountain ridge after another. The major canyons of the Middle Fork and main Salmon twist through the mountains, in places almost 7,000 feet deep! This is deeper than the Grand Canyon.

Long ago, a vast body of molten rock pushed up under central Idaho. It never reached the surface as lava. Instead, it cooled and crystallized into a complex of granitelike rocks—a batholith. Millions of years later this batholith was exposed to the elements and carved by wind, water, thawing and freezing, and glaciers into mountains and canyons. The rocks of the Idaho Batholith, one of the world's largest such igneous intrusions, underlie much of central Idaho, including much of the Frank Church–River of No Return Wilderness. When roads are blasted into its mountains, the soft, coarse-grained rock washes into the rivers, choking them with sand.

Most environmentally aware citizens are familiar with the Idaho Batholith. What is not so well known is that most of the southeastern part of the wilderness, as well as Big Creek, is instead a pile of volcanic rock, part of the vast Challis Volcanic Field. These mountains, too, are fragile with erosion after disturbance. Here the result is cloudy water as devastating to fish as the clear but sand-clogged streams from disturbed batholithic soils.

The undisturbed mountains and canyons of the wilderness are rich in wildlife, including elk, bighorn sheep, mountain goats, mule and white-tailed deer, cougar, black bear, and moose. Lynx, fisher, and wolverines exist in smaller numbers. The reintroduction of the wolf to central Idaho in 1995 and 1996 restored a top predator. The only missing large animal is the grizzly bear. As this edition goes to press, a furious battle is being waged over restoration of the grizzly to its Idaho home. The abundance of wildlife is due not to the area's fertility as much as to its untouched nature, especially the deep canyons that provide rare, undisturbed winter range for wild animals.

14 Bighorn Crags: Reflection Lake

This part of the Bighorn Crags hosts beautiful fishing lakes amid rugged scenery. There are fewer visitors than at the northern end of the Bighorn Crags.

Start: 35 linear miles west of Salmon, Idaho
Type of hike: Out-and-back
Total distance: 26 miles round-trip from Crags Campground
Approximate hiking time: 4-plus days
Difficulty: Moderate from the junction with Ship Island Lake Trail, 6.5 miles from Crags Campground
Best season: August
Trail surface: Dirt and rock
Land status: Frank Church–River of No Return Wilderness; Salmon–Challis National Forest
Canine compatibility: Not allowed
Fees and permits: None
Maps: USGS Hoodoo Meadows and Mt. McGuire ID

Trail contact: Salmon-Cobalt Ranger District; (208) 756-5200
Special considerations: As with the hike to Ship Island Lake (Hike 15), the access roads and probably part of this trail burned in the Clear Creek Fire of 2000. Check with the forest service for current information on rehabilitation of the access roads and trails. The area remained closed to recreational entry through the end of 2000. There is no reliable water for the first 4.7 miles.
Parking and trailhead facilities: Crags Campground is a large, developed fee site. There is a nearby stream, but don't count on potable water.

Finding the trailhead: There are two possible routes to the Bighorn Crags Campground and trailhead. From Salmon, drive 5 miles south on US 93 to the signed Williams Creek Road (FR 021) on the right (west). This good, 12-mile road climbs over the Salmon River Range for about 3,000 feet to the junction with Panther Creek Road (FR 055). At the junction turn left (south) and drive 10.5 miles up Panther Creek until you reach Porphyry Creek Road.

From Challis, drive 9 miles north on US 93 to the signed Morgan Creek Road turnoff. Turn left and follow Morgan Creek Road for 19.6 miles (pavement, then good gravel) to Morgan Creek Summit, where the road becomes Panther Creek Road. Drive north down Panther Creek for 14 miles to the signed turnoff at Porphyry Creek.

Porphyry Creek Road (FR 112) is graded and climbs 2,000 feet in 6 miles to a four-way junction. Take FR 113 to the right (north), and continue 8 miles to FR 114, which leads to Crags Campground in 2.5 more miles. You will have climbed another 800 feet and passed, on the right, the turnoff to FR 167. (Once the road has climbed out of Porphyry Creek, it keeps near an 8,500-foot ridgetop just 300 feet outside the wilderness boundary. The Blackbird Mountain USGS quad is useful for identifying sites from this impressive, sometimes white-knuckle road.) GPS: N45 6.25' / W114 31.47'

The Hike

Of the two Bighorn Crags hikes in this book, this is the less popular—though equally beautiful—traverse to the southwestern portion of the crags.

View from the pass above Welcome Lake. PHOTO BY LUKE KRATZ

As with the trail to Ship Island, begin at Crags Campground near Golden Trout Lake and climb the ridgeline, passing by Cathedral Rock and continuing to the junction with the Clear Creek and Waterfall Trails at 4.5 miles. On this trip, however, unlike the hike to Ship Island Lake, continue to the left on the Waterfall Trail to Welcome Lake at the trail junction at 7.0 miles.

At 6.5 miles from the trailhead, you come to a trail junction. The path to the right leads up into a tight cirque basin that shelters Harbor and Wilson Lakes, then over Fishfin Ridge and down to Birdbill and Gentian Lakes. Go left, following the sign to Welcome Lake. Welcome Lake is surrounded by peaks more than 9,500 feet high. This shallow, beautiful lake basin is filled with lush grass and marsh. It has plenty of campsites but is usually devoid of fish due to winter-kill. Mosquitoes can be a real threat here in the early summer, so be prepared to fend them off with repellent. As you approach Welcome Lake, a trail junction marks the way to Reflection Lake. This trail does not appear on USGS quadrangles. Take this trail.

The trail switchbacks six times in 0.5 mile up the steep ridge to the southeast to climb to an elevation of 9,000 feet. Follow the ridge to drop down a moderate grade. The trail takes three long switchbacks down, totaling nearly 3 miles in length. The mammoth basin below to the west is a beautiful timbered margin along the

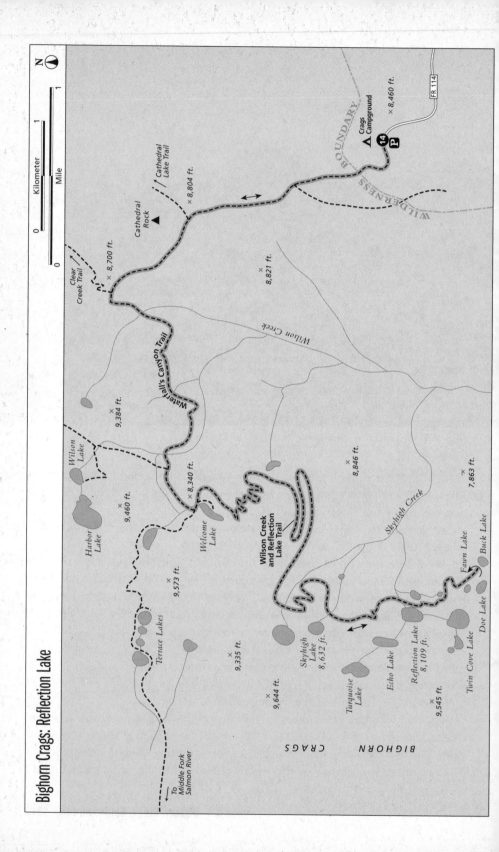

Bighorn Crags: Reflection Lake

N

0 Kilometer 1

0 Mile 1

Clear Creek Trail

× 8,700 ft.

Cathedral Rock ▲

Cathedral Lake Trail

× 8,804 ft.

× 8,460 ft.

Crags Campground ▲

14 🅿

FR 114

BOUNDARY

WILDERNESS

8,821 ft.

Wilson Creek

Waterfall's Canyon Trail

9,384 ft.

Wilson Lake

× 8,340 ft.

Harbor Lake

9,460 ft.

Welcome Lake

Wilson Creek and Reflection Lake Trail

8,846 ft.

Skyhigh Creek

7,863 ft.

9,573 ft.

Terrace Lakes

9,335 ft.

Skyhigh Lake 8,632 ft.

Buck Lake

Faun Lake

9,644 ft.

Turquoise Lake

Echo Lake

Reflection Lake 8,109 ft.

Doe Lake

Twin Cove Lake

9,545 ft.

BIGHORN CRAGS

To Middle Fork Salmon River

celebrated Bighorn Crags ridgeline. Eight lakes dot the nappy pine quilt of trees—Skyhigh, Turquoise, Echo, Reflection, Twin Cove, Fawn, Doe, and Buck. The area is also alive with wildlife, primarily deer, elk, goats, and bighorn sheep.

At mile 10 cross Skyhigh Creek, just below Skyhigh Lake. Descend, and gently switchback through the basin. Cross another small creek and follow the trail uphill to Reflection Lake at 12 miles. Reflection Lake is a good base camp. It contains numerous cutthroat and rainbow trout. The trail continues for another mile to Buck Lake and nearby Doe and Fawn Lakes. You can reach more lakes via cross-country ridge travel.

You may be able to get into this country by mid-July. It remains open until about mid-September. August is probably the best time.

—Philip Blomquist

Miles and Directions

0.0 Start at the Crags Campground trailhead (8,400 feet).

2.0 Pass the Frog Meadows side trail (8,667 feet).

3.5 Pass the Cathedral Lake cutoff (8,800 feet).

4.5 Take the Waterfalls Canyon Trail (8,720 feet).

4.7 Cross a stream (8,200 feet).

6.5 Take the Wilson Creek and Reflection Lake Trail (8,200 feet).

7.0 Reach Welcome Lake (8,332 feet).

7.5 Top the pass (9,000 feet).

10.0 Cross of Skyhigh Creek (8,500 feet).

12.0 Reach the Reflection Lake base camp (8,109 feet).

13.0 Arrive at Buck Lake (8,100 feet). Retrace your steps.

26.0 Arrive back at the trailhead.

15 Bighorn Crags: Ship Island Lake

This is one of the most spectacular areas in the Frank Church–River of No Return Wilderness. Witness stunning views of Ship Island Lake and the breaks country of the Middle Fork of the Salmon River, with spires, knobs, and the huge monoliths of rugged granite mountains. Many lakes have good fishing. The north and west sides of the Bighorn Crags are especially noted for bighorn sheep.

Start: 35 linear miles west of Salmon, Idaho
Type of hike: Loop to Harbor Lake
Distance: 22 miles
Approximate hiking time: 3-plus days
Difficulty: Moderate from the junction with Ship Island Lake Trail, 6.5 miles from Crags Campground
Best season: August
Trail surface: Dirt and rock
Land status: Frank Church–River of No Return Wilderness; Salmon–Challis National Forest
Canine compatibility: Not allowed
Fees and permits: None
Maps: USGS Hoodoo Meadows and Mt. McGuire ID; Frank Church–River of No Return Wilderness North Half forest map
Trail contact: Salmon–Cobalt Ranger District, (208) 756-5200

Special considerations: Be prepared for foul weather, including snow in August. Neither the USGS quads nor the forest maps show updated versions of many trails in the Bighorn Crags. Do not attempt Fishfin Pass until you're sure it's clear of horse traffic. When I hiked the trail in 2012, I noticed that the access roads had been slightly reworked due to the Clear Creek Fire of 2000. Check with the forest service for current information on rehabilitation of the access roads and trails. There is no reliable water for the first 4.7 miles.
Parking and trailhead facilities: Crags Campground is a large, developed fee site. There is a nearby stream, but don't count on potable water.

Finding the trailhead: There are two possible routes to the Bighorn Crags Campground and trailhead. From Salmon, drive 5 miles south on US 93 to the signed Williams Creek Road (FR 021) on the right (west). This good, 12-mile road climbs over the Salmon River Range for about 3,000 feet to the junction with Panther Creek Road (FR 055). At the junction turn left (south) and drive 10.5 miles up Panther Creek until you reach Porphyry Creek Road.

From Challis, drive 9 miles north on US 93 to the signed Morgan Creek Road turnoff. Turn left and follow Morgan Creek Road for 19.6 miles (pavement, then good gravel) to Morgan Creek Summit, where the road becomes Panther Creek Road. Drive north down Panther Creek for 14 miles to the signed turnoff at Porphyry Creek.

Porphyry Creek Road (FR 112) is graded and climbs 2,000 feet in 6 miles to a four-way junction. Take FR 113 to the right (north), and continue 8 miles to FR 114, which leads to Crags Campground in 2.5 more miles. You will have climbed another 800 feet and passed, on the right, the turnoff to FR 167. (Once the road has climbed out of Porphyry Creek, it keeps near an 8,500-foot ridgetop just 300 feet outside the wilderness boundary. The Blackbird Mountain USGS quad is useful for identifying sites from this impressive, sometimes white-knuckle road.) GPS: N45 6.25' / W114 31.47'

The Hike

Milton's words in *Paradise Lost* best describe this popular hiking and horse-packing area: "Heaven's high towers." It is a must for those who enjoy major excursions.

The hike to Ship Island Lake can be very demanding, depending on which route you take. If thunderstorms threaten, it's better to take Waterfalls Canyon Trail rather than the ridge route (see Options). The trail described here begins by climbing 500 feet along the ridge overlooking the basin of Golden Trout Lake, where cutthroat have displaced the California goldens. The climb continues for just less than a mile and 500 feet, then descends to a junction at the 2-mile point. From this ridgeline, you can see in the distant south the 9,045-foot granite Sugarloaf monolith.

The trail to the left (south) leads to Frog Meadows and Yellowjacket Lake. The trail on the right (northeast) is a horse route. Take the trail in the middle (northwest).

Now you climb again, 250 feet to the ridgeline. Below, on the left, is the deep Wilson Creek drainage. In the distance ahead is the Crags divide. At 3.5 miles, reach the base of another monolith called Cathedral Rock. Here a sign reads Cathedral Lake and points to the right. The lake is reached by a 0.3-mile route and offers an excellent view of Cathedral Rock and fishing for rainbow and cutthroat trout. Continuing on the main trail, begin a mile-long contour along the top of Wilson Creek Canyon. After this contour, 4.5 miles from the trailhead, you reach the junction of Waterfalls Canyon Trail on the left.

Waterfalls Canyon Trail descends in a long grade to Wilson Canyon. In 0.25 mile you come to the first and biggest stream. Although the map shows a second perennial stream in another 0.5 mile, this stream was almost dry in mid-August in a year of normal precipitation.

The trail continues for 1.75 miles west through forest, then turns north to head up Wilson Canyon. The trail to the left at the fork here, at the 6.5-mile point, leads left (west) to Welcome and Heart Lakes (see Hike 14, Bighorn Crags: Reflection Lake). The USGS map is off a bit here; just take the right fork and go north up to the headwaters of Wilson Creek. The trail gains about 400 feet in elevation as it tracks along the canyon rim about 100 feet above the creek (unlike the map, which shows it in the creek bottom). Follow the trail through this high alpine forest, where it gets lost a little way north of Peak 9,460. The trail, once found, is broad and obvious, leading to

Harbor and Wilson Lakes from Crags Trail. PHOTO BY JOSH KEELEY

Wilson and Harbor Lakes. Here, the USGS quad is seriously wrong. It puts the trail in the canyon bottom and crossing below the outlet of Wilson Lake. (There is a 120-foot waterfall at the outlet, a lovely meadow, and a headwall of spires and crags.) But this won't get you to Fishfin Pass without a struggle. Instead, stick to Harbor Lake Trail, which will take you up to the pass.

The trail down Fishfin Pass is along a vertical cliff and quite narrow. It spirals down about 280 feet on the right side of the canyon, then crosses to the left side. We could smell the carcass of a horse that had fallen from the pass. There is not enough room on Fishfin for hikers and equestrians to pass safely. At the bottom, you cross to the other side of the canyon, just above the creek, and gain about 80 feet to contour along the trail cut in the rock. From the pass, you can look down into Mirrow Lake but cannot see Gentian and Birdbill Lakes until you round the bend and rise again to drop down the rocky saddle into these lakes. They have small rainbow trout.

Near Gentian Lake you'll find an outhouse and a hitching post. The campsites in this high lake basin are heavily used, and this site is a major trail intersection. The northern route, recommended for horse traffic, comes in here.

Beyond Gentian Lake the trail climbs 160 feet on a low, slow horse trail and a traverse over the ridge into the huge Ship Island basin. At the top of the ridge, you can see both Airplane Lake and Ship Island Lake, as well as the massive granite cliffs backdropping the latter. It's about 2.5 miles to the eastern shore of Ship Island Lake, and a 1,000-foot drop from the pass. The trail in places is very eroded, exposing bare bones of rocks. The descent, outside of the 400 feet to Airplane Lake, is in heavy forest. (Horse traffic is not allowed beyond Airplane Lake.) Both lakes offer fishing for rainbow and cutthroat trout. From Airplane Lake, you can cut cross-country to Shoban and Sheepeater Lakes. It's 0.25 mile and a 200-foot climb to Shoban and another 0.5 mile and 250-foot climb to Sheepeater. Both have fishing.

The view at Ship Island Lake itself will take your breath away for a couple of months. The basin holding the lake is large and beautiful, hemmed in by rugged ridges of nearly 10,000 feet. You can hike down and around the east side of Ship Island Lake to its outlet. All told, it is about 1 mile to the lake outlet. The trail is at times faint and not maintained. The going is somewhat slow due to a huge amount of deadfall, the faintness of the trail, and the crossing of a boulder field.

The country on the right of the outlet is very rugged, and the trail, such as it is, through the smooth sheets of granite, is marked by only an occasional cairn. Stay to the right side on the rocks while you drop some in elevation to round the bend to the view down Ship Island Creek Canyon. At the outlet of the lake, immense granite spires line the canyon walls, and here Ship Island Creek begins to tumble down a steep, trailless canyon. It drops 4,500 feet in 5 miles to the Middle Fork of the Salmon River. Few have ever descended this canyon.

Options: To take the ridge trail from the Waterfalls Canyon Trail junction, continue for a short distance past the junction, making a climb of 120 feet. You will see Clear Creek Trail on the right. Clear Creek is the large, pristine drainage to the northeast, heavily fought over by the timber industry before it was included in the Frank Church–River of No Return Wilderness. Ironically, the Clear Creek Fire began in this general area. The fire burned 216,000 acres. First detected July 10, 2000, it was finally declared 100 percent contained on October 14. The 216,000 acres is hardly a total burn. Only 10 percent was judged to have been a severe burn. Many parts suffered ground fires only, and many areas inside its perimeter did not burn at all. Nevertheless, it was a humongous fire.

Pass this trail by unless you want to investigate. Instead, take the trail that continues climbing along the ridgeline. It is not on the Mt. McGuire topographic quadrangle or the Salmon National Forest map, but it is shown on the Frank Church–River of No Return forest map. Following this trail, climb up and around a granite knob of over 9,200 feet; then drop to a small saddle. From here you traverse over to Fishfin Pass. Do not take this demanding route if thunderstorms threaten. If you take this route, it is about 6 miles before you reach the first water.

—Jackie Johnson Maughan and Phil Blomquist

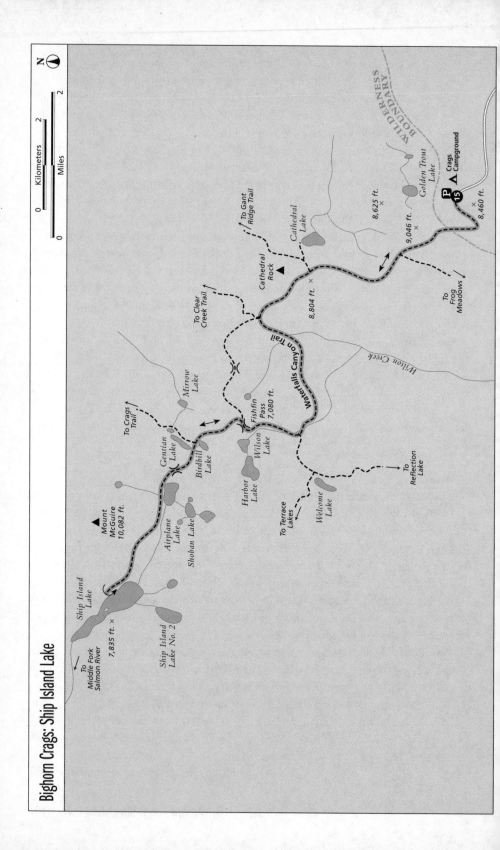

Bighorn Crags: Ship Island Lake

N

Kilometers
0   2

Miles
0   2

To
Middle Fork
Salmon River

Ship Island
Lake
7,835 ft. ×

Ship Island
Lake No. 2

Mount
McGuire
10,082 ft.

Airplane
Lake

Shoban Lake

To Crags
Trail

Gentian
Lake

Birdbill
Lake

Mirrow
Lake

To Clear
Creek Trail

Harbor
Lake

Wilson
Lake

Fishfin
Pass
7,080 ft.

Waterfalls Canyon Trail

Wilson Creek

To
Reflection
Lake

Welcome
Lake

To Terrace
Lakes

8,804 ft. ×

Cathedral
Rock

To Gant
Ridge Trail

Cathedral
Lake

8,625 ft.
×

9,046 ft.
×

Golden Trout
Lake

WILDERNESS
BOUNDARY

To Frog
Meadows

P
15
Crags
Campground

8,460 ft.
×

Miles and Directions

0.0 Start at the Crags Campground trailhead (8,400 feet).

2.0 Pass the Frog Meadows side trail (8,667 feet).

3.5 Pass the Cathedral Lake cutoff (8,800 feet).

4.5 Take the Waterfalls Canyon Trail (8,720 feet).

4.7 Cross a stream (8,200 feet).

6.5 Reach the Wilson Creek and Welcome Lake Trail junction (8,200 feet). Go right (north) toward Wilson Lake.

7.5 Pass Wilson Lake (8,920 feet).

8.0 Cross Fishfin Pass (9,000 feet).

9.0 Pass Birdbill Lake (8,680 feet).

10.0 Reach Airplane Lake (8,402 feet).

11.0 Reach Ship Island Lake (7,835 feet). Retrace your steps.

22.0 Arrive back at the trailhead.

16 Sheep Hill Area

Sheep Hill boasts mountain lakes and fishing with overviews of the Frank Church–River of No Return and Selway–Bitterroot Wildernesses.

Start: 80 road miles southeast of Grangeville, Idaho, and 72 road miles west of Conner, Montana, on the northern rim of the Frank Church–River of No Return Wilderness.
Type of hike: Out-and-back
Distance: 19 miles to Center Creek Lakes and back; other options possible
Approximate hiking time: 3–4 days
Difficulty: Moderately strenuous due to elevation loss and gain climbing into and out of lake basins
Best season: Mid-July–mid-September
Trail surface: Dirt and rock
Land status: Frank Church–River of No Return Wilderness; Nez Perce National Forest
Canine compatibility: Not allowed in within wilderness boundaries

Fees and permits: None
Maps: USGS Sheep Hill, Spread Creek Point, and Sabe Mountain ID; Frank Church–River of No Return Wilderness North Half forest map; Nez Perce National Forest map
Trail contact: Elk City Ranger Station, Red River Ranger District; (208) 926-4258
Special considerations: Check fire and weather conditions. The high-elevation access road is sometimes impassable into July and even August, and snow comes early in the fall. Chains and four-wheel drive may be needed. The road is rough, mountainous, and winding, with few places to pass other vehicles. It is not recommended for trailers and is definitely not accessible to RVs. Top off your gas tank.

Finding the trailhead: Road access is over the Magruder Corridor, also known as the Montana Road. It connects Red River Ranger Station on the west with Conner, Montana, on the east via a primitive, one-lane, 101-mile-long road. All major points along the road are well marked, perhaps as a preventive measure against years of conservationists' attempts to close it. If this closure had come to pass, the Selway–Bitterroot Wilderness and River of No Return Wilderness would have been joined in a continuous wilderness of mind-boggling size: over 3.5 million acres.

The Montana access leaves US 93 at Conner, where you turn west up the West Fork of the Bitterroot River on paved Road 473. The route crosses two major rivers and two mountain ranges before reaching the trailhead. After 13 miles on Road 473, you come to a junction on the right leading 18 paved miles to Nez Perce Pass to cross the Bitterroot Divide. A high-standard gravel road leads 15 miles from the pass to the Magruder Crossing bridge over the Selway River, a popular boat-launch site. From here the road becomes one lane, although with a good rock base. It climbs 3,000 feet and 12 miles to skirt Salmon Mountain. From here, it is 14 miles to the Dry Saddle Trailhead. An outstanding view of the Bitterroot Divide and deep forest are the redeeming qualities of this 72-mile passage.

From the west side out of Grangeville, take ID 13 west 9 miles to ID 14 on the right (south). From here, it is 31 miles to Elk City. Before Elk City, turn right onto paved FR 222 and continue 13 miles to Red River Ranger Station. Half a mile south of the station is a large sign warning of the hazards of driving the Montana Road (FR 468). Turn left. The road climbs steadily up the Salmon River–South Fork Divide to Mountain Meadows for a total of 7 miles. This area was scheduled for a controversial timber sale that would have destroyed prime elk summer range and caused untold damage to the pristine watershed of Meadow Creek, the largest tributary of the Selway River. This sale was dropped due to an administrative appeal led by the Idaho Environmental Council.

From Mountain Meadows, the road gradually drops into the headwaters of Bargamin Creek, passing Granite Springs and Poet Creek Campgrounds. It arrives, in 20.5 miles, at the Dry Saddle Trailhead. You will have traveled a total of 80 miles from Grangeville. GPS: N45 40.63' / W114 59.62'

Parking and trailhead facilities: The large, gravel Dry Saddle Trailhead has horse loading and a pit toilet, but no water. Developed campgrounds west of the trailhead are Poet Creek (6 miles), with four sites, pit toilets, no water; Granite Springs (11 miles), with four sites, pit toilet, potable water. Developed sites to the east are Magruder Crossing Campground (22 miles), with four sites, pit toilet, no potable water; and Deep Creek Campground (27 miles), with three sites, pit toilet, no potable water.

The Hike

This was the last place in the lower forty-eight to be mapped by the US Geological Survey, and good topo maps only became available in 1979. An up-and-down ridgeline hike positions you to drop into the fourteen lakes nestled below. Drops into the lakes are between 300 to 700 feet. Old and new fires have left their marks as part of the ecology of this region.

Spruce, subalpine fir, and whitebark pine cover most of the ridges, and none of the trail is above timberline. Wildlife, wildflowers, mountain lakes, and high-rent vistas make this trip worth the long road access. Bighorn sheep, black bear, elk, deer, and golden-mantled ground squirrels are common. Wolves do inhabit the area but are seen only occasionally. In mid-July and early August, the open ridges are covered with wildflowers, including bear grass, mountain pinks, penstemon, lupine, Indian paintbrush, heath, and shooting stars.

The main trail (Forest 575) follows the divide between Bargamin Creek and Sabe Creek to the junction to Sheep Hill lookout on the right or Bear Point on the left. The grades are not steep, but the trail is heavily used by pack stock in the hunting season. It is very well defined, and all intersections are signed.

Beginning with a slow drop into a saddle overlooking the Trilby Lakes, the first mile goes through timber. Trilby Lakes is a popular, although not especially good, fishing day hike, so expect to see other people.

At the Trilby Lakes junction, the trail climbs a moderate 350 feet to Spread Creek Point. Just before the final pitch, an unmarked fishing trail into Spread Point Lake

The Trilby Lakes. PHOTO BY LUKE KRATZ

meets the main trail at a high saddle. Spread Point Lake, a large lake, lies on the west side of the ridge. Several meadows at its outlet provide good big-game conditions.

From Spread Creek Point on, the trail rises into the open and becomes more scenic. Spread Creek Point, once a fire lookout, provides a good 360-degree view of the surrounding country. Beyond Spread Creek Point, the trail stays on top of the divide for about a mile to where the main ridge meets a spur coming up from Sabe Creek. Here, two side trails leave the ridge. Ring Creek Point Trail leads down into Sabe Creek, 5,000 vertical feet below the ridge, and into some beautiful country that rarely sees anybody. The other is a trail for fishers, which climbs down toward Saddle Lake and peters out.

At the Ring Creek Point Trail junction, the main trail begins its descent into Lake Creek Lakes. This drop is the longest on the hike but is well graded. Carefully observe the location of the three lakes on your way down if you plan to visit them, since they're in thick forest with no connecting trails. At the bottom of this grade is a sign marking a fishing trail that leads 0.25 mile down to the upper lake.

Lake Creek Lakes are heavily used, and you can expect to meet other parties. The upper lake generally produces the largest fish, while the lower lake, which has good natural reproduction, is the easiest from which to catch them.

At the Lake Creek junction, the main trail climbs 300 feet to a low saddle dividing Lake Creek from Rattlesnake Creek. Don't let the name throw you; all the rattlesnakes are at Rattlesnake Creek's lower elevations. At the saddle you'll meet trails

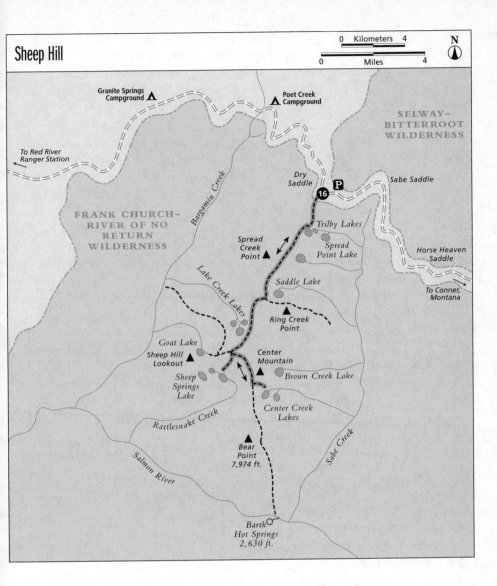

0   Kilometers   4

0   Miles   4

N

Granite Springs
Campground

Poet Creek
Campground

SELWAY–
BITTERROOT
WILDERNESS

To Red River
Ranger Station

Bargamin Creek

Dry
Saddle

16 P

Sabe Saddle

FRANK CHURCH–
RIVER OF NO
RETURN
WILDERNESS

Trilby Lakes

Spread
Creek
Point

Spread
Point Lake

Horse Heaven
Saddle

Lake Creek Lakes

Saddle Lake

To Conner,
Montana

Ring Creek
Point

Goat Lake

Sheep Hill
Lookout

Center
Mountain

Brown Creek Lake

Sheep
Springs
Lake

Center Creek
Lakes

Rattlesnake Creek

Sabe Creek

Bear
Point
7,974 ft.

Salmon River

Barth
Hot Springs
2,630 ft.

leading to three destinations: Bear Point to the left, Sheep Hill to the right, and Rattlesnake Lake in the middle.

Bear Point Trail climbs through open parks and clumps of whitebark pine to a saddle overlooking Ring Creek. Just past the saddle is a sign marking a fishing trail to Brown Creek Lake. This trail is faint and hard to follow in places. It continues around the face of Center Mountain, then generally follows the inlet down to the lake.

About 0.5 mile past the Brown Creek Lake sign, a well-marked trail leads down to the Center Creek Lakes. These lakes are also hard to find, but you can improve your odds by walking an extra couple hundred yards out Bear Point Ridge to where you can see them both.

After the Center Creek Lakes trail junction, it is another 1.5 miles to Bear Point. Bear Point offers a spectacular view of the Salmon River, 5,300 feet below. The area around Bear Point burned to sterile earth in 1989. As mentioned, wildfires are natural to this country, and so are bears. You may encounter both. Part of Center Creek burned in the big fire year of 2000.

Options: Back at the three-way fork above and south of the Lake Creek Lakes, the right fork heads toward Sheep Hill. It climbs gradually along a ridge for 320 feet and 0.9 mile to 8,000-foot Deadman's Saddle, where it meets a side trail dropping into Bargamin Creek. From Deadman's Saddle climb another 400 feet and 0.75 mile to the active Sheep Hill lookout. Near the lookout is a spring sometimes frequented by bighorn sheep. From this lookout you can see four small lakes surrounding Sheep Hill. All have fish, but they aren't as productive as some of the larger lakes. A good trail leads from the lookout down to Sheep Springs Lake, but the route into Goat Lake does not have a trail.

To access Rattlesnake Lake from the three forks, take the middle fork. It starts out as a very well-worn track that drops 0.5 mile directly into an outfitter's camp. From here the unmaintained trail becomes very faint. You'll have to pay close attention to blazes cut into the trees. It contours along an east-facing slope to end with a 150-foot drop to the lake. Be cautious not to lose your elevation as you walk along the east-facing slope. If you do, you'll drop down into Rattlesnake Creek and end up headed toward the Salmon River. Once you get to Rattlesnake Lake, you may wish to explore Upper Rattlesnake Lake. To do so, follow the inlet on the northwest side of lower Rattlesnake for about 0.5 mile.

—H. W. W. "Blue Moose" Johnson

Miles and Directions

0.0 Start at the Dry Saddle Trailhead (7,720 feet).

1.0 Pass the Trilby Lakes Trail (7,560 feet).

2.5 Pass the Spread Point Lake Trail (7,720 feet).

3.0 Pass Spread Creek Point (8,190 feet).

5.0 Pass the Saddle Lake fishing trail (8,000 feet).

5.2 Pass the Ring Creek Point Trail (8,000 feet).

6.5 Pass the Lake Creek Lakes Trail (7,560 feet).

7.0 Pass the Sheep Hill Lookout Trail (7,520 feet).

9.0 Take the Center Creek Lakes Trail (8,000 feet).

9.5 Reach Center Creek Lakes. **Option:** Hike 1 mile to Bear Point (7,974 feet). Retrace your steps.

19.0 Arrive back at the trailhead.

17 Sleeping Deer Mountain

In this high mountain wilderness, you'll find lovely scenery, nice camping, and decent fishing in small, subalpine cirque lakes. There is a long but very scenic and inspiring road trip to the trailhead.

Start: At the end of a long improved dirt road deep in the Frank Church–River of No Return Wilderness, about 39 road miles from Challis

Type of hike: Out-and-back

Distance: 11 miles

Approximate hiking time: 2 days

Difficulty: Moderately easy to Cache Creek Lakes, except in the early summer. Moderate to the more distant West Fork Lakes.

Best season: Mid-July–mid-September

Trail surface: Dirt and rock

Land status: Frank Church–River of No Return Wilderness; Salmon–Challis National Forest

Canine compatibility: Not allowed

Fees and permits: None

Maps: USGS Sleeping Deer Mountain ID; Frank Church–River of No Return Wilderness

South Half forest map; Middle Fork, Yankee Fork, Challis, and Lost River Ranger Districts/ Challis National Forest map

Trail contact: Challis Ranger District; (208) 879-4100

Special considerations: Access road is suitable for trucks, marginal for sedans, and unsuitable for RVs and horse trailers. Check weather and fire conditions.

Parking and trailhead facilities: The trailhead, located at the end of the road and perched on a ridgetop high above Rock Lakes at 9,300 feet, has room for about four vehicles. In the unlikely event that it is full, you must go back 0.5 mile. There is a hillside outhouse with a view, but no water.

Finding the trailhead: This access road—perched on a wilderness ridgetop for 18 miles—is as impressive as the hike. The boundary of the Frank Church–River of No Return Wilderness is just 300 feet away on either side, and all drains into the Middle Fork of the Salmon River. The road is improved dirt for a total of 28 miles to the Sleeping Deer Trailhead.

To reach the trailhead from Challis, turn right (north) from Main Street onto the Challis Creek county road. Follow this paved road through farmland in lower Challis Creek Canyon for 8 miles. It eventually becomes gravel. Soon thereafter, take a right onto the improved dirt Bear Creek Road (FR 086). The road passes through some recreational homesites, then climbs 3,200 feet and 9 miles to a pass at 9,190 feet between the cone-shaped Twin Peaks, which rise to well over 10,000 feet. There is an active fire lookout on the southern peak.

From the pass, the road follows a ridgeline to the trailhead. You pass a number of trailheads that lead down into the wilderness canyons 3,000 to 5,000 feet below. There are also a number of primitive campsites along the road (no water).

From Twin Peaks, it is 3.5 miles to Spider Creek. The road has been improved to the Spider Creek helispot for firefighting deployment, but this is still a 15-miles-per-hour drive. The 15 miles beyond the helispot have a number of rocky spots but do not require four-wheel drive. At times the road is paint-scratching narrow, and you must back up anywhere from several hundred feet to 0.5 mile if you encounter another vehicle. GPS: N44 45.21' / W114 40.78'

The Hike

This is a strikingly beautiful area—exciting, rugged, and not heavily used, with a number of lakes that present camping options. Sleeping Deer (9,881 feet) is one of the highest mountains in the wilderness and the highest in this area.

One of the great victories of the political fight to establish the Frank Church–River of No Return Wilderness was to include not just the area from Sleeping Deer Mountain westward to the Middle Fork of the Salmon River but also all of the canyons to the east of this striking mountain. The forest service felt this addition was "just too much wilderness." However, this area—more than 500,000 acres to the east and south of the old Idaho Primitive Area—was just as wild as the primitive area itself and did indeed become part of the wilderness.

Like many routes in the Salmon River Mountains, this one goes up and down, up and down, from pass to basin, from basin to pass. In all, you'll cross four passes, two of which are notable: Sleeping Deer and Woodtick. None of these pulls is long. In fact, the trailhead is the highest elevation of the trip.

From the trailhead, the trail immediately swings around a ridgetop and contours high above Cabin Creek to Sleeping Deer Pass just southeast of beautiful Sleeping Deer Mountain. The views, framed by contorted whitebark pine, are outstanding. At the pass, a trail fork to the left takes you quickly thousands of feet down into Cabin Creek. Straight ahead a trail climbs to the Sleeping Deer fire lookout, still used in emergencies.

Take the trail to the right, which descends in seven switchbacks to the cirque just below Sleeping Deer Mountain at the head of Pole Creek. This descent is fairly easy except early in the summer, when snow makes it dangerous.

At the bottom of the switchbacks is an intersection; the trail to the right leads down Pole Creek Canyon. Stay to the left. The trail traverses the rocky head of Pole Creek basin (directly below the cliffs of Sleeping Deer Mountain) to the easy pass between Pole and Cache Creeks. This section, from the trailhead to the top of Cache Creek, gets a lot of weather because it's high and exposed. It is dangerous during lightning storms. In addition to keeping an eye on the weather, however, look for bighorn sheep.

From the divide, you descend 400 feet on a rocky, eroded trail to the first of the four trail-accessible Cache Creek Lakes. Near the lake's inlet on the right side is a pretty little spring. Despite its beauty, in July it might be mosquito-ridden because it is flanked by an extensive wet meadow. Several big horse camps are also situated in this area. Although we saw little wildlife here in late

Sleeping Deer Mountain. Photo by Josh Keeley

August, we did see and hear many pikas and marmots, as well as a lot of grouse in the wooded areas. The grouse whortleberries (the smallest of the blackberries) were ripe. We also found the fishing here good for brook trout (6 to 12 inches).

The trail drops down past a cabin and continues north. Losing little elevation, it passes three more lakes. They lie about 100 feet below on a shelf above dramatic Cache Creek Canyon. The second lake is the largest. The third one loses much of its water by midsummer and so contains no fish. The fourth lake is within the burned area of the 1988 Battle Axe Fire. There are six more Cache Creek Lakes scattered about the area. Access to them is cross-country.

Just past the third lake, you enter the Battle Axe burn. Here you must look carefully for the trail junction on the right, which takes you to Woodtick Summit. If you find yourself descending to the lake, you've missed the junction. You can spot the correct trail up on the flank of Woodtick ahead.

From the junction, the trail climbs over a corner of Peak 9,488 to Woodtick Summit at 8,863 feet. The elevation gain is only about 300 feet. This entire portion of the route lies within the Battle Axe burn. The area near the trail burned twice in forty years, so it ought to remain a generally open slope providing fine views of Sleeping Deer Mountain and the basin at the head of Cache Creek.

Sleeping Deer Mountain

0   Kilometer   1

0   Mile   1

N

8,863 ft.

Woodtick
Summit

To Camas
Creek

West Fork
Lakes

SALMON–CHALLIS
NATIONAL FOREST

To Cache
Creek

Cache Creek Lakes

Cache Creek

× 9,574 ft.

× 9,471 ft.

× 9,340 ft.

× 8,558 ft.

8,685 ft. ×

× 9,753 ft.

Sleeping
Deer
Mountain
9,881 ft.

× 9,574 ft.

Pole Creek

To Cabin
Creek

× 9,301 ft.

9,503 ft. ×

WILDERNESS
BOUNDARY

Rock
Lakes

17 P

Rock Creek

× 9,323 ft.

To Challis
(39 miles)

Woodtick Summit is not notable for the presence of ticks. At the summit is a trail junction. Take the fork to the right, which descends two steep switchbacks and then contours across the head of Woodtick Creek. From here you have fine views down heavily forested Woodtick Creek. After a mile or so, this rocky trail leads to a grassy divide between Woodtick Creek and the West Fork of Camas Creek. From the divide, you get a good view of three of the West Fork Lakes. At the trail junction on the pass, take the trail in the middle that descends into the West Fork. The descent of 500 feet is steep, and the trail is at times worn and rocky.

At the bottom, you're on the north side of the largest of the West Fork Lakes. Take the right fork of the trail here, and continue until you've crossed over the stream, which is the inlet. We found this largest of the lakes to be the only one to have fish—a few large trout we were unable to catch. We saw plentiful elk sign and much pika activity as well as a bighorn sheep.

The lowest of the West Fork Lakes has increased considerably in size due to beavers, which have dammed the outlet. Their large lodge is visible in the lake. The lakeshore has an eerie quality—swamped, dead timber and marsh grass.

—Jackie Johnson Maughan and Ralph Maughan

Miles and Directions

0.0   Start at the Sleeping Deer Trailhead (9,300 feet).

0.8   Pass the Sleeping Deer lookout and Cabin Creek Trails (9,300 feet).

1.0   Pass the Pole Creek Canyon Trail (8,880 feet). Stay left.

1.3   Summit the Pole and Cache Creeks pass (8,960 feet).

2.0   Reach Cache Creek Lakes (8,635 feet).

3.5   Stay right on the Woodtick Summit Trail (8,600 feet).

4.0   Top the Woodtick Summit (8,863 feet).

5.0   Take the West Fork Lakes Trail (8,600 feet).

5.5   Reach the West Fork Lakes (8,295 feet). Retrace your steps.

11.0   Arrive back at the trailhead.

18 Soldier Lakes-Patrol Ridge Loop

This nostalgic hike is known for good fishing in numerous subalpine lakes and breathtaking views into the Middle Fork of the Salmon River canyon and out to the distant peaks of the Frank Church–River of No Return Wilderness.

Start: 42 road miles north of Stanley
Type of hike: Lollipop loop
Distance: 16.5 miles
Approximate hiking time: 3–4 days
Difficulty: Moderately easy to Soldier Lakes. Doing the entire loop is moderately strenuous.
Best season: July–mid-September
Trail surface: Dirt and rock
Land status: Frank Church–River of No Return Wilderness; Salmon–Challis National Forest
Canine compatibility: Not allowed within wilderness
Fees and permits: None

Maps: USGS Soldier Creek and Big Soldier Mountain ID; Frank Church–River of No Return Wilderness South Half forest map; Middle Fork, Challis, Yankee Fork, and Lost River Ranger Districts/Challis National Forest map
Trail contact: Challis Ranger District, (208) 879-4100
Special considerations: Patrol Ridge is a long stretch exposed to lightning.
Parking and trailhead facilities: Scenic Josephus Lake is actually two lakes separated by a short stream. It is heavily used by fishers. There is room for about five vehicles at this well-shaded trailhead.

Finding the trailhead: Drive northwest from Stanley on ID 21 for 18.6 miles, and turn left (north) onto the gravel road. Turn right again, almost immediately, onto another gravel road. From here it is 21 miles to the trailhead at Josephus Lake. This road quickly crosses Marsh Creek, and 100 yards past the bridge there is yet another fork. Stay to the left and follow this road over Vanity Summit. The gravel road is wide and in good condition until the climb to Vanity Summit. As you begin the ascent, it turns to large (rocky) gravel but remains two lanes wide. The right side of the road burned in 1999 all the way to Vanity Summit (elevation 7,813 feet).

Descend from Vanity Summit on a graded dirt road that stays high above the creek. The road has one and a half lanes, as well as many tight (often blind) curves; it's steep but not very rocky. About 16 miles from ID 21, you reach the junction with Float Creek Road and the road down Rapid River. Stay left and follow the graded Float Creek dirt road on a 5-mile, 1,100-foot climb to Josephus Lake. All of these junctions are well signed. GPS: N44 33.01' / W115 8.56'

The Hike

This hike covers a popular area of lake and high ridge country in the southern part of the Frank Church–River of No Return Wilderness. It ranges from forest to approximately the alpine zone at 9,000 feet. The trail begins at 7,100 feet at Josephus Lake on Float Creek and passes by, or near, more than a dozen lakes and along a high ridge with tremendous views as it traces a rough horseshoe shape. Most of the lakes are fishable for cutthroat trout.

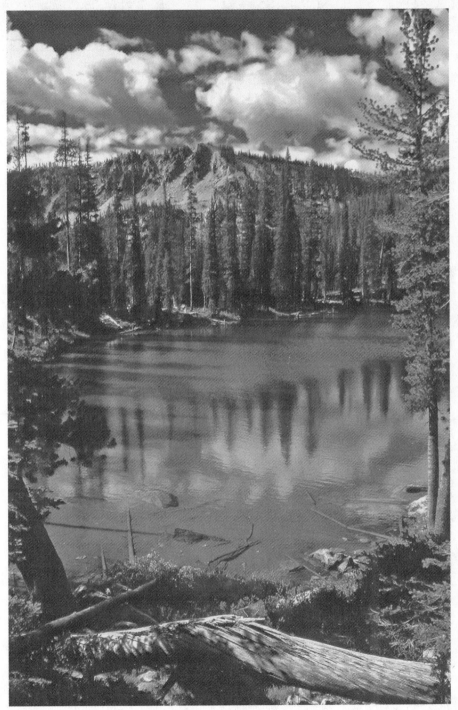

The Major Lake at the foot of Patrol Ridge. PHOTO BY RALPH MAUGHAN

The lakes are in two groups: Soldier Lakes and Cutthroat Lakes. Both lie in large basins beneath the long Patrol Ridge, which sports numerous rugged, but short, peaks. The ridge is unnamed on most maps. The more popular and perhaps the more scenic of the two groups is the Soldier Lakes, nestled beneath Patrol Ridge at the headwaters of Soldier Creek. Each of the Soldier Lakes is named after a military rank. The Cutthroat Lakes are generally unnamed (except a large one named Cutthroat Lake). They lie under Patrol Ridge at the head of Muskeg Creek.

The north side of Patrol Ridge, which overlooks the lakes, is precipitous. Its opposite side is steep but smooth, plunging several thousand feet into the Middle Fork of the Salmon River Canyon. The trail on the ridge keeps close to the top and offers outstanding views of both sides.

The trail leaves from the heavily timbered trailhead just above lower Josephus Lake, but soon breaks out into the open at the marshy and very scenic upper end of Josephus Lake. Here, you can see not only the lake but a number of rocky peaks just to its south and southeast, including Mount Mills.

After this short stretch with a view, the trail heads into deep forest and quickly reaches the Frank Church–River of No Return Wilderness boundary. You'll then climb steadily through forest and a few openings to reach pretty Helldiver Lake after 2 miles. There are a few springs along the trail to Helldiver Lake early in the summer. Mushroom Springs, about 1 mile from the trailhead, usually flows all summer. Float Creek remains far below the trail.

Past Helldiver Lake, a climb of 400 feet in 0.5 mile puts you on a pass between Float Creek and the Soldier Creek drainage. Climbing 30 yards up the north slope from the pass will give you a fine view. This pass also marks the spot where Greyhound Ridge joins Patrol Ridge.

The trail drops steeply, but briefly, down from the pass and past a pond to a trail junction. At the junction, follow Soldier Lakes Trail to the left. The trail soon breaks into the open as it begins to cross the head of Soldier Creek Canyon, whose thickly timbered bottom spreads below. After less than a mile, drop down to the first of the Soldier Lakes: First Lieutenant. Immediately after that comes Colonel Lake and a trail junction. A right goes to other Soldier Lakes, and to the Cutthroat Lakes. A left goes to more Soldier Lakes and then to the top of Patrol Ridge, the route described here. Most people end their trips near this junction.

On Patrol Ridge Trail, you quickly come to a pretty blue-green lake called The General. From The General, an unmarked trail climbs briefly to the biggest of the lakes, The Captain. The main trail circles The General, then circles a lake with no fish called The Major, after which it begins a steep 400-foot ascent to the top of Patrol Ridge.

Once you are on the ridge, views are few at first and the trail is quite narrow, but both conditions soon improve, and after 0.5 mile the trail follows the very top of the ridge, offering dramatic views of the Soldier Lakes below and down toward the Middle Fork in the opposite direction. In July the ridge is covered with flowers between the scenic clumps of whitebark pine.

As the trail follows the ridge, it gradually climbs, offering views of the Cutthroat Lakes below and finally, to the south, the headwaters of the Middle Fork, where Marsh Creek and Bear Valley Creek run together. You see not just the canyon but the actual river. You also see the results of the huge Deadwood Fire of 1987.

The trail reaches its highest point (about 9,000 feet) as it bends northward and traverses under Peak 9,107. Here, as you cross the head of Lincoln Creek (which bears a lake far below), the trail grows quite narrow, with a very steep slope down into Lincoln Creek. It is not so treacherous, however, as to prevent its use by horses (which, prudently, should be walked).

Soon there comes a saddle that may appear to be the one on the map, which shows the loop trail dropping eastward off Patrol Ridge back to the Soldier Lakes. This is not the case. The correct saddle is 0.25 mile farther north. This saddle is broader than the first (wrong) one. There may or may not be a sign marking Muskeg Creek Trail, but the track is obvious if you walk to the edge of the saddle-top meadow.

The trail leaves the saddle to contour directly under the cliffs of Patrol Ridge. For about a mile, as it contours around the head of a tributary of Muskeg Creek, it is rocky, narrow, and somewhat difficult. Soon, however, it begins to ramble through forest and meadow as it approaches the Cutthroat Lakes. In the last mile before reaching Cutthroat Lake, it descends 900 feet.

Cutthroat Lake is at the base of Peak 8,996 on Patrol Ridge. A small cascade tumbles into the lake on its west side. At a junction 0.5 mile above Cutthroat Lake, a fork leaves to the left down Muskeg Creek, Soldier Creek, and eventually the Middle Fork of the Salmon River.

From this junction to Colonel Lake, the trail you follow is called Cutthroat Trail. It generally climbs, sometimes steeply, and fails to go close to most of the Cutthroat Lakes. About 2 miles past Cutthroat Lake, the trail drops into the Soldier Creek drainage and passes two beautiful and large Soldier Lakes—Staff Sergeant Lake and Sargeant Lake. Soon thereafter, you complete the loop at the junction at Colonel Lake. From that point, retrace your steps to the trailhead.

Options: From the Patrol Ridge pass, which connects with Muskeg Trail, you can make a side trip along the ridge to its terminus at Big Soldier Mountain. This is a 3-mile round-trip to Big Soldier lookout, which is used for emergency fire detection.

Big Soldier Mountain 8,984 ft.

GREYHOUND RIDGE

Cutthroat Lakes

Soldier Creek Trail

Josephus Lake

008

Float Creek

Rapid River

P 18

9,107 ft.

PATROL RIDGE

Helldiver Lake

Colonel Lake

Soldier Lakes

Mount Mills 9,185 ft.

Vanity Creek

008

Vanity Summit

Middle Fork Salmon River

SALMON–CHALLIS NATIONAL FOREST

Bear Creek

Burn from 1999

To 21

You will have views of all of the southern part of the Frank Church–River of No Return Wilderness. You can't see the actual Middle Fork from the lookout, but you can see it on your way to the lookout, as well as glimpse the Dagger Falls boat put-in on the river.

—Ralph Maughan and Jackie Johnson Maughan

Miles and Directions

0.0 Begin at the Josephus Lake trailhead (7,100 feet).

2.0 Arrive at Helldiver Lake (7,720 feet).

2.5 Cross the Float Creek and Soldier Creek Pass (8,088 feet).

3.0 Reach the Soldier Lakes Trail (7,020 feet). Go left.

4.0 Reach the Patrol Ridge Trail (7,900 feet).

5.0 Hike along Patrol Ridge (8,600 feet).

7.0 Reach Peak 9,107 (9,000 feet).

8.0 Reach the junction with the Muskeg Trail (8,520 feet).

10.0 Take the Cutthroat Trail (7,880 feet).

10.7 Arrive at Cutthroat Lake (7,560 feet).

12.0 Reach Staff Sergeant Lake (7,960 feet).

12.8 Close the loop at Colonel Lake (7,900 feet).

16.5 Arrive back at the Josephus Lake trailhead (7,100 feet).

19 Stoddard Lake

Here we have spectacular vistas of the Middle Fork of the Salmon River's Impassable Canyon and the Bighorn Crags. The hike to Stoddard Lake is a challenging yet rewarding trip into remote parts of the Frank Church–River of No Return Wilderness.

Start: 40 miles northwest of Salmon, 7 miles from the end of the Salmon River Road, and just beyond the mouth of the Middle Fork of the Salmon River
Type of hike: Out-and-back
Distance: 22.6 miles
Approximate hiking time: 4–5 days
Difficulty: Very strenuous
Best season: Mid-July–early September
Trail surface: Dirt and rock
Land status: Frank Church–River of No Return Wilderness; Salmon–Challis National Forest
Canine compatibility: Not allowed
Fees and permits: None
Maps: USGS Butts Creek Point, Cottonwood Butte, and Long Tom Mountain ID; Frank Church–River of No Return Wilderness North Half forest map is preferable to the Salmon National Forest map.
Trail contact: North Fork Ranger District; (208) 865-2700

Special considerations: Stoddard Lake is no weekend hike. Route-finding skills required. The trip needs to be planned according to scarce water sources. Although Stoddard Lake is situated on the edge of the Chamberlain Basin—a gentle 300,000-acre plateau in the middle of the giant, 2.4-million-acre Frank Church–River of No Return Wilderness—getting here is a physical challenge. You begin by climbing out of one of the world's deepest canyons. The trailhead is at the Stoddard Pack Bridge, 3,000 feet in elevation. It climbs to no less than 8,800 feet, and most of the climb (more than a mile in altitude change) is immediate. You will climb 5,400 feet in one day.
Parking and trailhead facilities: Parking only. One mile back, at the Middle Fork Trailhead, are toilets and horse loading but no developed overnight camping sites. Ebenezer Bar Campground, 6 miles back, is a developed overnight site. Bring your own water since sources at campgrounds are not reliable.

Finding the trailhead: Drive about 11 miles north from Salmon on US 93 to North Fork. Leave the highway and follow the paved Salmon River Road left (west) to Shoup for some 19 miles, as the road follows the winding path of the Salmon River. From Shoup, the road becomes gravel; continue for another 21 miles to the mouth of the Middle Fork of the Salmon River. Just beyond this is the Middle Fork Trailhead and, in another 0.5 mile, the trailhead at Stoddard Pack Bridge. GPS: N45 17.96' / W114 35.72'

The Hike

Here, where the Middle Fork flows out of the Impassable Canyon into the Main Fork of the Salmon River, there used to be a sign that read Yonder Lies the Idaho Wilderness. Fortunately, one of the major battles for Idaho wilderness was won here in 1980, so although the sign no longer exists, the wilderness does.

Parts of this trail have been reconstructed recently, and some of the bad sections have been improved. On the other hand, substantial forest fires have burned areas near the trail.

The pack bridge is 0.5 mile downstream from the confluence of the Middle Fork on the Main Fork of the Salmon River. Cross the bridge, carrying plenty of drinking water. The trail immediately begins climbing up the face of the Salmon River Canyon. In 12 switchbacks, you climb from the river's elevation of 3,000 feet to 4,613 feet. At this point you round a ridge and continue climbing in the company of excellent views of Middle Fork Canyon, with the river chewing its way ever deeper into the bedrock of the Idaho Batholith.

The trail is now above the breaks of the Middle Fork, and you continue to climb but less steeply. At an altitude of 5,800 feet, reach a saddle where the trail crosses a small, grassy park. This is an excellent place to stop for a rest, with a very photogenic view of both the canyon and the Bighorn Crags on its opposite side.

Color Creek is 4 miles from the trailhead, at 6,414 feet in elevation. Just 0.25 mile past Color Creek, watch for the cutoff trail leading to the right to Nolan Mountain. Take this cutoff trail; it is unmarked but fairly easy to find. Here you depart from the well-built Stoddard Trail, leaving it to wander along the side of the Middle Fork's canyon. (Stoddard Trail does lead to Stoddard Lake, but it's a two-day horse ride.)

Now on the trail to Nolan Mountain, you'll have to switchback steeply uphill. As you near the top (a climb of about 1,000 feet from Color Creek), the trail worsens and deadfall may be a problem. At various times Nolan Mountain becomes prominent on the skyline, and before too long you are on top of the mountain next to what's left of the lookout tower (four steel corner brackets).

Fire damage has taken out the trail downhill to a spring. The spring is used for a campsite by hunters in the fall and is a good place to rest.

From the spring, the trail runs along the top of the ridgeline. However, its path deteriorates and is easily lost in the deadfall. This is no great matter, however, since you are on a high ridge with only one way to go: west toward the 9,000-foot Twin Peaks massif. Soon you'll find the trail again; however, just as it seems to improve, it

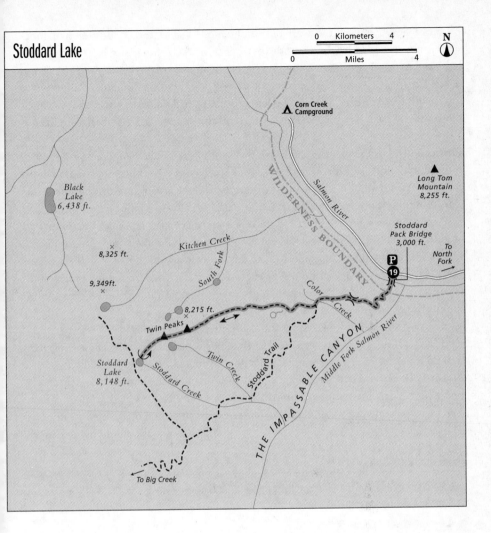

0 Kilometers 4

0 Miles 4

N

Corn Creek
Campground

WILDERNESS BOUNDARY

Salmon River

Long Tom
Mountain
8,255 ft.

Black
Lake
6,438 ft.

Stoddard
Pack Bridge
3,000 ft.

To
North
Fork

× 8,325 ft.

Kitchen Creek

South Fork

9,349ft. ×

P
19

8,215 ft. ×

Color Creek

Twin Peaks

THE IMPASSABLE CANYON

Middle Fork Salmon River

Stoddard
Lake
8,148 ft.

Stoddard Creek

Twin Creek

Stoddard Trail

To Big Creek

ends. It ends just as the topographic map shows—at a magnificent saddle that certainly looks like the bighorn sheep country it is. The best, and really the only, way to go is onto the saddle and straight up the mountain. It is not a technical climb, but you'll have to contend with loose rocks.

Once you get to the top of the first point of the Twin Peak massif (9,108 feet), descend to the saddle between it and ascend to the second point (9,258 feet). The top of the second and highest point is really interesting, and you can get a feel for how large sections of the mountain slough off over time and ultimately fall. There is also a large cairn on top, which is home to about a gazillion little flies.

◀ *Bridge to Stoddard Lake Trail.* PHOTO BY LUKE KRATZ

From here descend due west 0.25 mile and 400 feet to an outfitter trail (not shown on maps), which leads south to a camp on the southwest edge of Stoddard Lake and to good cutthroat fishing. It is another mile, and 700 feet of switchbacking, to the lake.

From Stoddard Lake, trails lead deep into the primal wilderness to Papoose Lake, Cottonwood Lake, Basin Lake, Black Lake, and the vastness of Chamberlain Basin.

Options: To fish the two larger lakes in the South Fork of Kitchen Creek, follow the outfitter trail northeast for about 2 miles and 500 feet of elevation gain. The trail then switchbacks downhill steeply to join the upper lake near its outlet on the northeast side. Camping is not recommended because of deadfall and a lack of level spots.

You can follow Stoddard Trail to make a loop back to the trailhead, but count on at least two hard days. You will also need the Aggipah Mountain and Papoose Peak USGS quads. If you are tempted to take any other route back to the main Salmon River, other than the one that crosses the Stoddard Pack Bridge, remember that you'll have to swim across this major river to get back to Salmon River Trail. There are no other bridges within hiking distance.

If you decide to do the loop, a trail leads due west from Stoddard Lake to Stoddard Trail. This trail is somewhat hard to find, but it makes the steep climb (750 feet in 0.25 mile) easier. A water source and a good stopping place are located where the North Fork of Stoddard Creek joins Stoddard Creek. Make certain to stock up on water here. There are two small, human-made places by Reese Creek to pitch a tent. Make sure to replenish water here also. The rest of the terrain is too steep for camping.

—Philip Blomquist and Mark Leininger

Miles and Directions

0.0   Start by crossing the Stoddard Pack Bridge (3,000 feet).

3.0   Reach a saddle (5,800 feet).

4.0   Cross Color Creek (6,414 feet).

4.3   Reach the Nolan Mountain junction (6,800 feet). Go right on the cutoff trail.

5.8   Reach the Nolan Mountain lookout site (8,215 feet).

6.0   Pass the spring (8,000 feet).

8.0   Reach the saddle before the Twin Peak massif and the end of the trail (8,400 feet).

10.0 Pass the second Twin Peak (9,258 feet).

10.3 Pass the outfitter trail to Stoddard Lake (8,800 feet).

11.3 Reach Stoddard Lake (8,148 feet). Retrace your steps.

22.6 Arrive back at the trailhead.

20 West Yankee Fork–Crimson Lake

Crimson Lake is one of the finest lakes in the Frank Church–River of No Return Wilderness. It has a rugged setting, colorful peaks, and big trout. The long hike to the lake itself is worth it.

Start: About 15 miles northeast of Stanley. The lakes are in the Frank Church–River of No Return Wilderness, but most of the hike is in a roadless area that was left out of the wilderness designation.

Type of hike: Out-and-back

Distance: 20 miles

Approximate hiking time: 3–4 days

Difficulty: The West Fork of the Yankee Fork is moderately easy. The climb to Crimson Lake is moderately strenuous.

Best season: Mid-July through mid-September

Trail surface: Dirt and rock

Land status: Frank Church–River of No Return Wilderness; Salmon–Challis National Forest

Canine compatibility: On leash to wilderness boundary; not allowed in wilderness

Fees and permits: None

Maps: USGS East Basin Creek, Knapp Lakes, Mt. Jordan, and Sunbeam ID

Trail contact: Challis Ranger District; (208) 879-4100

Special considerations: Take wading shoes. Bring rope to hang your food away from bears.

Parking and trailhead facilities: The partially shaded trailhead has a loading ramp and a latrine, as well as room for about ten vehicles. The trail is the gated road. Follow it downhill to your right. The hike is open to trail machines for 6 miles, but I have not found their numbers oppressive.

Finding the trailhead: Drive 13 miles east of Stanley on ID 75 or, from the other direction, drive 41.5 miles west on ID 75 from its junction with US 93 just south of Challis. In either case, turn off at Sunbeam to head northward up the Yankee Fork of the Salmon River on a narrow, paved two-lane road. The pavement ends in 3 miles, just about where you will see the burn of the Rankin Creek forest fire, which dates from August 2000. The fire burned west to east across the road but did not burn out your destination.

Drive north on what is now a good gravel road that goes through the ruins left by gold dredge mining some fifty to seventy-five years ago. The Yankee Fork of the Salmon River Canyon is quite wide through here.

Turn left onto a dirt road (FR 074) at the ghost town of Bonanza, a cluster of log cabins 7.5 miles north of Sunbeam. A sign here indicates that your destination, West Fork Trail, is 1 mile. It also says Bonanza G.S. 0.1; Bonanza Cemetery 0.5; Boot Hill (Cemetery) 1.3. Pass by the forest service guard station, and at the fork follow the road signed for the cemetery or Boot Hill Cemetery. Avoid the road that goes to West Fork Campground. Follow the road downhill about a mile to the trailhead in an old clear-cut. The road continues down the hill to a gravel pit, but this part is usually gated. GPS: N44 23.23' / W114 44.69'

The Hike

I first wondered about this area when I was in the Sawtooth Range, weary of the streams of people passing by on the trail. I noticed that across the Stanley Basin and to the northeast, a clump of jagged peaks rose that looked a lot like the Sawtooths and, I thought, seemed a lot less crowded. These peaks didn't seem to have a name, and I couldn't find anyone who had been there. But during the public hearings on the River of No Return Wilderness, people began referring to them as the Tango Peaks since many of them cluster about the head of Tango Creek.

Years later, now familiar with the area, along with many others, I helped push the headwaters of Loon Creek and Tango Creek into the wilderness classification. Included in this addition were the Crimson Lake and the Knapp Lakes basins, even though they do not drain directly into the Middle Fork of the Salmon River (which was the official justification for including the headwaters of Loon and Tango Creeks in the wilderness). The colorful Crimson Lake area, however, contained mineralized rock. I hope I helped stop a nasty mine there, similar to the Grouse Creek Mine in nearby Jordan Creek, which destroyed a mountain and produced gold for about one year before shutting down for good.

The old road/trail leads down toward the canyon; avoid an ATV trail that soon leaves to the left. Rather than reaching the canyon bottom, the trail soon comes to a gravel pit. Cross the pit; West Fork Trail (Trail 155) leaves on the other (west) side. The trail quickly climbs 300 feet up the mountainside to avoid a short gorge that constricts the West Fork. Beyond the top of the climb, the trail quickly drops down to the floor of West Fork Canyon, which, by south-central Idaho standards, is quite lush. After the climb and descent of the first mile, the trail is easy all the way to the confluence of Cabin Creek, about 3 more miles. As soon as you descend to the West Fork of the Yankee Fork, you'll find many small meadows among the conifers. The grade of the trail is essentially flat. If you camp in this canyon, you may find it to be amazingly cold in midsummer. I have seen it freeze hard on a day when, in the afternoon, the temperature was over 80 degrees. The canyon seems to collect cold air in its bottom.

You quickly come to the Deadwood Creek Trail junction. Deadwood Creek Trail leaves to the left, fords the West Fork, and goes up into Deadwood Creek, which burned in the Rankin Creek forest fire. Next comes the trail up Lightning Creek. West Fork Trail passes by an impressive volcanic rock face and swings up into the mouth of Lightning Creek Canyon; Lightning Creek Trail (Trail 156) leaves to the right. Then West Fork Trail crosses Lightning Creek with a bridge for better crossing.

West Fork Trail continues upstream for 2 more miles, passing through forest and willow thicket and occasional meadows that give views of pink-colored Red Mountain ahead. The willows look like a good place to meet a bear, and they are. There are lots of black bears in this country.

Turn right onto the Cabin Creek Trail, and head up Cabin Creek (alternatively, a hike to the head of the West Fork is pleasant as well). You are now on Trail 156. The

Majestic Crimson Lake. Photo by Luke Kratz

trail up Cabin Creek soon crosses the creek to its west side and heads up a linear meadow. About 0.75 mile from the start of Cabin Creek Trail, the path may disappear under avalanche debris (it depends on the year and how recent maintenance has occurred). Cross to the east side of the creek here, where you'll pick up the trail again. As you continue up the canyon, each open area gives you a closer view of the rugged gray mountain at what appears to be the head of Cabin Creek. Actually, Cabin Creek bends to the west and then to the south, to where it begins at Crimson Lake. The gray mountain is really a wall of the canyon. As you reach its base, avoid any side trails that leave to the left.

Staying on the right, cross the stream (the "north fork" of Cabin Creek) and begin to climb. At the west edge of the bend in the big switchback, Crimson Lake Trail leads to the left. The main trail (Trail 113) continues to the right, climbing 1,400 feet to drop into Pioneer Creek in the Frank Church–River of No Return Wilderness. Climb instead to the left, up Cabin Creek on the rough Crimson Lake Trail (Trail 202, which isn't shown on the USGS quadrangle). Soon you'll hear the creek crashing below you in a gorge. A short step off the trail gives a good view of the gorge, of the north side of Red Mountain, and down Cabin Creek.

The trail continues in a rocky fashion, crossing over slides and through sparse forest with fine views of the rugged and increasingly colorful mountains. Soon you pass

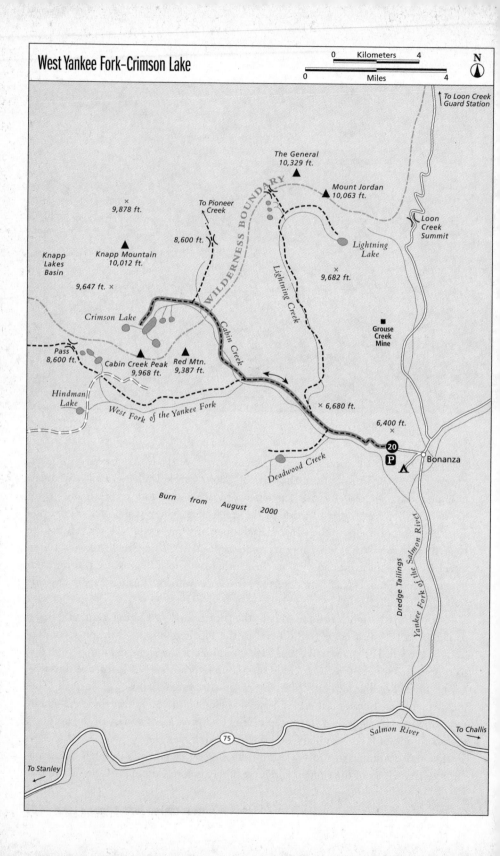

into the Frank Church–River of No Return Wilderness and drop down to Cabin Creek, cross a tributary, and labor the last 0.3 mile and 600 feet up to Crimson Lake. This lake, large, deep, and full of cutthroat trout (some of them quite large), rests on top of crimson-colored rock. Rough, jagged peaks of reddish orange rise above the lake, with the two-toothed spires of Cabin Creek Peak providing a contrasting gray color. As I climbed between the two teeth of the peak, a large billy left the other mountain goats and watched me for half an hour, his legs straddling the narrow, but very deep, crack.

The unnamed lake at elevation 8,565 feet, above and southeast of Crimson Lake, is also full of large cutthroat. However, the lake in the small cirque above and southwest of Crimson is windswept and barren. Still, from this barren lake you can walk to the top of the mountain for a grand view of the Knapp Lakes below. There are more than twenty of these lakes, all barren and completely pristine except for the largest and lowest lake, which is full of rainbow trout. Beyond are the typical endless ridges of the River of No Return Wilderness. A descent to the Knapp Lakes from this mountain requires an exciting ride down a moving talus slope—rock glissading. I enjoyed it, but do not recommend it.

If you camp in the area, please dismantle fire rings and don't create new ones.

Options: Lightning Creek trail has been removed due to excessive burns. There is also a good trail up the West Fork of Cabin Creek that eventually meets a jeep trail.

—Ralph Maughan

Miles and Directions

0.0 Start at the trailhead (6,580 feet).
0.2 Cross the gravel pit (6,450 feet).
0.6 Reach the top of the climb to avoid the gorge (6,750 feet).
1.3 Pass the Deadwood Trail junction (6,480 feet).
2.5 Make the Lightning Creek ford or cross the bridge (6,550 feet).
4.8 Reach the Cabin Creek–West Cabin Creek confluence (6,690 feet).
7.2 At the trail junction, go left to Crimson Lake (7,220 feet).
10.0 Reach the Crimson Lake outlet (8,330 feet). Retrace your steps.
20.0 Arrive back at the trailhead.

Lick Creek Mountains

The Lick Creek Mountains are a big subrange of the vast Salmon River Mountains. The canyon of the South Fork of the Salmon River is generally regarded as the east side of the Lick Creek Mountains. Long Valley, which contains the towns of McCall and Cascade, is the western boundary.

The range's mostly granitic rock has been intensely carved by ice age glaciers into a variety of scenic peaks and cirque basins filled with subalpine or alpine lakes. About 150,000 acres of this area burned in fire the summer of 1994, and more again in the summer of 2000. Vast areas of these mountains now have regenerating forests. Hikers should understand the dangers (such as falling snags) and the joys (wildflowers) of walking through burns with standing dead trees and new forests.

A large portion of the Lick Creek Mountains is roadless, perhaps 200,000 acres. Idaho conservationists have for years sought wilderness protection for this area, but without success.

—Ralph Maughan

Granite cliffs are common in the Lick Creek Mountains. PHOTO BY LUKE KRATZ

21 Box Lake

Lovely granite mountains and a large subalpine lake radiate within burned areas and new growth.

Start: 13 road miles northeast of McCall
Type of hike: Out-and-back with the option of a longer hike requiring a shuttle
Distance: 8 miles
Approximate hiking time: 2 days
Difficulty: Moderate due to elevation gain of 1,860 feet in 3 miles, followed by a 350-foot descent to Box Lake
Best season: August–mid-September
Trail surface: Dirt and rock
Land status: Payette National Forest
Canine compatibility: On leash
Fees and permits: None

Maps: USGS Box Lake and Fitsum Summit; McCall and Krassel Ranger Districts, Payette National Forest map
Trail contact: McCall/Krassel Ranger District; (208) 634-0400 (McCall); (208) 634-0600 (Krassel)
Special considerations: Wading shoes needed in June and July.
Parking and trailhead facilities: Black Lee Trailhead is mostly in the shade under big conifers. It has an outhouse and room for five or six vehicles. A sign at the trailhead reads Box Lake 4.

Finding the trailhead: Where ID 55 reaches Payette Lake from the south, it makes an abrupt left turn. This is downtown McCall, where you'll part with ID 55. Make a right turn here, and take Park Street to Davis Street to the signed Lick Creek Road (FR 48). The road is paved for 3 miles as it travels along the north shore of Little Payette Lake. The road gradually turns north into Lake Fork Canyon. Broken pavement, which contains some impressive holes, continues for about 3 more miles. At the end of the pavement, you are fully in Lake Fork Canyon. The road is all-weather gravel, one and a half to two lanes wide, but it is also rough and busy. The canyon is very scenic. Thirteen miles from the beginning of the signed road back in McCall, you reach the Black Lee Trailhead. GPS: N44 59.35' / W115 57.25'

The Hike

This hike provides a good introduction to the Lick Creek Mountains, which form part of the westernmost portion of the massive Idaho Batholith. Glaciers filled the valleys in the Box Lake area during the Pleistocene (ice age) era, and left many tarns (glacial lakes) when they receded. These mountains are also characterized by steep river breaks with shallow soils. Much more recently (1994), a large portion of the Lick Creek Mountains burned in the hot Blackwell Fire. The fire burned part of this trail, including Box Lake itself. The area is still scenic, and the fire recovery is under-way, even in the areas where the fire was so hot it sterilized the soil.

Box Lake is one of the largest in the Lick Creek Mountains—about a mile long and a third of a mile wide. You can reach it most years by late June, but you will slog through some snow and the fords might be difficult. August is best, with many

Box Lake post-burns. PHOTO BY LUKE KRATZ

wildflowers. September has beautiful foliage, and the biting flies and mosquitoes have disappeared by then.

The trail (Trail 110) heads northwest from the trailhead and immediately begins to climb steeply on switchbacks up a steep slope into the canyon of Black Lee Creek. This steep section is in the shade of large Douglas fir and Engelmann spruce. Black Lee Creek tumbles to your left not far below the trail. The trail then levels out a bit, enters the burn, and meanders through several meadows after a ford of Black Lee Creek. Here you'll find yellow columbine, red Indian paintbrush, blue penstemon, yellow composites, and much bear grass, which blooms mid-July through mid-August. Before reaching the summit, the trail crosses Black Lee Creek three more times.

The rest of the way to the summit, the trail passes in and out of the burn several times. The burn has opened up the views of the impressive walls and peaks of granitic rock. The trail climbs steeply in places, and this part of the climb is usually in the sun. The trail was well cleared, but because the

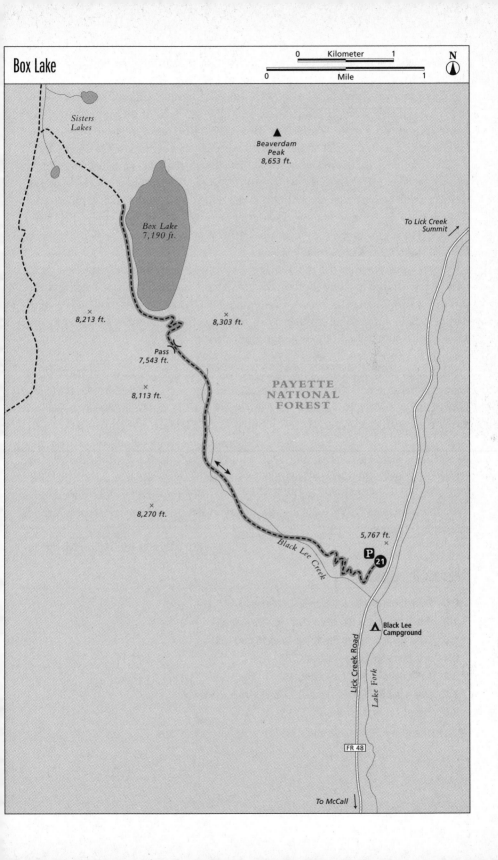

Box Lake

Kilometer

Mile

N

Sisters
Lakes

Beaverdam
Peak
8,653 ft.

Box Lake
7,190 ft.

To Lick Creek
Summit

× 8,213 ft.

× 8,303 ft.

Pass
7,543 ft.

× 8,113 ft.

PAYETTE
NATIONAL
FOREST

× 8,270 ft.

5,767 ft.
×

Black Lee Creek

P 21

Black Lee
Campground

Lick Creek Road

Lake Fork

FR 48

To McCall

burned snags will be falling for some time, trail maintenance crews will have to cut the trail frequently to keep it in good condition.

The summit is gentle and broad, with very nice meadows through which course the rivulets that become Black Lee Creek. At the very end of the summit area, you come abruptly to a steep overlook of Box Lake. There are also good views of the granite ridges around you. The fire burned especially hot right near the overlook.

The trail descends from the overlook 350 feet to the lake, switchbacking down first to the right and then to the left (west) side of the lake. It follows the west side of the lake to its broad outlet area. Although the trail is close to the lake, getting to the shore is not easy because it is lined with boulders. The outlet area, where Box Lake Creek begins, is marshy, but there is a beach as well as an old dam, which has raised the lake slightly from its natural level.

Upon your return to the trailhead, be sure to stop near the top of the first set of switchbacks on the trail and look southward down the classic U-shaped valley of the North Fork of Lake Fork Creek. To the right is Slick Rock, an 800-foot-high vertical slab of granite. From here, looking down this canyon that now has a road in it, you can imagine how truly wild this country once was.

Options: Beyond Box Lake, a backpacking trip can continue past the marshy Sisters Lakes to Crestline Trail (Trail 109). Here, you can proceed north-northwest to marshy Heart Lake (2 miles), Brush Lake (2.7 miles), or Pearl Lake (4.5 miles). This is all in burned, but scenic, glaciated granite country. You could extend the hike farther west to the junction with Wagon Creek Road (7 miles) or 5 miles along the road in the Pearl Creek drainage. This should bring you out at the North Fork of the Payette River. You'll need the Granite Lake USGS quadrangle to route this part of the hike, plus a shuttle vehicle since you'll come out at a different trailhead. Unfortunately, Trail 109 is open to ATVs, reducing the quality of what could otherwise be a hike of statewide importance.

—Jerry Dixon and Ralph Maughan

Miles and Directions

0.0 Start at the Black Lee Trailhead (5,680 feet).

1.2 Reach the end of the steep climb (6,480 feet).

1.6 Make the first ford of Black Lee Creek (6,550 feet).

2.7 Reach the Box Lake overlook (7,543 feet).

3.2 Arrive at Box Lake (7,190 feet).

4.0 Reach the Box Lake outlet (7,190 feet). Retrace your steps.

8.0 Arrive back at the trailhead.

22 Lava Butte Lakes

This trail offers spectacular scenery and solitude, the sublime Lava Ridge, and chances to see wildlife.

Start: 25 linear miles north of McCall in the Salmon River Mountains
Type of hike: Out-and-back with good base camp possibilities
Distance: 8.4 miles
Approximate hiking time: 2-plus days
Difficulty: Moderate
Best season: Mid-July–mid-September
Trail surface: Dirt and rock
Land status: Payette National Forest
Canine compatibility: On leash
Fees and permits: None
Maps: USGS Hazard Lake, Hershey Point, and Patrick Butte ID; Weiser, Council, and New

Meadows Ranger District–Payette National Forest map
Trail contact: New Meadows Ranger District; (208) 347-0300
Special considerations: The topographic quadrangles are badly out of date and show almost none of the roads or trails in the right places.
Parking and trailhead facilities: The Clayburn Trailhead has a latrine and space to park many cars. Camping (fee) is available at Hazard Lake Campground, 4 miles back down Goose Lake Road.

Finding the trailhead: From McCall, drive 6 miles west on ID 55, and turn right on FR 257, the paved road to Brundage Mountain ski resort. At 3 miles, bear left at the turnoff to the resort, and continue north on FR 257, which quickly becomes a good, but sometimes washboarded, dirt road. At 6 miles bear left at a Y junction and continue north on FR 257. The road parallels the long shores of Goose Lake and continues climbing. You pass Hard Creek Guard Station at 19 miles, and Hazard Lake Campground at 22 miles, before reaching the road's end and turnout at the Clayburn Trailhead at 26 miles. GPS: N45 10.61' / W116 10.72'

The Hike

This is a beautiful hike that takes you up and over the incredible ramparts of Lava Ridge in the Patrick Butte–French Creek unprotected roadless area. Timber companies have been chipping away at this roadless area for years, with the compliance of the Idaho congressional delegation and the USDA Forest Service. The abundant old growth that this area contains makes it highly coveted by extractive interests.

This hike can be done as an overnight backpacking trip, although you could spend several days exploring this magnificent area.

From the trailhead, descend 100 yards to a signed junction indicating that Trail 505 heads (right) east. The main trail, Trail 347, is a closed road that has become popular with off-road vehicle enthusiasts. It continues straight (north).

The trail starts to climb immediately. It is faint and difficult to follow, at times going through open meadows. If you lose it, just head east to Clayburn Creek. You can pick the trail up again where it crosses the creek.

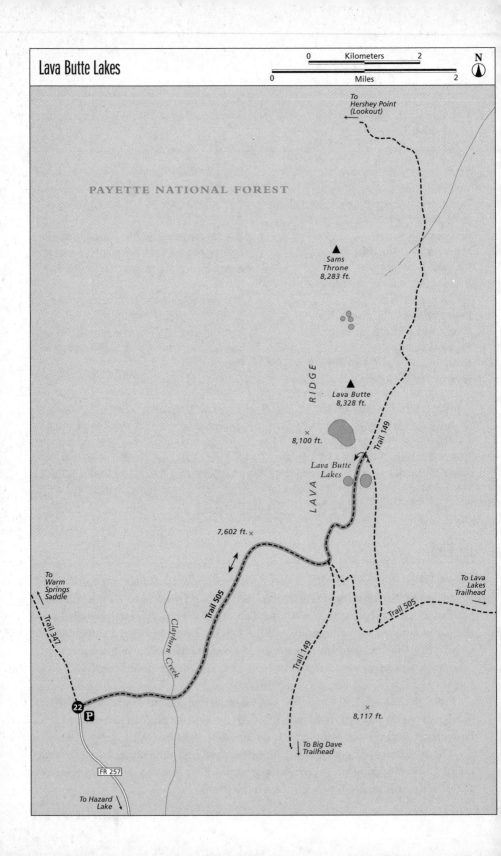

Lava Butte Lakes

To
Hershey Point
(Lookout)

PAYETTE NATIONAL FOREST

▲
Sams
Throne
8,283 ft.

R I D G E

▲
Lava Butte
8,328 ft.

× 8,100 ft.

Trail 149

Lava Butte
Lakes

L A V A

7,602 ft. ×

Trail 505

To
Warm
Springs
Saddle

Trail 347

Clayburn Creek

To Lava
Lakes
Trailhead

Trail 505

Trail 149

× 8,117 ft.

22
P

FR 257

To Big Dave
Trailhead

To Hazard
Lake

Once you reach the creek, the trail climbs in earnest to Lava Ridge and the junction with Trail 149, which it reaches at 2.7 miles. Trail 149 traverses Lava Ridge. Turn left here and follow Trail 149.

Lava Ridge is a unique feature. It represents an overlap of Columbia River basalt with the granitic rock of the Idaho Batholith. Lava Ridge itself is aesthetically similar to the limestone Scapegoat massif or Chinese Wall of the Bob Marshall country in Montana. It is an imposing feature, continually demanding attention.

On top of Lava Ridge, the views of the surrounding country are incredible. To the west, the Seven Devils tower magnificently above Rapid River, the Little Salmon River, and the Salmon River, while massive Patrick Butte dominates the foreground. To the north, beyond the Salmon River, is the Gospel–Hump country. To the east are the great peaks in the Secesh unprotected roadless area, highest in the Payette National Forest. So much of this country remains unprotected. Continued support for roadless area preservation will be necessary to save what you see from destruction.

From here, the trail soon descends to the eastern side of the ridge, reaching the lovely Lava Butte Lakes at 4.2 miles.

Options: From the Lava Butte Lakes, you can explore the lofty heights of Lava Ridge. Lava Butte, Sams Throne, and Hershey Point all provide spectacular views. You could spend a couple of days gazing at some big and remote mountain country.

—Lee Mercer

Miles and Directions

0.0 Start at the Clayburn Trailhead (7,000 feet).

2.7 Reach the junction with Trail 149 (7,600 feet). Go left on Trail 149.

3.4 Reach the trail's high point (7,980 feet).

4.2 Reach Lava Butte Lakes (about 7,600 feet). Retrace your steps.

8.4 Arrive back at the trailhead.

Boise Mountains

The Boise Mountains are located north and east of Boise and cover a vast area south of the Salmon River Mountains. These mountains are more great examples of Idaho Batholith granite and its history of uplifting and carving through faulting and waterways.

The area is heavily forested and receives more rainfall than most of the central Idaho ranges. Most of the evergreen forests are mixes of ponderosa pine, grand fir, Douglas fir, Engelmann spruce, lodgepole pine, and subalpine fir. The mountains contain large numbers of big-game species, including mule deer, elk, and black bear.

The 2,612,000-acre Boise National Forest manages much of the land in the Boise Mountains, as well as in the Salmon River ranges in Idaho. The district offices are located at Emmett, Garden Valley (Emmett Ranger District), Boise (Mountain Home Ranger District), Mountain Home, Lowman, Idaho City, and Cascade. Contact the forest service for information on many more hiking opportunities available within hours of the Boise area.

Anderson Ranch Reservoir in the Boise Mountains. PHOTO BY JOHN KRATZ

23 Jennie Lake

Jennie Lake is a beautiful mountain lake nestled in the Boise Mountains.

Start: 27 miles southeast of Lowman; 69 miles northeast of Boise
Type of hike: Out-and-back
Distance: 9 miles
Approximate hiking time: 2 days
Difficulty: Moderate
Best season: July–September
Trail surface: Dirt and rocks

Land status: Boise National Forest
Canine compatibility: Voice command
Fees and permits: None
Maps: USGS Jackson Peak and Bear River, Boise National Forest map
Trail contact: Lowman Ranger District; (208) 259-3361

Finding the trailhead: Take ID 21 east from Boise for 55 miles, past Idaho City. Fourteen miles before you reach Lowman, turn right onto the well-marked FR 384. Stay on this good gravel road for 6.2 miles until it forks. Take the left fork, FR 348, for 7.6 miles before reaching the 0.1 mile turnoff to the well-marked Jennie Lake Trailhead. GPS: N43 59.49' / W115 27.09'

The Hike

This is a great opportunity for residents of the large, growing, urban area of Boise to visit a pristine lake. Due to its proximity (a little over an hour) to such a populated area this trail is quite popular, and special consideration to preserve this delicate area should be considered.

The trail begins by following Bear Creek upstream. It gently climbs, skirting flowery hillsides and meadows and thick fir forests typical of the Boise mountains. It is well suited for any hiking ability and there are plenty of resting spots near the creek. After 3 miles the trees thin out slightly and the trail moves away from the creek to more open sage and meadow terrain. Nice views of colorful forest pockets along the slopes can be enjoyed with the changing seasons. The trail then veers south and climbs toward the lake.

Jennie Lake is nestled among nice granite outcroppings at the foot of Wolf Mountain. There are plenty of places to set up camp. Please do not form new campfire rings. The lake area serves as a nice jumping off point for cross-country exploring and scrambling opportunities.

Options: The Crooked River Trail is a popular hike near FR 384's turnoff from ID 21. Farther along FR 348 is the Bear River Trail, and eventually the North Fork of the Boise River Trail, which both provide extended backcountry experiences. Boise National Forest has numerous named and unnamed trails along the sides of the forest roads. Always look for the nonmotorized signs!

Jennie Lake

Miles and Directions

0.0 Start at the Jennie Lake trailhead (5,943 ft).

3.2 The trail curves westward.

4.2 The trail begins its final ascent.

4.5 Arrive at Jennie Lake. Retrace your steps.

9.0 Arrive back at the trailhead.

Trinity Mountains

The Trinity "Alps" are a small, scenic subrange of the Boise Mountains that rise just west of Anderson Ranch Reservoir on the South Fork of the Boise River. The subrange harbors about twenty scenic subalpine lakes. Trinity Mountain is also the name of the high point in the range. At 9,451 feet, it seems a bit higher because one of Idaho's most picturesque fire tower lookouts sits on top.

Most of the big lakes in the range are accessible by truck, and even sedan if driven carefully. Big Trinity, Little Trinity, Big Roaring, and Little Roaring Lakes all have busy campgrounds because they are set in very scenic locations just north of Trinity Mountain itself.

A number of trails climb the flanks of the Trinity Mountains, but the most popular by far is Rainbow Lakes Trail, which takes you on a nonmotorized route to a ring of subalpine lakes in a big cirque on the east side of Trinity Mountain.

—Ralph Maughan

Wildflowers on slopes in the Boise Mountains. Photo by Luke Kratz

24 Rainbow Lakes

The basin has beautiful scenery, including nine fishable lakes close together.

Start: About 50 linear miles north of Mountain Home

Type of hike: Out-and-back

Distance: 9 miles to Hideaway Lake

Approximate hiking time: 2-plus days

Difficulty: Moderate due to elevation gain and loss

Best season: July and August

Trail surface: Dirt and rock

Land status: Boise National Forest

Canine compatibility: Voice command though leash recommended

Fees and permits: None

Maps: USGS Little Trinity Lake and Trinity Mountain; Boise National Forest map.

Trail contact: Mountain Home Ranger District; (208) 587-7961

Special considerations: The drive is long and, at Anderson Ranch Reservoir, somewhat hazardous.

Parking and trailhead facilities: The well-developed parking lot on the east side of Big Trinity Lake has an outhouse and room for about twenty vehicles, but no potable water.

Finding the trailhead: It is a long drive to Trinity Mountain. From I-84 at Mountain Home, turn northeast onto US 20 and follow it 20 miles up into the mountains to the signed turnoff to Anderson Ranch Reservoir Dam. This road is paved for 3.5 miles, until it descends into the canyon of the South Fork of the Boise River to Anderson Ranch Dam. It is a steep, 2-mile descent to the dam (washboard road), but you cross the dam on a paved road. Across the dam at the road fork, turn right and follow the gravel road (FR 113) 8.5 somewhat treacherous miles to Fall Creek. The road winds above the reservoir the entire distance. There are many blind curves and no guardrails. Many folks drive big RVs on the road, so be very careful.

At Fall Creek, turn left onto FR 123, heading up Fall Creek. From here, it is 19 miles on gravel and dirt to Big Trinity Lake. FR 123 is gravel and follows Fall Creek for 5 miles to a junction where FR 123 ends. At the junction, take FR 129. In 2 more miles there is another junction. Turn right. Now the road gets steeper, narrower, and rougher, but it can be negotiated by a small sedan.

The road eventually climbs out of Fall Creek. Most problematic is the switchback ascent across the face of Peak 9,037. Snowslides from the winter sometimes block the pass here until mid- or even late July. Views are dramatic as you reach the pass at 8,500 feet. Especially intriguing is nearby Trinity Mountain. At 9,451 feet, it is the highest mountain in the area. On its top is a fire tower, one of the highest in Idaho. This mountain will dominate your view for most of the hike.

From the pass, descend to a number of pretty lakes with motorized campgrounds. It is 2 miles from the pass to the campground and trailhead at Big Trinity Lake. The main road continues on, eventually leading to Featherville, an alternative but longer route to the Trinity Mountain area. GPS: N43 37.50' / W115 25.52'

The Hike

Rainbow Lakes Trail is well signed and obvious as it leaves southward from the trailhead. It is open to foot traffic only—no horses or mountain bikes. There is no forage or room at the lakes for horses.

Green Island Divide. PHOTO BY LUKE KRATZ

The trail climbs moderately up a mostly open slope with great views to the northwest of unnamed lesser peaks in the Trinity Mountain area. Wildflowers are exceptional from July to mid-August, with mountain sorrel especially prominent. The trail levels out and then makes a steep final climb to the divide into the Rainbow Lakes basin. From the divide, you immediately see Trinity Mountain, and Green Island Lake 450 feet below.

The trail switchbacks down into the basin and soon reaches the side trail leading down to Green Island Lake. This is the first of many such trails to the lakes. Except for this one, all are short climbs up to the lakes. The main trail passes directly by only one lake—Little Rainbow. The shortest side trail is to Little Lookout Lake.

Every lake is scenic, and all have small rainbow and brook trout, except Hideaway, which has far fewer, but bigger, rainbow trout.

A sign marks every side trail to every lake with an estimate of the distance to that lake. All creeks have good log bridges. The main trail is well maintained to Little Rainbow Lake, after which the quality of tread and frequency of maintenance decline.

After passing Little Rainbow Lake and then two ponds, which are not on the topo quad, the trail fades but is quite easy to find. Soon you climb steeply to the divide between the Rainbow Lakes basin and Parks Creek. One steep section harbors a snow patch well into July.

At the divide, a faint trail proceeds down the left side of meadowy Parks Creek. The trail to Hideaway, on the other hand, is more obvious and climbs steeply right up the ridge to the south (topped by Peak 8,916). Follow this steep trail for about 0.2 mile; it then swerves just to the right of the ridge and leads into the basin that holds Hideaway Lake. There is an unmapped pond just below Hideaway and a creek between the two.

Options: The side trail to Big Rainbow Lake (8,126 feet) continues past the lake and on to Trinity Mountain, where it joins the road to the lookout at 9,300 feet.

—Ralph Maughan

Miles and Directions

0.0 Start at the Big Trinity Lake trailhead (7,790 feet).

1.0 Reach the Rainbow basin divide (8,410 feet).

1.3 Pass the Green Island Lake Trail (8,150 feet).

3.5 Reach Little Rainbow Lake, the basin's low point (7,790 feet).

4.2 Cross the Rainbow basin and Parks Creek divide (8,340 feet).

4.5 Reach Hideaway Lake (8,420 feet). Retrace your steps.

9.0 Arrive back at the trailhead.

Hells Canyon

Many claim that Hells Canyon is the deepest gorge on earth. Some hold that it is "merely" the deepest gorge in North America. However, relief and exposure are only one aspect of the precarious balance of Hells Canyon and the surrounding glacier-carved canyon country that reaches west to Oregon and Washington's Blue Mountains and east to Idaho's Little Salmon River Valley: In terms of geologic, botanic, scenic, ecological, and historical significance, the Hells Canyon country is a story unto itself.

The Hells Canyon ecosystem rests at the geographic heart of the vast Columbia River basin. It is literally the hub of the wheel in terms of the large wildland and ecosystem complexes in the Pacific Northwest. Its wildlands are a veritable conduit for genetic interchange, including the migration of large mammals, throughout the region.

In the era before full occupation by settlers (a mere 125 years ago), the Hells Canyon environs were home to the Joseph band of the Nez Perce tribe, led in its latter years by the renowned Chief Joseph. In modern times, the native civilization is not to be found in Hells Canyon. (The Nez Perce tribe was driven out in 1877 by the US Cavalry in one of the saddest chapters in Native American history.) Yet artifacts and homesites remain. The Hells Canyon country is identified as one of the most significant archaeological sites in the American West. Part of the area is designated as a National Archaeological Sensitivity Area.

The canyon bottom is a furnace of inversion-induced heat in summer: lower in elevation, warmer, and climatically isolated from the cold, snow-mantled upland regions. At the floor of Hells Canyon, 100 miles of the Snake River is still free flowing, 67 of which are designated under the National Wild and Scenic Rivers Act. This section of river represents the largest watercourse still in a predominantly wilderness condition in the lower forty-eight states. Including the adjoining Wallowa Mountains in Oregon, well over a million acres of roadless land remain, about half of which is designated wilderness. Most of these protective classifications are a result of the 1975 Hells Canyon National Recreation Area Act, which established the 652,000-acre Hells Canyon National Recreation Area (HCNRA) in recognition of the need to protect the unique and irreplaceable values of Hells Canyon.

Wildlife is diverse and abundant, mainly due to the diversity of vegetation and climate in a relatively concentrated area and also because of the predominantly wild character of the landscape. In addition to supporting one of the two largest elk herds in North America, this is the habitat of a healthy predator population: a wide variety of hawks and other birds of prey, including ospreys and bald and golden eagles, which winter in the depths of the canyon. Peregrine falcons have been reestablished on the canyon's west rim. Relatively large numbers of predatory mammals exist, including black bears, cougars, martens, and fishers. There have even been sightings of grizzly bears in the Lord Flat area on the Oregon side. (These were thought to have been extinct in Oregon for more than fifty years.) In recent years wolves may have crossed from Idaho into Oregon by way of Hells Canyon.

Endangered salmon and steelhead, greatly diminished from historic levels, retain a precarious hold despite interference from numerous downstream impoundments and habitat degradation from logging and livestock grazing. Good potential for increased anadromous fish runs exists, provided the habitat is maintained. In addition, prehistoric giant white sturgeon also inhabit the Snake River. A variety of other rare or infrequent species, such as the great gray owl, bighorn sheep, and Franklin's grouse, find a haven in Hells Canyon.

Despite the bounty, grace, and unique features of Hells Canyon, the rush to consume and develop it has been almost overwhelming. The latter-day struggles that have taken place over the fate of these lands have been nearly as hard-fought and bitter as the wars between the Nez Perce and the US Cavalry. The initial controversies began in the late 1950s and raged over the "use" and "ownership" of the Hells Canyon country. Conservationists, recreationists, and Native Americans engaged the hydro and resort developers and timber companies in administrative and legal skirmishes.

The timber companies covet the old-growth ponderosa pine, while the hydro developers had varying visions of huge dams that would have flooded the remainder of the free-flowing Snake. The proposed sites of these dams are still in evidence via painted inscriptions imposed high on the canyon walls. They remain as a reminder to those who were involved in the initial controversies of the narrowly avoided doom, which culminated with the passage of the Hells Canyon National Recreation Area Act.

The act protected 67 miles of the Snake River and 26 miles of the Rapid River from dams, as well as designated 194,000 acres of wilderness. It also set restrictions on developmental activities among goals aimed at protecting and maintaining the myriad natural phenomena within the HCNRA. Yet while the victory of 1975 was tremendous, the controversy is far from over. The forest service, entrusted with management of the HCNRA, has instead instigated enthusiastic programs of timber extraction, motorized recreation, and livestock grazing within the HCNRA, ignoring the stewardship obligation of the HCNRA Act.

These timbering, livestock, and motorization priorities in the HCNRA have completely overshadowed the pursuit of legislatively mandated goals for protection of fish, wildlife, wilderness, scenic, and unique ecological values. Logging and road-building projects in the HCNRA are concentrated in the most critical strongholds of ecological integrity.

Unfortunately, the prospect looms of having to "reprotect" what was presumed protected when the HCNRA Act was passed. Current management practices in the HCNRA have inspired litigation and calls for new legislation. Discussion of legislative proposals is proceeding. Chief among alternative proposals is the application of National Park and Preserve status, an option that could more fully protect the area and still allow traditional activities such as hunting to continue. This option would entrust management of the Hells Canyon ecosystem to the National Park Service instead of the forest service.

The Hells Canyon Preservation Council (HCPC), formed in 1965 to preserve the qualities that define the deepest gorge on earth and its surrounding terrain, continues the effort to keep Hells Canyon intact. For additional information regarding Hells Canyon, or to become part of this nonprofit organization, please contact the HCPC. (See Appendix A.)

　　　—Ric Bailey, former executive director, Hells Canyon Preservation Council

25 Seven Devils Loop

Circumnavigate the rugged and well-named Seven Devils Mountains. This 25-mile-plus loop offers magnificent views into Hells Canyon with some thirty lakes and abundant wildlife.

Start: 17 miles west (and far above) Riggins, in the Hells Canyon Wilderness
Type of hike: Loop
Distance: 23.5 miles for the featured loop; 29 miles if you include the side mileage to Dry Diggins fire lookout and Echo, Baldy, and Lower Cannon Lakes.
Approximate hiking time: 4–7 days plus
Difficulty: Strenuous
Best season: Mid-July–mid-September
Trail surface: Dirt and rock
Land status: Hells Canyon National Recreation Area and wilderness
Canine compatibility: Not allowed within wilderness

Fees and permits: None
Maps: USGS He Devil and Heavens Gate ID; Hells Canyon National Recreation Area map
Trail contact: Hells Canyon National Recreation Area; (208) 628-3916; www.fs.usda.gov/wallawallawhitman
Special considerations: Lots of elevation gain and loss. To camp by a lake usually means a 400-foot, 1-mile climb off the main trail.
Parking and trailhead facilities: The trailhead is located at Windy Saddle Campground, but Seven Devils Campground (0.5 mile farther) is nicer and has more cover; there are ten units at Seven Devils and five at Windy Saddle. No water.

Finding the trailhead: The access road climbs 5,400 feet in 17 miles. From US 95 just south of Riggins, take the signed FR 517 on the right (west), which leads to the Seven Devils. This road is oiled to control dust for 5 miles, to the national forest boundary. At the boundary, it becomes a gravel road, but the last 7 miles are rough, with much embedded rock. It requires high clearance but not four-wheel drive. It is not an acceptable road for trailers or RVs. GPS: N45 20.96' / W116 30.75'

The Hike

This is an excellent loop hike because each day offers fine views and each night a lake to camp by. The terrain is rugged with a good deal of elevation loss and gain.

The Seven Devils create their own weather, as storms sweep off Lord Flat on the Oregon side of Hells Canyon and recirculate over these pinnacled mountains. The west side is where one encounters the fiercest weather, including hailstorms.

Hells Canyon is visible from points on the west side of the range. It is approximately 8,000 feet deep, measuring from the top of the Seven Devils to the canyon bottom. The Hells Canyon National Recreation Area Act established the 223,000-acre Hells Canyon Wilderness. Although inclusion of the Seven Devils proper in the wilderness was never contested, privately owned domestic sheep grazing on federal land here have passed a fatal disease on to wild bighorn sheep. On the Oregon side, the beautiful Lord Flat, visible for much of this hike, is still under threat from logging and road building.

There is scarring from forest fires that have burned in the past on or near the loop, most extensively near the head of the Rapid River.

I recommend doing the loop counterclockwise, saving the easiest part (Lower Cannon Lake to the trailhead) for last and taking the toughest part (Windy Saddle to Bernard Lakes) first.

The trail starts by dropping 480 feet through forest into the East Fork of the Sheep Creek valley. It then climbs 1,000 feet to cross the northern spur of the Seven Devils range. Here you can look back and see the Heavens Gate lookout at 8,407 feet. As the trail skirts west and then south, it drops 1,300 feet to a log crossing at the West Fork of Sheep Creek. In this section, the Devils Tooth monolith dominates the weird and wild-looking terrain. The trail goes west, contouring the head of the West Fork for approximately 1 mile, then climbs yet again for 400 feet to Iron Phone junction. So far you have covered 5 miles but climbed some 1,200 feet.

Portions of the old downed telephone line still lie abandoned near the four-way Iron Phone junction. Most people take Sheep Lake Trail on the extreme left, which leads into the heart of the Seven Devils and to a cluster of six lakes. Sheep Lake Trail also forks in 0.5 mile to lead on the right (west) to Hibbs Cow Camp, where you'll pick up the continuation of the loop described here.

However, to see Hells Canyon from Dry Diggins fire lookout, continue straight ahead on the trail to the Bernard Lakes. It is a little over a mile, and 300 feet in elevation gain, to the second of the Bernard Lakes. Just past this lake is a lily-covered pond. Here, keep to the right in a confusing and unsigned web of trails. This will lead you up 500 feet and another 0.25 mile to the lookout. The Snake River and Hells Canyon lie 6,500 feet below in a sloping descent through forest and old burns. You may also see mountain goats.

Back down on the main trail, continue to your right (south) for a little over a mile through open, then sparsely wooded country. Do not take the trail on the left, which leads to Sheep Lake. Instead, continue for 0.3 mile to the signed Potato Hill and Little Granite Creek Trails above Hibbs Cow Camp. Stay to the left, which will put you on Potato Hill Trail and eventually the trail leading to Echo Lake. This part is confusing, but stay to the left and you'll be okay. The basic idea is to hug the toe of the range and not wander too far downhill into Little Granite Creek.

The Seven Devils Mountains. PHOTO BY LUKE KRATZ

From the Dry Diggins lookout junction to the turnoff to Echo Lake is 2 miles. Little Granite Creek and others in Hells Canyon have seen massive forest fires in recent years. This forested lake is about 300 feet above and a rocky 0.5 mile from the main trail. Its rocky cirque basin is headed by the He Devil, at 9,393 feet the highest in the range.

Back on the main trail, it is about 1.5 miles to the cutoff trail to Baldy Lake. The trail drops 160 feet west through forest, then contours generally south to cross the southernmost fork of Little Granite Creek. It is a steep (500-foot), 1-mile climb to Baldy Lake, one of the more heavily used sites. Baldy Lake itself is splendid. Here you are able to see the He Devil, Mount Belial, the Devils Throne, and the Twin Imps. This country might remind you of the "Night on Bald Mountain" segment of Disney's classic *Fantasia*.

From this point to the Cannon Lakes, the trail is not heavily used. It is about 4.5 miles and 1,280 feet of elevation gain to the southern end of the range and the Horse Heaven junction. This is probably the most outstanding section of the loop because of the eagle's view as you head due south above timberline for almost the entire trek.

Once past Horse Heaven, you begin a slow, easy downhill walk. After you turn north, you're on Boise Trail. The aspect of the land changes dramatically as you descend into old-growth forest, and this looks like the good black bear habitat that it is. While there are many lakes on this side of the range, we found trails to only one. Although the USGS quad shows a trail to Dog Lake, we could not find it. It is another 7.5 miles to Hanson Creek. There is one trail (about 1 mile before Hanson Creek) that leads down to the Rapid River. Stay to the left, but consider the Rapid River hike as a possible, even larger loop for those who just can't get enough wild country.

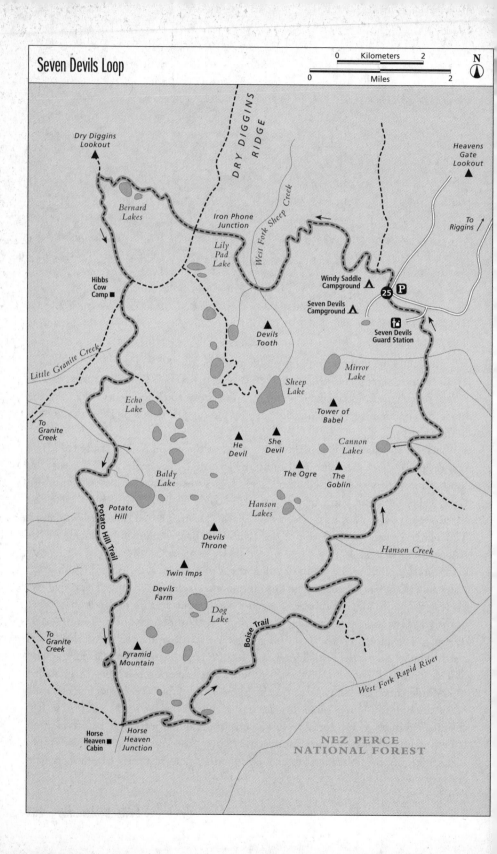

Hanson Creek itself is not remarkable. The land is slumping and full of deadfall, and the creek is difficult to access. It is another easy 2 miles of contour through forest cover and occasional deep woods to the Cannon Lakes. The trail to this popular area leaves on the left (west) and climbs 240 feet in less than a mile to Lower Cannon Lake. The peaks surrounding the Cannon Lakes are the Goblin, the She Devil, and the Tower of Babel.

The hike from the Cannon Lakes to the trailhead is 2.5 miles, in good condition, and rises about 240 feet. For more than a decade, much of the trail work in the Seven Devils has been accomplished through annual service trips conducted by the Sierra Club. If you would like to participate in these adventures, contact the Sierra Club Outings department (see Appendix A).

Options: To get a full view of this country, you might want to take Heavens Gate Road to the Heavens Gate fire lookout. The road is nicely graded for the first two-thirds but then is rocky, almost requiring four-wheel drive. From the end of the road, it is a 0.25-mile walk to the top.

—Jackie Johnson Maughan

Miles and Directions

0.0 Start at the Windy Saddle trailhead (7,600 feet).

0.8 Pass the East Fork Sheep Creek Trail (7,200 feet).

2.0 Reach the northern end of the Seven Devils (8,000 feet).

3.5 Reach the West Fork Sheep Creek (6,900 feet).

5.0 Arrive at the Iron Phone junction (7,310 feet). Continue straight.

6.0 Reach the upper Bernard Lake (7,400 feet).

6.5 Arrive at the Dry Diggins Fire Lookout Trail (7,560 feet). **Option:** Hike 0.5 mile to the Dry Diggins fire lookout (7,828 feet).

8.0 Pass the Sheep Lake Trail (7,310 feet).

8.2 Arrive at Hibbs Cow Camp and the junction with the Little Granite Creek Trail (7,400 feet). Continue on the Potato Hill Trail.

8.5 Pass the Echo Lake Trail (6,920 feet). **Option:** Hike 0.5 mile to Echo Lake (7,243 feet).

10.5 Pass the Baldy Lake Trail (6,880 feet). **Option:** Hike 1 mile to Baldy Lake (7,200 feet).

14.0 Arrive at the Horse Heaven junction (7,840 feet). Head north on the Boise Trail.

18.0 Pass the Rapid River Trail (7,014 feet).

19.0 Cross Hanson Creek (6,800 feet).

21.0 Pass the Cannon Lakes Trail (6,800 feet). **Option:** Hike 0.75 mile to Lower Cannon Lake (7,320 feet).

23.5 Arrive back at the trailhead.

Sawtooth Mountains

Perhaps the most famous mountains in Idaho, the Sawtooth Range rises abruptly on the west side of the beautiful and spacious Sawtooth Valley and nearby Stanley Basin. Near the southern end of the Sawtooth Valley, the Sawtooths give way to the Smoky Mountains, which then extend southward all the way to the Snake River Plain.

The core of the Sawtooth Range is composed of beautiful pink granite, which originated as a molten intrusion—a pluton—into the already emplaced igneous formation called the Idaho Batholith, which covers most of central Idaho. Unlike the mostly gray granitic rock of the Idaho Batholith, the Sawtooth Batholith is noted for its pink or even apricot color, the result of high concentration of potassium feldspar (a granitic mineral) in the rock. The hard pink granite, sculpted into walls, peaks, and spires by ice age glaciers, is a mecca for climbers. Parts of this range indeed resemble sawteeth.

The 216,000-acre Sawtooth Wilderness protects the core of the Sawtooth Mountains and is Idaho's best-known designated wilderness area. Use of the east side of this fairyland of rock is heavy. The western side is relatively uncrowded, and the vast unprotected roadless country that adjoins it is virtually unused.

The entire wilderness is well served with good trails. Access to the trailheads is easy on the east side of the wilderness, which has all-weather gravel or paved roads and mostly well-developed trailheads. The west side, however, involves longer drives, mostly on dirt or gravel roads.

Anglers can discover more than 300 stunning alpine and subalpine lakes, sixty or so of which support fisheries. The most common game fish is the brook trout. Unfortunately, many of these brook trout populations consist only of small fish due to overpopulation and the inherent low productivity of these high, granite-bound lakes.

Wildlife is varied, with most of the Rocky Mountain game species represented except grizzly bears. The Sawtooth Range is a stronghold for wolverines. Despite all the variety, however, the density of wildlife is low. The growing Idaho wolf population has found the White Cloud Mountains on the east side of the Sawtooth Valley more to its liking.

At the base of the Sawtooth Mountains are a number of large, moraine-dammed lakes. Alturas, Pettit, Redfish, and Stanley Lake are the largest. Redfish Lake was named for the color of the tens of thousands of salmon returning to spawn in the lake and die. Sadly, dams on the Columbia River and the Snake River in Washington State have caused the extinction of many salmon runs, almost including that of the Snake River sockeye, which spawn in these lakes and adjacent creeks. The grimmest year was 1989, when just one sockeye salmon returned to Redfish Lake. (He was

The jagged-edge scenery of the Sawtooths. PHOTO BY ANNE KRATZ

nicknamed "Lonesome Larry.") Since then, a very expensive effort to save the Snake River sockeye run has slowly resulted in a partial restoration of the run. Between 1991 and 1999, sixteen wild and seven hatchery-produced adults returned to Idaho. In the fall of 2000, 257 hatchery-produced adults had returned—making it the best sockeye return for Idaho since 1977. The run won't be considered recovered until more than 2,000 fish return each year. Good runs of more than 1,500 sockeye occurred in 2010 and 2011, but the numbers declined in 2012 and are still not self-sustaining.

Adjacent to the Sawtooth Wilderness, to the west, northwest, and south, are 320,000 acres of unprotected de facto wilderness. Outdoor lovers want to add it to the Sawtooth Wilderness, increasing the size of the protected country to 536,000 acres. This would be one of America's biggest wildernesses. A considerable portion of the country to the west and southwest (including part of the existing Sawtooth Wilderness) burned in the Rabbit Creek Fire of 1994, and more burned in the Trail Creek Fire of 2000. There is no timber resource left to cut, and due to the slow growth rate of trees in these mountain lands, there never was one unless the logging was fueled by taxpayer subsidies.

The Sawtooth Wilderness is part of the larger Sawtooth National Recreation Area (SNRA), which also gives protection to the pastoral beauty of the Sawtooth Valley and the Stanley Basin. The act of Congress that created the SNRA in 1972 also gives limited protection to the wild character of the White Cloud and Boulder mountain ranges, which lie on the SNRA's east and southeast sides. In recent years, however, the SNRA has suffered from lack of funding. One result is a charge to hike at almost all trailheads. You can purchase a pass for several days or, for just a bit more, for the entire season.

—Ralph Maughan

26 Bench Lakes

This beautiful ridgeline walk above Redfish Lake leads, to five-plus lakes nestled below Mount Heyburn.

Start: Redfish Lake area 5 miles south of Stanley

Type of hike: Out-and-back

Distance: 8 miles

Approximate hiking time: 2 days

Difficulty: Easy to moderate

Best season: Summer, fall

Trail surface: Sand along the ridge; dirt and rock

Land status: Sawtooth Wilderness; Sawtooth National Recreation Area

Canine compatibility: Not allowed in wilderness

Fees and permits: Check with the forest service. Some years require a Sawtooth National Recreation Area (SNRA) trailhead fee. In addition, a free wilderness permit (available at the trailhead) is needed. Parties of eight or more must get a wilderness permit from the SNRA headquarters or the Stanley office of the SNRA.

Maps: USGS Mt. Cramer and Stanley ID; Sawtooth National Recreation Area–Sawtooth National Forest map

Trail contact: Sawtooth National Recreation Area–Stanley Office; (208) 774-3000

Finding the trailhead: On ID 75 at 4.1 miles south of Stanley, turn at the sign for Redfish Lake. Follow this road until another sign indicates Redfish Trailhead. If you reach the lodge, you've gone too far. GPS: N44 8.84' / W114 55.19'

The Hike

Park at the Redfish Trailhead and follow the path across the road to where the Fishhook Creek Trail begins. At 0.6 mile there is a junction with the Bench Lakes Trail. Turn left here and follow the trail across a bridge over Fishhook Creek. The trail winds up the ridge overlooking Redfish Lake until it finally maintains a straight path parallel to the lake. This stretch is an enjoyable walk. On the right (west) are views of Sawtooth peaks: Heyburn Mountain, Horstmann Peak, and the Grand Mogul. On the left (east), overlooking the deep, blue Redfish Lake, are views of Castle Peak and the White Clouds.

After nearly 2.5 miles you reach another junction with the Bench Lakes Trail. Head right here into the Sawtooth Wilderness, where you must obtain a permit. Begin the climb up gentle switchbacks to the first lake. The waters are pristine, with a more intimate view of the Sawtooth Peaks than normally encountered. The second lake is a mere stroll from the first. The third lake takes a little more time—the trail diminishes and you must follow the lake's outflow. A good-size fourth lake also can be reached by hiking 0.5 mile cross-country from the third. A fifth lake is even farther, tucked high in the crags; this may take some climbing to access. These all lie at the

Bench Lakes

0 Kilometer 1

0 Mile 1

N

SAWTOOTH
NATIONAL FOREST

Fishhook Creek Trail

Fishhook Creek

To 75

26
P

Redfish Lake Rd.

Lodge

Redfish
Lake
Visitor
Center

Point
Campground

Redfish Lake Trail

Redfish
Lake

Bench Lakes

1
2
3
4
5

Bench Lakes Trail

Heyburn
Mountain
10,200 ft.

Grand Mogul
9,733 ft.

The First Bench Lake with Heyburn Mountain in the background. PHOTO BY LUKE KRATZ

base of the castlelike Heyburn Mountain; this and McGown, Regan, and the Grand Mogul are some of the most scenic mountains in the state.

Options: Continue on Fishhook Creek Trail or Redfish Inlet Trail for more multi-day backcountry opportunities.

Miles and Directions

0.0 Start at the Redfish Lake trailhead (6,600 feet).

0.6 Turn right at the Bench Lakes trail junction.

1.1 Reach the ridgeline above Redfish Lake (7,100 feet).

3.5 Turn left at second Bench Lakes trail junction toward the mountains (7,500 feet).

3.7 Pass the Sawtooth Wilderness boundary.

4.0 Reach the third Bench Lake (7,800 feet).

8.0 Arrive back at the trailhead.

27 Toxaway-Pettit Loop

This is a classic backpacking trip in the Sawtooth Mountains. There are alpine lakes, waterfalls, and views of some of the most jagged of the Sawtooths.

Start: 15 miles south of Stanley
Type of hike: Loop
Distance: 18 miles
Approximate hiking time: 3–5 days, depending on options
Difficulty: Moderately strenuous due to elevation gain and possible early-season snowfield crossing (mid- to late July)
Best season: Late July–mid-September
Trail surface: Dirt and rock
Land status: Sawtooth Wilderness; Sawtooth National Recreation Area
Canine compatibility: Dogs on leash July 1–Labor Day
Fees and permits: Check with the forest service. Some years require a Sawtooth National Recreation Area (SNRA) trailhead fee. In addition, a free wilderness permit (available at the trailhead) is needed. Parties of eight or more must get a wilderness permit from the SNRA headquarters or the Stanley office of the SNRA.
Maps: USGS Mt. Everly and Snowyside Peak ID; Fairfield and Ketchum Ranger Districts and Sawtooth National Recreation Area–Sawtooth National Forest map
Trail contact: Sawtooth National Recreation Area Headquarters; (208) 727-5000
Special considerations: Snow can make Snowyside Pass, Sand Mountain Pass, and Imogene Divide tricky until late July or even August. Campfires not allowed.
Parking and trailhead facilities: This is a major trailhead, with room for perhaps thirty vehicles at the well-developed, gravel parking lot, which is mostly in the shade of lodgepole pine. The trailhead has a nice restroom and a bulletin board.

Finding the trailhead: Turn off ID 75 about 45 miles north of Ketchum onto the signed road to Pettit Lake. Follow this much-used, but often badly washboarded, road about 2 miles to a T intersection at Pettit Lake's outlet. Take the road to the right. At the next fork, turn left and go about 0.5 mile to the obvious parking area at the trailhead. Signs guide the way. GPS: N43 59.05' / W114 52.33'

The Hike

The 18-mile loop begins and ends at Pettit Lake, a large moraine lake on the valley floor. The loop encounters all the features that have made the Sawtooths famous: toothed peaks, glacial boulders, large and small mountain lakes, avalanche runs, talus slides, granite cliffs, mountain meadows, waterfalls, cascading streams, and dense stands of lodgepole pine.

A brief walk down the trail brings you to the junction with the trail that goes up Pettit Lake Creek (straight ahead) and the trail leading up into Yellow Belly Creek (to the right). It's best to take the right fork and climb over into Yellow Belly Creek, making Pettit Lake Creek the last leg of the hike. The prospect of climbing over the

Elegant Sawtooth backcountry. PHOTO BY JOSH KELLEY

550-foot-high moraine between the two drainages is more inviting on the first day, when you're fresh, than on your last.

At the trail junction, begin the switchbacking ascent of the moraine amid grass, sage, and flowers. The dark blue waters of Pettit Lake sparkle behind you. After about 0.3 mile you'll reach the edge of the forest. Giant, weathered, outlying Douglas firs quickly give way to dense lodgepole thickets as you continue to climb. You'll have to find some other inspiration besides anticipation of the view to egg you on: There is no view at the top. From the top, switchback down into the canyon of Yellow Belly Creek, continuing through lodgepole forest. You arrive at the bottom of the canyon 2.7 miles from your vehicle and join the trail that comes up Yellow Belly Creek. Just a few yards down this trail is McDonald Lake, a somewhat marshy lake with a burn on its south side from a 1981 fire. Larger Yellow Belly Lake, another 0.5 mile down-canyon, has a burn from a 1982 fire.

Continuing on the main trail, head up the canyon, walking almost on the level through more lodgepole forest. After about a mile you climb a short hill and then cross Yellow Belly Creek.

Just 0.2 mile past the stream crossing, you begin the 600-foot climb to Farley Lake. After 0.75 mile the trail goes past a small, thundering waterfall on Yellow Belly Creek. Then, in another 0.5 mile, you cross through a grassy scrub timber basin through which the creek cascades. Soon you're at Farley Lake (about 1.75 miles from the start of the climb). This pretty lake is full of brook trout, a very common fish in the Sawtooths.

For the next 1.5 miles, the trail climbs moderately, but erratically, through small meadows and scrub timber and past large boulders and rock slabs.

At 6.5 miles from the trailhead, you come to a junction. The trail to the right leads to Edith Lake, then over a 9,200-foot pass and down to lovely Imogene Lake, which rests in the Hellroaring Creek drainage. Stay on the trail to the left. Soon you'll pass an elongated pond at an elevation of 8,165 feet. Continue past this and a smaller pond, then past small Bowknot Lake. One mile and about 150 feet above the junction with Edith Lake Trail, you finally reach big, beautiful Toxaway Lake. Gorgeous peaks rise above the lake at the head of the canyon. The lake itself is a mile long, making it one of the biggest in the Sawtooth Mountains. You'll generally find good fishing in Toxaway for brook trout of up to a foot—pretty large for Sawtooth brookies.

On the north side of the lake is a trail that climbs over Sand Mountain Pass, providing access to Vernon, Edna, and Virginia Lakes (all on the other side of the Sawtooth crest) at the headwaters of the South Fork of the Payette River. The trail over Sand Mountain is also an alternative route to Edith Lake and then down into the Hellroaring drainage to Imogene Lake. To continue on the loop to Twin and Alice Lakes in the Pettit Lake Creek drainage, continue around Toxaway Lake. The trail has been completely rebuilt since the Snowyside USGS quadrangle was published in 1964, so the map is incorrect. You can't get lost, however.

It's a 1,000-foot climb and about 1.5 miles from Toxaway to Snowyside Pass (9,390 feet). The trail rounds big Toxaway Lake and climbs up into a steep canyon that harbors three small lakes. The scenery is absolutely sublime as you switchback to the pass. Note that snow often remains here, on the northeast-facing slope of 10,651-foot Snowyside Peak, until late July.

From the notch at the pass, start down into the Pettit Lake Creek drainage by following the trail that is lodged into the wide part of a steep wall. Right below, 500 feet down, is the upper of the Twin Lakes. The trail loops around the north side of the cirque and descends to the Twin Lakes, two sapphire pools situated just below timberline in a wonderful pink cirque. Rugged peaks rise all around these fish-filled lakes, which are separated by only a narrow rock band.

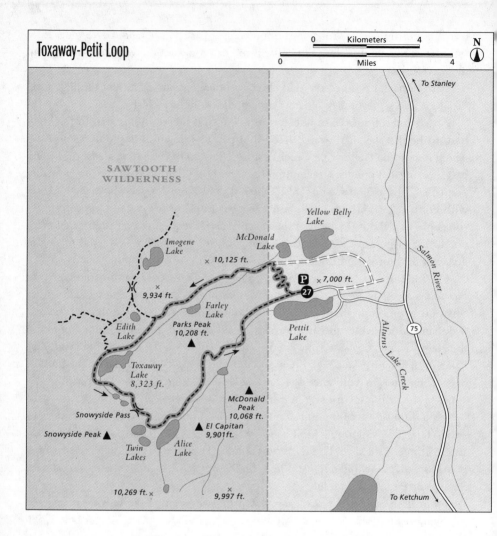

0   Kilometers   4

0   Miles   4

N

To Stanley

SAWTOOTH
WILDERNESS

Yellow Belly
Lake

Imogene
Lake

McDonald
Lake

× 10,125 ft.

Salmon River

×
9,934 ft.

Farley
Lake

P
27

× 7,000 ft.

Edith
Lake

Parks Peak
10,208 ft.

Pettit
Lake

Alturas Lake Creek

75

Toxaway
Lake
8,323 ft.

McDonald
Peak
10,068 ft.

Snowyside Pass

Snowyside Peak ▲

El Capitan
9,901 ft.

Twin
Lakes

Alice
Lake

10,269 ft. ×

9,997 ft.

To Ketchum

From Twin Lakes, head east over a saddle and switchback down to Alice Lake, another large lake, fully the size of the Twin Lakes together. Alice is a scintillating blue, bejeweled with small rock islands and surrounded by subalpine fir struggling through the granite. El Capitan thrusts up on the lake's east side, looking somewhat similar to its namesake in Yosemite National Park. The serrated crest of the Sawtooth Range forms the skyline to the south and southwest and shows why these mountains are called the Sawtooths.

Past Alice Lake, heading down Pettit Lake Creek, walk on the level past two small lakes, then begin a moderate descent through open forest to a creek ford 0.5 mile below the last of the two small lakes. Descend, now at a steeper angle, for 0.3 mile to a bridged crossing of Pettit Lake Creek. Continue to descend, switchbacking at times, as the right (northwest) wall of the canyon becomes very rugged and convoluted.

After 2 miles you'll pass under the rugged cliffs and reach the floor of the lower canyon. Here the atmosphere is moister, and the trail can be muddy after a summer thundershower. Cross the creek twice, but you can probably get across on logjams or foot logs without having to wade. There is a lush flat at the inlet of Pettit Lake.

Once you reach the shore of Pettit Lake, follow the trail on its north side for another mile, passing in and out of timber. Here you can take a classic photo of the lake waters and 10,068-foot McDonald Peak rising to the southwest.

Options: You can climb over Imogene Divide (9,270 feet) into Hellroaring Creek and visit Imogene Lake. Or you can climb over Sand Mountain Pass (9,400 feet) and visit the lakes in the South Fork of the Payette headwaters: Vernon, Edna, and Virginia Lakes. They are all beautiful.

—Ralph Maughan

Miles and Directions

0.0 Start at the Pettit Lake Trailhead (7,000 feet).

0.1 At the trail junction, go right toward Yellow Belly Creek.

0.9 Top the Pettit Lake and Yellow Belly divide (7,570 feet).

1.7 At the trail junction in bottom of Yellow Belly (7,100 feet), turn up the canyon toward Farley Lake.

2.7 Cross Yellow Belly Creek (7,190 feet).

4.2 Reach Farley Lake (7,750 feet).

6.5 At the Edith Lake Trail junction (8,200 feet), stay left on the trail to Toxaway Lake.

7.8 Pass the trail junction to Sand Mountain Pass at Toxaway Lake (8,380 feet).

9.3 Head over Snowyside Pass (9,390 feet).

10.0 Reach the first Twin Lake (8,854 feet).

11.2 Reach Alice Lake (8,600 feet).

12.2 Cross Pettit Lake Creek (8,580 feet).

14.2 Pass under a rugged cliff (7,800).

16.4 Reach the west shore and inlet of Pettit Lake (7,000 feet).

18.0 Arrive back at the trailhead (7,000 feet).

Boulder and White Cloud Mountains

Salmon River Mountains is a nonspecific name applied to a 30,000-square-mile maze of high ridges and deep canyons in central Idaho. From the edges of this mountain fastness radiate other mountains, identifiable as separate ranges.

One such string of mountains, consisting of hundreds of 10,000- to 11,000-foot peaks, runs southward from the Salmon River Mountains to form the east side of the Sawtooth Valley, then it humps farther south, past Ketchum, Hailey, and Bellevue, to end in the basalt of the Snake River Plain.

Although this is one continuous mountain range, over the years the string has been broken into three separate groups in people's minds. To the north, against the Salmon River Canyon and Salmon River Mountains, they are known as the White Clouds. This was originally a local name, limited to just one magnificent ridge of high, often white, peaks. Today, all mountains between Salmon River Canyon on the north, Germania and Pole Creeks on the south, and the East Fork of the Salmon River to the east bear this name.

The next mountains in this string are not pearls but boulders. The Boulder Mountains are perhaps the least known and visited of the three mountain groups, especially their eastern flank, which is beginning to take on the name Herd Peak Highlands.

Finally, the southernmost and highest are the Pioneer Mountains. In average elevation, they are the second highest range in the Gem State. One peak, Hyndman Peak, just tops 12,000 feet. The Boulders, it is generally agreed, end at Trail Creek Gorge. Here, the Pioneers more than take up the slack of the colorful Boulders with their glistening gray peaks, speckled tarns, and gorges thundering with cascades. The Pioneer Mountains are described in detail in the next section of this guide.

The White Clouds became celebrities in the late 1960s, when a group of hikers found then-lonesome Willow Lake, the first of the Boulder Chain Lakes, under siege. The waters of the lake were normally perfectly clear, reflecting the rainbow colors of a nearby peak. But the hikers found the waters full of "mud" from a driller's bit. One side of the lake had been stripped bare of trees to make room for mining exploration. One of Idaho's most famous conservation battles ensued. Before the dust would settle, there would be a new conservation-minded governor (Cecil Andrus) in the

Boulder and White Cloud Mountains from the East Fork area. PHOTO BY ANNE KRATZ

statehouse, with a whole new outlook and the political clout to back it. The legacy of Andrus, and his allies Frank Church and John Evans, lasted an entire generation before it devolved to the present group of anti-environmental politicians.

When the hikers protested the destruction, the now-famous retort was, "Don't worry, when we're done there won't be a lake. Hell, there won't even be a mountain!" The mountain they were referring to was none other than Castle Peak—at 11,810 feet the highest by far of the White Clouds, ruler of the range. This giant is now one of the best known mountains in Idaho. Back then, however, Castle Peak was pretty obscure, despite its exciting, towering beauty. It just didn't tower over any highways— or even dirt roads, for that matter.

Dedicated Idaho conservationists and the public were not convinced by talk of temporary jobs from the proposed mine or of the "critical" need for molybdenum in the economy—a metal that is now in extreme surplus.

Persistence led to creation of the Sawtooth National Recreation Area (SNRA) in 1972. This not only withdrew the White Clouds, most of the Boulders, and the Sawtooth Mountains from the filing of further mining claims but also provided the means to clean up the subdivisions sprouting like mushrooms in a cowpie in Sawtooth Valley. It also reclassified the old Sawtooth Primitive Area into the new, larger, and better Sawtooth Wilderness.

Ironically, while the White Clouds heralded the victory for many other successful battles, they themselves still lack wilderness designation today, despite the best efforts of the Idaho Conservation League and the Boulder–White Clouds Council. ATVs rip through too many high meadows, and bands of sheep beat some places to dust while threatening the native wildlife, such as the wolves that have recently reinhabited these mountains.

The White Clouds have many subalpine and alpine lakes. These see the most use, while the lower mountains to the north and west are where you will find the most solitude.

The Boulder Mountains rise in full view of ID 75 in the SNRA, but this face is too steep for much hiking. The good hiking portion requires a longer drive to the back-side (northeast side). The southwestern flank of the Boulders fronts the Ketchum–Sun Valley area, and they get a lot of use—usually by cheerful, fit, environmentally conscious, and well-educated folks. The comparatively lakeless Boulders offer rugged cliffs, booming waterfalls, and colorful rock.

Both ranges have much wildlife—elk, deer, mountain goats, pronghorn antelope, black bear, mountain lion, bighorn sheep, one or two wolf packs, and, of course, coyotes.

The White Clouds and part of the Boulders are a congressionally mandated Wilderness Study Area of about 200,000 acres. Idaho conservationists propose a 500,000-acre White Clouds–Boulder Wilderness. This is one of the largest remaining legally unprotected roadless areas in the United States. Idaho is lucky to have it, but the state's present congressional delegation doesn't see it that way. This delegation, financed by every moneyed special interest group in the alphabet (from AMAX to Zinc), thinks that the wilds of Idaho are a mote in the eye of humanity. But the decision is up to all American citizens. Will we prevail?

—Ralph Maughan

Even with deadlock in Congress to preserve this area, there is still a push to form the 571,276 acre Boulder–White Cloud National Monument. This would have to be an effort based on a coalition of many different Idaho groups, with a unified goal to recognize the ecological and economical benefits from preserving such an area. While it may not completely restrict grazing and off-road vehicles, as a wilderness area would, this plan would provide for single management of the entire area and balanced access for users of the backcountry. National monument status would also allow consistent coordination in protecting the wilderness character of the area and generate national interest and support to keep the area unchanged. Please contact the Idaho Conservation League and voice your support and opinions!

—Luke Kratz, 2014

28 Boulder Chain Lakes

Hike to a string of lakes with many small rainbow trout and access many other lake basins. This is a well-used and absolutely beautiful trail.

Start: In the White Cloud Mountains of the Sawtooth National Recreation Area (SNRA), about 35 miles southwest of Challis
Type of hike: Out-and-back
Distance: 20 miles
Approximate hiking time: 3–5 days
Difficulty: Moderate
Best season: Mid-July–August
Trail surface: Dirt and rock
Land status: Sawtooth National Recreation Area
Canine compatibility: Dogs on leash July 1– Labor Day
Fees and permits: None

Maps: USGS Boulder Chain Lakes and Livingston Creek; Fairfield and Ketchum Ranger Districts and Sawtooth National Recreation Area–Sawtooth National Forest map
Trail contact: Ketchum Ranger District; (208) 622-5371. Sawtooth National Recreation Area Headquarters; (208) 727-5000.
Special considerations: The trail is at high altitude with variable snowpack.
Parking and trailhead facilities: In most years and in most vehicles, you won't be able to drive clear to the trailhead but will have to stop 0.25 mile before. A site crowded with many vehicles is not uncommon.

Finding the trailhead: From Challis, take US 93 south to its junction with ID 75 on the right. Follow ID 75 about 16 miles south to where it bends right (west) toward Clayton. Before reaching Clayton, turn left (south) onto the signed and paved East Fork of the Salmon Road. It is 17 miles (the last 3 are gravel) until the turnoff on the right (west) onto the dirt Livingston Mill Road (FR 667). Another 5 miles brings you to the trailhead. GPS: N44 07.85' / W114 30.80'

The Hike

This hike will confirm everything you may have heard about the beauty of the White Clouds and Castle Peak. It has just about every lure for the outdoorsperson: deep, cool forests, mountain springs, lakes to fish or swim, mountains to climb, and a conservation battle to get you out of your armchair. (See the Boulder and White Cloud Mountains overview.)

Although this area gets heavy use, you lose about half the traffic early on when the trail forks to the Big Boulder Lakes. You lose another half after Frog Lake, because trail machines are not allowed into the Boulder Chain Lakes.

The first 0.5 mile of the trail is an old jeep road that ascends Big Boulder Creek canyon. After the road disappears in a slide, you'll pass briefly through a lodgepole pine and spruce forest. The trail is good throughout, and you should have no navigation problems. After the section of forest, you'll come out into a willow flat. Here you cross a bridge over Big Boulder Creek. Shortly thereafter, the trail forks. The right fork leads to the Big Boulder Lakes.

Two of the lakes in the Boulder Chain. Photo by Luke Kratz

The left fork (the one you follow) immediately leaves Big Boulder Creek and begins the long climb to Red Ridge, which involves about 4 miles and a gain of 1,900 feet of altitude. The trail was rebuilt to accommodate horse and off-road vehicle traffic; therefore, it has many more switchbacks than appear on the topographic quad. After you've climbed about a quarter of the way to Red Ridge, you'll encounter a good, heart-stopper view out over Big Boulder Creek's timber, its meadow, and the high peaks that rein it all in. Shortly after this view is a side trail on the left (south) leading to Little Redfish Lake.

Now you're stuck with the rest of the long pull to the top of Red Ridge. You'll make slow progress but then finally reach the pass. Big Boulder Creek lies behind you, creating a magnificent view. Below Railroad Ridge to the northwest, not quite in sight, is Livingston Mill. On the other side of the pass, Castle Peak rises ahead, framed by the ridge's wind-lashed whitebark pine. Below are the two Frog Lakes in a meadow of marsh grass.

The trail descends toward the Frog Lakes in seven long switchbacks. We tried fishing here, but the only things jumping were the frogs. From Frog Lakes, you can see the northeast face of Castle Peak and, in front of it, Merriam Peak (10,920 feet). Dr. John Merriam was an economist who was extremely influential in saving the White Clouds and establishing the SNRA. Upon his death in a hypothermia-drowning accident, Merriam Peak was named after him.

You'll leave Frog Lakes as the trail turns in a westerly direction to traverse a sage-brush hill. An excellent view accompanies you as you walk into the Little Boulder Creek drainage below.

The hike from Frog Lakes on is pure joy. After a brief trek through sagebrush, you'll enter forest and lake country. The trail crosses the outlet of Willow Lake, where the forest has mostly reclaimed itself after the debacle that first aroused concern for this area. Just past the lake outlet is a trail junction. Take the right fork; the left leads down into the Little Boulder Creek drainage.

After Willow Lake the trail climbs steadily from lake to lake, each one jumping with little trout. Once you turn south to skirt the edge of Hourglass Lake, the country becomes more alpine. The next lake up is Lake 9,643. To the south, you'll see a boul-der slope that you ascend to get to Windy Devil Pass. From the lake, it looks more difficult than it is. Once you start up the trail, it's easy and obviously marked.

The pass welcomes you with a great view. A few hundred yards beyond the pass is a wonderful view of Serrate Ridge as it merges with Castle Peak. The nameless peak on the east side of the pass is Peak 10,296.

Options: Little Boulder Creek access to the Boulder Chain Lakes is about a mile shorter than from Livingston Mill, but less pleasant. The first 2 miles climb 1,000 feet through sagebrush. However, there are excellent, classic views of Castle Peak on this route. To access the route, continue 3 miles past Livingston Mill Road. There is no room to park at the trailhead, so you must walk the last 0.3 mile. This route is open to motorcycles until it meets Boulder Chain Lakes Trail.

If you want close-up views of Castle Peak, a traverse can be done with a shuttle (long) or by two parties exchanging vehicle keys after meeting in the middle.

From the west—the Sawtooth Valley side—enter via a 12-mile drive on Pole Creek Road to the Germania Creek Trailhead. The last 4 miles are rough and may require four-wheel drive if the road is muddy and the stream is high. Germania Creek Trail is open to trail machines.

From the trailhead and Germania Creek, you can get to the Chamberlain Lakes either by taking Washington Creek Trail (easier and shorter) or by continuing up Ger-mania Creek for 5 miles to Chamberlain Lakes Trail (marked by a cairn). About 0.5 mile before this junction, not visible from the trail but audible, is Germania Creek Falls.

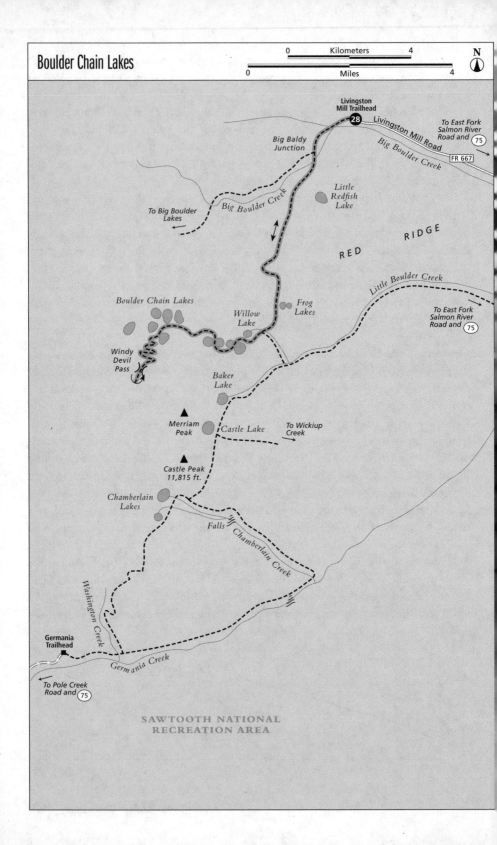

Boulder Chain Lakes

From the east side, Germania Creek Trail from the East Fork of the Salmon River to Chamberlain Creek is a moderately difficult, 5-mile hike on a well-defined trail. It begins with a steep 0.5-mile climb up to wide meadows that gradually narrow over the next 1.5 miles. You will then be treated to a panoramic view of a willow- and aspen-filled valley framed by high, rugged ridges and peaks.

The trail then descends into the valley and intersects Chamberlain Creek Trail in about 3 miles. You will cross the creek twice about 0.5 mile before this intersection. Be prepared to remove your boots for these crossings.

The junction with the trail up Chamberlain Creek to the lakes is steep (a 2,000-foot climb) and little used. It is marked by only a cairn. The trail itself disappears in places. Good navigation skills are required. In its upper reaches are the spectacular Chamberlain Creek Falls (visible from the trail). They are your reward for taking the harder route.

From Chamberlain Lakes, skirt around Castle Peak to a 10,000-foot divide between the Chamberlain basin and the Boulder Creek drainage. The trail (Castle Peak Divide) is a bit rocky, with fairly steep switchbacks. It is another 2.5 miles through forest to Little Boulder Creek Trail, and another mile after that to the trail into the Boulder Chain Lakes. Navigating the part between Baker Lake and the trail junction with Little Boulder Creek can be tricky because you're down in the trees and encounter myriad old mining roads and trails. As you work your way northeast for a mile along the base of Slickenslide Ridge, look and listen for the well-used motorcycle trail coming in from Little Boulder Creek to the right (east). This will take you north and over Slickenslide to connect with Boulder Chain Lakes Trail.

—Jackie Johnson Maughan

Miles and Directions

0.0 Start at the Livingston Mill Trailhead (7,200 feet).

1.0 Reach the Big Boulder Lakes junction (7,700 feet). Stay left on the trail to Boulder Chain Lakes.

5.0 Top the Red Ridge Pass (9,600 feet).

6.5 Pass Frog Lakes (8,800 feet).

7.3 Pass Willow Lake (8,735 feet).

9.0 Pass Hourglass Lake (9,500 feet).

10.0 Top Windy Devil Pass (10,000 feet). Retrace your steps.

20.0 Arrive back at the trailhead.

29 Fourth of July Creek to Born Lakes

Stunning views of the White Cloud peaks abound, with numerous subalpine lakes to explore.

Start: On the west side of the White Cloud Mountains, 25 miles northwest of Ketchum
Type of hike: Out-and-back with base camp possibilities
Distance: 8 miles
Approximate hiking time: 2–4 days
Difficulty: Moderate, unless early in the season when snowfields must be crossed on the last leg of the hike to the Born Lakes
Best season: Mid-July–early September
Trail surface: Dirt and rock
Land status: Sawtooth National Recreation Area
Canine compatibility: Dogs on leash July 1–Labor Day

Fees and permits: No fees; self-issued permits
Maps: USGS Boulder Chain Lakes and Washington Peak ID; Fairfield and Ketchum Ranger Districts–Sawtooth National Forest map
Trail contacts: Sawtooth National Recreation Area Headquarters; (208) 727-5000
Special considerations: About a mile of this trail is near the top of a ridge or in a high treeless basin, making lightning a threat.
Parking and trailhead facilities: The trailhead is a large gravel parking lot with loading ramps, a restroom, and room for about thirty vehicles. It has partial shade but no water except the nearby creek.

Finding the trailhead: Finding the trailhead is easy. Turn off ID 75 in the middle of the Sawtooth Valley, 15 miles south of Stanley. Follow this gravel side road directly up into the White Cloud Mountains. You reach the trailhead in 11 miles. The road narrows to one lane but is gravel all the way, suitable for a sedan. There are no side roads that would cause you confusion. GPS: N44 02.82' / W114 39.46'

The Hike

This is a busy hike, especially the first 1.4 miles to beautiful Fourth of July Lake.

The trail to Fourth of July Lake is open to all but ATVs and full-size vehicles. The trail from there to the Born Lakes is closed to motor vehicles. The first leg of the trail to Fourth of July Lake has modest scenery, but many use it because the trailhead gives high elevation and deep access into the White Cloud Mountains. The lake itself is very pretty, with meadows all around it. Big, bold Patterson Peak (10,872 feet) rises just to the lake's east.

The wide trail is easy to find and leaves directly east of the trailhead. You quickly cross a good bridge over Fourth of July Creek and then come to the Phyllis Lake jeep road, which the trail crosses at a right angle.

The trail climbs at a moderate pace all the way to Fourth of July Lake. The first third of the route is a pleasant, willowy meadow to the left of the trail. You get glimpses of the high peaks but cannot really see any of them unless you hike off the trail and search for a viewpoint. Most of this short hike is through forest.

Fourth of July Lake. Photo by Luke Kratz

Just before the lake, you encounter a signed trail junction. The fork to the Born Lakes is to the left, but before you take it, continue another 100 yards to the right (on what is now the trail to the Washington Lakes) and walk to the outlet of Fourth of July Lake. It is a beautiful scene, with the lake framing Patterson Peak. Otherwise, you will miss seeing the lake until you are high above it.

On Born Lakes Trail, you quickly come to a sign indicating that no motor vehicles are allowed. The trail narrows but is readily evident and easy to follow. You'll begin to climb more steeply, rapidly gaining more than 300 feet in 0.3 mile. The trail levels out, and you pass an unnamed, pretty lake with a view of all of the west-facing ramparts of Patterson Peak.

The trail climbs to the ridgetop, slanting to the northwest, without switchbacks. This climb through open forest gains just over 200 feet in 0.5 mile. Through the trees, you get excellent views of Fourth of July Lake, Fourth of July Creek canyon, Patterson Peak, and an unnamed, triangular-shaped, light brown mountain across the canyon to the south (elevation 10,713 feet), and—off to the southwestern distance—Washington Peak (elevation 10,519 feet) and surrounding summits. The summits around Washington Peak are gray and stand in sharp contrast with brownish Peak 10,713 before you.

The trail attains the ridgetop divide and follows it briefly. It does not cross at a pass. On the divide, you get a splendid view in three directions. To the south are the peaks just described. To the west, the high point on the ridge is Blackman Peak (10,300 feet). In the far west rises the jagged Sawtooth Range. Directly below you to the north is meadowy Antz Basin, with a few trees and a pond. All around this side of the ridgetop rise the summits that were originally named the White Cloud Mountains in the years before the entire mountain range between the Salmon River on the north and Pole Creek on the south had that name affixed. Each of the peaks you see has a different shape and color. One in particular, Peak 11,314, can be described as light silver, almost white in some lighting conditions. Other peaks are shades of pink, gray, and brown, all of which change as the sun makes its daily transit across the sky.

These peaks are built mostly of granite, although some of the white peaks are formed of a kind of marble (metamorphosed limestone). I found it difficult to describe what color the granite really was. For example, it may appear pinkish at 100 feet. When you examine the rock closely, you find it is made of many crystals of differing colors: neutral transparent, white, orange-red, black, pink. These are combinations of quartz, feldspar, mica, hornblende, and other minerals. The color your eye perceives is the product of the balance of all of these as illuminated by the color of the sunlight at a given time of day.

Geology lesson over: You drop quickly off the ridge, switchbacking down to Antz Basin. If you attempt this hike too early, this is where you will encounter your greatest problem. Early in the season (for example, late June), this slope will be covered with a steeply inclined snowfield.

As you reach the sod of Antz Basin, the well-worn tread of the trail vanishes. To find it again, walk east-by-northeast and you will soon see the tread leading up into some trees at the basin's edge. From here it drops into the headwaters of Warm Springs Creek, which is the big canyon between Antz Basin and the White Cloud peaks.

The trail is not shown on the Washington Peak topographic quadrangle but on the adjacent Boulder Chain Lakes quad and in the wrong place. Trail traffic has changed a great deal since these maps were compiled in the 1960s.

Soon the trail passes high above the first of the Born Lakes, a pond in a grassy meadow. Keeping high, just above the timber, the trail leads to the other lakes. It is hard to say when you have arrived because there are many Born Lakes (they were named after Boren, a prospector) scattered about in the timber just below the rock line. They are of varying shapes and sizes and number perhaps ten in all. I estimate the distance to the last and highest of the lakes to be about 4 miles from the trailhead.

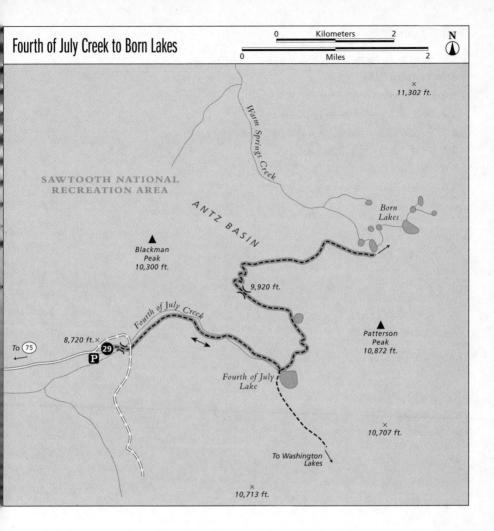

Kilometers

Miles

N

SAWTOOTH NATIONAL
RECREATION AREA

Warm Springs Creek

× 11,302 ft.

ANTZ BASIN

Born Lakes

Blackman Peak 10,300 ft.

× 9,920 ft.

Fourth of July Creek

Patterson Peak 10,872 ft.

8,720 ft. ×

To 75

29

P

Fourth of July Lake

× 10,707 ft.

To Washington Lakes

× 10,713 ft.

The entire area is very scenic, situated as it is beneath the north flank of Patterson Peak and other rugged peaks—nameless and with no exact elevation recorded, but all well over 10,000 feet.

If you wish, you can locate an old trail down Warm Springs Creek. You are at its very head. It is the longest canyon in the White Cloud Mountains. In recent years, this has been summer range of a large wolf pack.

Options: Back at Fourth of July Lake, if you take the right fork of the trail, it leads over a low divide (9,560 feet) to the large, scenic Washington Lakes in just 1 mile. This is a busy trail, even more so than the one to Born Lakes.

From Born Lakes, you can also scramble over the crest to the east to Four Lakes Basin. This is rugged off-trail hiking, not for those with unsteady balance.

—Ralph Maughan

Miles and Directions

0.0 Start at the Fourth of July Trailhead (8,720 feet).

0.2 Cross the Phyllis Lake jeep road.

1.4 Reach Fourth of July Lake (9,365 feet).

1.7 Pass an unnamed lake (9,660 feet).

2.2 Reach the ridgetop divide, with a great view (9,920 feet).

2.5 Arive in Antz Basin (9,580 feet).

4.0 Reach the highest of the Born Lakes (9,700 feet).

8.0 Arrive back at the trailhead.

Pioneer Mountains

The Pioneer Mountains, the second highest range in Idaho, rise east of Ketchum and Hailey, south of the Boulder Mountains, west of the Lost River Range, and immediately north of the Snake River Plain. Part of this range consists of the widespread and colorful Challis Volcanics. The core of the range consists, however, of intruded granitic rocks on the eastern side and a great variety of metamorphic rocks on the western side—very hard rocks polished to perfection by glaciers.

This is a complicated mountain range, roughly oval in shape and very mixed in composition. There are a score of subalpine and alpine lakes, including Idaho's highest—Goat Lake.

On the south, it consists of tall hills, or low mountains, that are almost bare save for groves of aspen overlooking the basaltic Snake River Plain. On the east these mountains are obscured by the somewhat lesser White Knob Range. To the north, they merge imperceptibly with the Boulder Mountains. On the west, they present a large area of ever-rising ridges that top out along a big north–south trending crest of eye-opening peaks, arêtes, and pinnacles. The crest is somewhat similar to the Sawtooth Range but higher (topping 12,000 feet at Hyndman Peak). However, the glaciated peak zone is less extensive than in the Sawtooths.

The Pioneers have almost no commercial timber. The major objection to protecting them as wilderness in their roadless heights has been raised by the sheep and cattle industry. These livestock are increasingly well controlled on the western (or Hailey-Ketchum) side of the range, but on the east, save for a few drainages like Fall Creek, you will find cattle or sheep to timberline and beyond, such as standing beside Idaho's highest lake—Goat Lake—and defecating in its icy waters. Because of livestock overuse, we have ignored some popular hikes, such as Broad Canyon, Bellas Lakes, Bear Canyon, and others. These mountains are a real favorite of hikers, backpackers, climbers, and mountain bikers.

Where the livestock are under control, wildlife is abundant, including pronghorn antelope, deer, elk, black bear, mountain goats, and an occasional moose. In the spring of 2000, the first wolf pack formed in the heights of the Fall Creek–Wildhorse Creek–Summit Creek area.

—Ralph Maughan

30 Fall Creek

Hike through glaciated mountain scenery, with access to alpine lakes and impressive erosion scars from a great flood in 1984. Several waterfalls are also available to explore.

Start: 20 miles northeast of Ketchum
Type of hike: Out-and-back
Distance: 14 miles to the head of Fall Creek
Approximate hiking time: At least 3–4 days
Difficulty: Moderately easy to the Left Fork; difficult to the head of Fall Creek
Best seasons: Mid-June–mid-July to Left Fork; August–mid-September to the head of the canyon
Trail surface: Dirt and rock
Land status: Salmon-Challis National Forest
Canine compatibility: On leash
Fees and permits: None

Maps: USGS Standhope Peak ID; Middle Fork, Challis, Yankee Fork, and Lost River Ranger Districts–Challis National Forest map
Trail contact: Lost River Ranger District; (208) 588-3400
Special considerations: Hiking beyond the maintained trail's end requires strong boots.
Parking and trailhead facilities: The developed site offers access for people with disabilities to Fall Creek Falls Nature Trail and the trail described here, which goes up Fall Creek Canyon. The trailhead has parking for many vehicles, loading ramps for horses, and an outhouse, but no water or shade.

Finding the trailhead: From downtown Ketchum, turn east and take the road to Sun Valley. Continue eastward past Sun Valley up Trail Creek Canyon. Just as the canyon begins to narrow and the road begins to climb, it turns to rough gravel. Climb on a precipitous ledge above Trail Creek Gorge all the way to Trail Creek Summit. Although hundreds of vehicles travel this road every day, it is winding, washboarded, narrow in places, and without guardrails. Safely past Trail Creek Summit, continue on down gentle Summit Creek until you are 22 miles from Ketchum. Then turn right onto Copper Basin Road.

From Mackay or Challis, turn west off US 93 near the base of Mount Borah onto the paved county highway. Take this road due west across the valley, reaching the Big Lost River as the road enters low, bare, red-rock mountains. At this point the pavement ends, but the road is good gravel. Turn left onto Copper Basin Road 18.5 miles from U.S. 93.

Follow the gravel Copper Basin Road for 2.5 miles, then turn right and go up Wildhorse Creek on Wildhorse Creek Road. Lower Wildhorse Creek is typical Challis Volcanic terrain: steep, low, reddish mountains fronted by sagebrush bottoms. But up-canyon, toward the head of Wildhorse Creek, stand pointed peaks that stun most tourists. These giants are not your destination, however. Instead, 3.5 miles up Wildhorse Creek, turn off Wildhorse Creek Road onto the gravel Fall Creek Road. Drive 0.3 mile to the obvious trailhead at the mouth of Fall Creek Canyon. GPS: N43 51.15' / W114 04.68'

The Hike

This hike can be a relatively easy overnighter to the edge of beautiful, rugged scenery, or a two-plus night rugged trip to the seldom-visited head of Fall Creek Canyon, with its granite walls and alpine meadows harboring elk, mountain goats, bears, and wolves. The trail also provides access to three other splendid trails—up the Left Fork of Fall Creek, the Right Fork of Fall Creek, and to Surprise Valley.

Although the mouth of Fall Creek is not impressive, this modest entrance is deceptive. After about 1.5 miles, the trail enters big mountain country. Here, glacier-sculpted peaks, horns, and arêtes rise around you. Some peaks are almost 12,000 feet high. The three forks of Fall Creek are textbook examples of hanging valleys.

Almost half the trailhead traffic is for the wheelchair-accessible trail to the lowest of Fall Creek's several waterfalls. This trail is self-evident and not described here.

Cross the pack bridge, and you quickly come to a buck-and-pole fence with a gate to keep out the cattle. The trail sign indicates horses and foot traffic only. The welcome closure of Fall Creek to livestock came in 1998 and has reaped great rewards in improved aesthetics and an increase in wildlife.

The trail follows an old jeep two-track that has now largely faded but that actually had vehicles on it in the 1970s when I first visited. The trail is always obvious as it climbs moderately about 480 feet in 1.5 miles and then drops a bit as it reaches the Left Fork of Fall Creek. The trail crosses on a makeshift log bridge. At this point you can see a giant horn that guards the Right Fork, another that guards the entrance to Surprise Valley, and pyramidal, 11,878-foot Standhope Peak. The confluence area is also the largest flat spot in Fall Creek and its forks. On the way to the Left Fork junction, Fall Creek courses 100 feet below the trail. You do not see the waterfall, but the creek is visible from time to time.

The faint Left Fork Trail leaves at a ninety-degree angle immediately after crossing Left Fork Creek. The main trail continues up Fall Creek Canyon with very little grade until you approach some of the erosion from the great 1984 thunderstorm flood. Although the scars have softened, they are still obvious when their origin is known. A black cloud settled over the heads of Fall Creek, Wildhorse Creek, and the East Fork of the Big Wood River on August 9, 1984. In just a few hours, it dropped 10 inches of rain on this uplift of jagged granite peaks. The volume of Fall and Wildhorse Creeks grew to rival that of the Snake River in flood, uprooting trees, washing away meadows, cutting out streamside cliffs, and accomplishing several hundred years of erosion in a few hours.

About 0.4 mile past the Left Fork, the trail crosses (and also splits and goes above) a huge cutbank from the flood. From here on, it climbs gently until you reach the junction with Right Fork Trail. Right Fork Trail is actually the wider of the two, and for years a sign

Fall Creek and Right Fork of Fall Creek

0   Kilometers   4

0   Miles   4

N

30 and 32
P

Paved trail

Fall
Creek
Falls

Left Fork

Fall Creek Trail

SALMON–CHALLIS
NATIONAL FOREST

×
10,354 ft.

32

30

Right Fork Trail

Right Fork

Fall Creek

Surprise Valley Trail

× 8,980 ft.

Moose
Lake
9,345 ft.

Lower Lake

×
10,832 ft.

9,455 ft. ×

×
11,376 ft.

×
10,083 ft.

Angel Lake
10,278 ft.

▲

×
11.687 ft.

×
11,316 ft.

Upper Lake
10,148 ft.

on a large conifer has pointed to it, reading "trail," as if the trail up the main fork were some improper route.

Ignore the sign and keep left. The trail now climbs through a dense forest growing amid incredible boulders and dead fallen timber, much of both the result of the great flood. It took a long time to recut the trail through this stretch of the canyon. The area has a very wild, untamed atmosphere. After about 0.3 mile, you reach the junction with Surprise Valley Trail, which is usually signed. This time, stay to the right.

The trail continues to climb through the wild forest and boulders. The horn that guards the Right Fork now appears as what it really is—the beginning of the rugged west wall of Fall Creek Canyon. Early in the season, you can see a number of waterfalls on the west wall, one from Angel Lake. A number of small waterfalls and many cascades rumble just out of sight on Fall Creek itself.

You reach the end of the maintained trail 4.2 miles from the trailhead, where you cross the outlet stream from Surprise Valley, but the route continues on. From here on, the trail is maintained mostly by elk. It goes through forest but soon breaks out above a willow patch for your first view of the great headwall of Fall Creek, all of it well above 11,000 feet, with a number of peaks, all of them nameless. A large patch of snow lingers most of the summer beneath the headwall.

The trail continues to the head of the canyon. In places it is easy, but it crosses a number of boggy springs, willow meadows that hold plenty of water in June and July, rockslides, and some deadfall. If you lose the trail, you can soon pick it up again by heading upslope or downslope a bit.

While the beauty of the stream itself is somewhat marred by the erosion scars from the flood, the scenery is tremendous, and you will be alone except for the wildlife. In August, the wildlife especially favor the head of the canyon.

—Ralph Maughan

Options: Surprise Valley is a great trail. The junction is well-defined at 3.3 miles from the main trailhead. The trail climbs through meadows and high pine forests for 3 miles, visiting two small lakes and a gorgeous outflow gushing down the mountainside.

—Luke Kratz

Miles and Directions

0.0 Start at the Fall Creek Trailhead (7,240 feet). Shortly, cross a pack bridge over Fall Creek.

0.1 Pass a buck-and-pole fence and gate.

1.8 Pass the trail up the Left Fork of Fall Creek (7,683 feet).

3.0 Pass the Right Fork Trail junction (7,820 feet).

3.3 Pass the Surprise Valley Trail junction (8,100 feet).

4.2 Reach the end of the maintained trail (8,480 feet).

7.0 Reach the head of Fall Creek (9,500 feet). Retrace your steps.

14.0 Arrive back at the trailhead.

31 Left Fork of Fall Creek

The Left Fork holds rugged mountain scenery with more wildlife and geological variety than most Pioneer Mountain areas.

Start: 20 miles northeast of Ketchum
Type of hike: Out-and-back
Distance: 8.4 miles from the junction with the main Fall Creek Trail to the end of the meadow and back (12 miles total round-trip)
Approximate hiking time: 2 days
Difficulty: Moderate due to elevation gain and some route finding
Best season: July–mid-September
Trail surface: Dirt and rock
Land status: Salmon–Challis National Forest
Canine compatibility: On leash

Fees and permits: None
Maps: USGS Big Black Butte and Standhope Peak ID; Middle Fork, Challis, and Lost River Ranger Districts–Challis National Forest map
Trail contact: Lost River Ranger District; (208) 588-3400
Parking and trailhead facilities: The developed site offers access for people with disabilities to Fall Creek Falls Nature Trail and the trail described here. The trailhead has parking for many vehicles, loading ramps for horses, and an outhouse, but no water or shade.

Finding the trailhead: From downtown Ketchum, turn east and take the road to Sun Valley. Continue eastward past Sun Valley up Trail Creek Canyon. Just as the canyon begins to narrow and the road begins to climb, it turns to rough gravel. Climb on a precipitous ledge above Trail Creek Gorge all the way to Trail Creek Summit. Although hundreds of vehicles travel this road every day, it is winding, washboarded, narrow in places, and without guardrails. Safely past Trail Creek Summit, continue on down gentle Summit Creek until you are 22 miles from Ketchum. Then turn right onto Copper Basin Road.

From Mackay or Challis, turn west off US 93 near the base of Mount Borah onto the paved county highway. Take this road due west across the valley, reaching the Big Lost River as the road enters low, bare, red-rock mountains. At this point the pavement ends, but the road is good gravel. Turn left onto Copper Basin Road 18.5 miles from U.S. 93.

Follow the gravel Copper Basin Road for 2.5 miles, then turn right and go up Wildhorse Creek on Wildhorse Creek Road. Lower Wildhorse Creek is typical Challis Volcanic terrain: steep, low, reddish mountains fronted by sagebrush bottoms. But up-canyon, toward the head of Wildhorse Creek, stand pointed peaks that stun most tourists. These giants are not your destination, however. Instead, 3.5 miles up Wildhorse Creek, turn off Wildhorse Creek Road onto the gravel Fall Creek Road. Drive 0.3 mile to the obvious trailhead at the mouth of Fall Creek Canyon. This trail begins where Fall Creek Trail crosses the Left Fork of Fall Creek. Look for it at a 90-degree angle to the Fall Creek Trail. It is a bit faint at first. GPS (Left Fork turnoff): N43 50.73' / W114 02.88'. GPS (trailhead parking): N43 51.15' / W114 04.68'

The Hike

Of the three splendid forks of Fall Creek located in the jagged Pioneer Mountains, the Left Fork is the least often seen. This is probably because, from the start of the trail, the country ahead is not nearly as scenic as the view up the Fall Creek Valley or the

View near the junction with the wild Left Fork of Fall Creek. Photo by Luke Kratz

horn-guarded Right Fork. In reality, the Left Fork of Fall Creek is very similar to the main Fall Creek in its form, with an unimpressive entrance that eventually turns to the south to head into beautifully ice-sculpted granite. However, the Left Fork is more varied geologically and has more wildlife than the rest of Fall Creek and its tributaries.

The faint but very easy-to-follow trail leaves Fall Creek where Fall Creek Trail crosses the Left Fork. Just beyond the Left Fork, find the trail at a ninety-degree angle from the main trail. You'll climb steeply, switchbacking several times into the hanging valley of the Left Fork. As you climb in the open, you have a good view across the main canyon toward the Right Fork's hanging valley. The trail does not follow the creek for this first steep section. The creek instead cascades in a minor gorge below and to the left.

After climbing 500 feet in just 0.6 mile the grade lessens, and a welcome spring runs across the trail out of the willows. The trail then fords the Left Fork to climb to the left (north) bank. This ford is easy in mid- to late summer but can be swift when the creek is higher (late June). Now you are in the stream valley, and the creek moves lazily below the trail through a maze of short willows.

The trail wanders across the open hillside and through patches of silvery quaking aspen and sagebrush that adorn the slope, which is made of reddish-brown volcanic rock. Flowers wink at you here early in the summer. A few small springs run across the trail throughout most summers. Across the stream valley, the opposite slope is covered with a dense forest of conifers.

Bare crags of volcanic rock made of the widespread Challis Volcanic Formation poke into the sky above the trail. Soon, the trail contours along a steep sidehill just above a willowy meadow. Be careful here because the tread is narrow for about 0.2 mile.

At 1.5 miles from the trail's start, you begin to climb up the mountainside and away from the stream valley. The topographic maps show the trail continuing directly over the mountain and down the other side to Copper Basin, but this trail no longer exists. Instead, the trail leads out over a broad sage- and grass-covered platform and up the Left Fork valley. Here, the valley begins a big bend toward the south. At first you see, on your left, the talus slopes that form the backside of the Big Black Dome (11,353 feet), a chunk of sedimentary rock lodged between the volcanics to the north and the hard, crystalline, intruded rock to the south. Ironically, this side of the mountain is neither black nor domelike. The rock is light brown, dark brown, and pinkish brown, depending on the angle of the sun. Just below these amazingly smooth talus slopes grow flowers, short willows, and photogenic patches of spruce, fir, and whitebark pine. There are a number of springs, and you often find pronghorn antelope and elk here in the heat of the day.

As you complete the turn to the south, you'll see the rugged, gray, mostly unnamed granite peaks at the head of the canyon. The most prominent is Peak 11,281. The topo map shows 11,628-foot Pyramid Peak, but you can't really see this peak well unless you leave the trail and climb up onto the talus of the Big Black Dome.

Once you turn the corner of the canyon, the trail becomes intermittent, showing up alternately on both sides of the valley. Numerous small springs feed the dense low willows next to the creek. Low flow makes these springs poor sources of water. However, as you continue and enter the land underlain by the hard quartz monzonite of the Pioneer core area, the streamside becomes less mushy and the springs, though fewer, have a better flow.

In the upper canyon, there are increasingly alpine meadows. Game trails are so numerous and well used they appear to have been constructed. You can follow them right up to the hard rock of the peaks. Although this has always been a good canyon for wildlife, since the cows have been booted out the wildlife has exploded. There are many elk, mule deer, pronghorn antelope, and even some moose, black bear, cougar, and mountain goats. Beginning in 2000 a wolf pack began to inhabit the area. I heard them howl for five minutes.

Despite a plentitude of moisture and perfect altitude, the trees grow only in isolated clumps in this canyon. Almost all of the hike is in the sun unless you seek out a tree. My hypothesis is that avalanches from the Big Black Dome keep continuous forest from growing.

—Ralph Maughan

Left Fork of Fall Creek

Miles and Directions

0.0 Start at the Fall Creek Trailhead. The Left Fork Trail begins where Fall Creek Trail crosses the Left Fork (7,683 feet), about 1.8 miles from the trailhead.

0.7 Ford the Left Fork (8,210 feet).

1.3 Pass a narrow contour above meadow (8,600 feet).

1.5 The trail climbs to a sagebrush bench and begins to follow the bend of the canyon (8,900 feet).

3.0 The canyon begins to climb much more steeply (9,380 feet).

4.2 The meadow ends and rock begins at base of Pyramid Peak (10,240 feet). This is the turnaround.

8.4 Return to the trail junction with the main Fall Creek Trail. Retrace your steps. The total round-trip distance from the trailhead parking area is 12 miles.

32 Right Fork of Fall Creek

This popular trail heads into rugged mountain scenery and passes two alpine lakes.

See map on page 186 (Fall Creek).
Start: 20 miles northeast of Sun Valley
Type of hike: Out-and-back
Distance: 10 miles to Moose Lake and back (from the junction with the main Fall Creek Trail)
Approximate hiking time: 2 days
Difficulty: Moderately difficult due to a steep climb, but the distance is not great
Best season: July–mid-September
Trail surface: Dirt and rock
Land status: Salmon-Challis National Forest
Canine compatibility: On leash

Fees and permits: None
Maps: USGS Standhope Peak ID; Middle Fork, Challis, Yankee Fork, and Lost River Ranger Districts–Challis National Forest map
Trail contact: Lost River Ranger District; (208) 588-3400
Special considerations: None
Parking and trailhead facilities: The developed site offers access for people with disabilities to Fall Creek Falls Nature Trail and the trail described here. The trailhead has parking for many vehicles, loading ramps for horses, and an outhouse, but no water or shade.

Finding the trailhead: From downtown Ketchum, turn east and take the road to Sun Valley. Continue eastward past Sun Valley up Trail Creek Canyon. Just as the canyon begins to narrow and the road begins to climb, it turns to rough gravel. Climb on a precipitous ledge above Trail Creek Gorge all the way to Trail Creek Summit. Although hundreds of vehicles travel this road every day, it is winding, washboarded, narrow in places, and without guardrails. Safely past Trail Creek Summit, continue on down gentle Summit Creek until you are 22 miles from Ketchum. Then turn right onto Copper Basin Road.

From Mackay or Challis, turn west off US 93 near the base of Mount Borah onto the paved county highway. Take this road due west across the valley, reaching the Big Lost River as the road enters low, bare, red-rock mountains. At this point the pavement ends, but the road is good gravel. Turn left onto Copper Basin Road 18.5 miles from U.S. 93.

Follow the gravel Copper Basin Road for 2.5 miles; then turn right and go up Wildhorse Creek on Wildhorse Creek Road. Lower Wildhorse Creek is typical Challis Volcanic terrain: steep, low, reddish mountains fronted by sagebrush bottoms. But up-canyon, toward the head of Wildhorse Creek, stand pointed peaks that stun most tourists. These giants are not your destination, however. Instead, 3.5 miles up Wildhorse Creek, turn off Wildhorse Creek Road onto the gravel Fall Creek Road. Drive 0.3 mile to the obvious trailhead at the mouth of Fall Creek Canyon. GPS (Right Fork turnoff): N43 49.95' / W114 02.64'. GPS (trailhead parking): N43 51.15' / W114 04.68'.

The Hike

The Right Fork of Fall Creek is yet another hanging valley that drops, along with the Left Fork and Surprise Valley, into Fall Creek. The Right Fork is the only one of these three valleys that has a lake with fish—Moose Lake. Therefore, it is by far the busiest

Moose Lake. PHOTO BY LUKE KRATZ

of the hikes in Fall Creek described in this book, and the lake area can look a bit beaten out.

The hike to Moose Lake is short from where the trail leaves the Fall Creek valley, but the elevation gain is considerable: 1,545 feet. The trail is well constructed, however, and easy to follow.

Begin at a junction in the trail up the main fork canyon, about 1.2 miles above the mouth of the Left Fork of Fall Creek. You merely stay on the most heavily used trail, and it soon leads down to Fall Creek, which you must probably ford, although a rather tricky log has been in place across the creek for some time. The ford is no problem in late summer, but it is rather deep earlier on.

On the other side, you begin the steep climb, making several long switchbacks that are not shown on the topographic map.

A big horn guards the entrance to the canyon on the left, and a less rugged big mountain stands to its right. Once you arrive at the cirque, you'll find the horn is really the end of a mile-long spiny ridge. As you climb through forest and rock, you'll get occasional glimpses of the view back down across Fall Creek to the cream-colored, ribbed wall of the canyon's east side.

As you enter the hanging valley, the grade diminishes, but the trail is still anything but level. The two sides of the valley contrast sharply: The left side is made of the rugged igneous rock of the Pioneer Window, while the right is composed of the softer, sedimentary rock of the Copper Basin Formation.

Just before you reach the lake, you'll wander through meadows near the outlet. Above the lake, a smaller, shallow lake nestles in the rocks. All of this is set in a large, high basin, dominated by nameless Peak 11,667 at its head. The only route out of the cirque, besides the way you came, is a rough cross-country hike to Angel Lake, a large, scenic gem that barely hangs on to the side of Fall Creek Canyon. You can spend a day exploring the cirque or drop over to Angel Lake. Otherwise, side hikes are limited.

Moose Lake is overly full of brook trout, and some rainbows, too.

Option: You can scramble to Angel Lake from the Right Fork Lakes.

—Ralph Maughan

Miles and Directions

0.0 The Right Fork Trail begins where Fall Creek Trail splits (7,820 feet). This is about 3 miles from the formal Fall Creek Trailhead.

0.1 Ford Fall Creek (7,800 feet).

2.0 Reach Moose Lake (9,345 feet). This is the turnaround. Option: Hike 0.2 mile to an unnamed upper lake (9,455 feet).

4.0 Arrive back at the junction with the main Fall Creek Trail. Retrace your steps, arriving back at the main trailhead for a total of 10 miles round-trip.

33 Iron Bog Lake

Several lakes and ponds lie among scenic peaks and uplands.

Start: In the southern part of the Pioneer Mountains, about 40 road miles northwest of Arco

Type of hike: Out-and-back, unless you choose the Muldoon Canyon option, which requires a shuttle

Distance: 3.2 miles

Approximate hiking time: 2–3 days

Difficulty: Moderately easy

Best season: July

Trail surface: Dirt and rock

Land status: Salmon–Challis National Forest

Canine compatibility: On leash

Fees and permits: None

Maps: USGS Smiley Mountain ID; Middle Fork, Challis, Yankee Fork, and Lost River Ranger Districts–Challis National Forest map

Trail contact: Lost River Ranger District; (208) 588-3400

Special considerations: You'll be walking in high-altitude sun with little shade. Make sure you have good sun protection.

Parking and trailhead facilities: The undeveloped trailhead has room for about ten vehicles.

Finding the trailhead: Drive 10.5 miles north of Arco on US 93, and turn onto Antelope Creek Road. This road is paved for the first 4 miles; then it's 23 miles of gravel and dirt to the trailhead, which is on the Left Fork of Iron Bog Creek. Just after Iron Bog Campground is a fork in the road. Take the left fork, FR 220. The right fork gives access to a trail to Brockie Lake, another nice hike, but the road requires four-wheel drive. It is about 1 mile from the turnoff to the trailhead. The road is rough but has been improved a bit so that two-wheel-drive access is not difficult. GPS: N43 39.56' / W113 49.19'

The Hike

The southern portion of the Pioneer Mountains consists of rugged, glaciated peaks with numerous cirques, many with lakes. Despite their height and cool weather, these mountains have very sparse forests. Although this sometimes makes it hard to get out of the high-elevation sun, it does provide for almost constant, scenic views into the distance.

Iron Bog and nearby Fishpole Lakes have a reputation as being among Idaho's prettiest. Iron Bog has a big black mountain (Peak 10,149) rising from its west shore. The hiking distance to the two lakes is not great. These two aspects—scenery and relative ease—make the area a bit crowded sometimes. Fortunately, off-road vehicles have been excluded for the past fifteen years or so, and some of the localized areas of overuse have healed. Nevertheless, violations continue to take place. Please report violations in both Iron Bog and Muldoon Canyon to the Lost River Ranger District in Mackay.

Iron Bog Lake. Photo by Luke Kratz

The well-defined, reconstructed trail climbs the slope to the right of the trailhead. There are several springs in the early season along the trail. The trail has fine views of the Left Fork of Iron Bog Creek below.

Due to overuse, please avoid the campsites right on the lake. Less sensitive spots are available just before and beyond the lake. There is a tiny lake above Iron Bog (off the trail) and two small lakes on the way over to the Fishpole cirque (the second being very scenic).

There are fish in Iron Bog and Fishpole Lakes. Mule deer and coyote, as well as elk, are present in the area, and pronghorn antelope are surprisingly common despite the high elevation. Prior to seeing antelope here, I had been told they do not range higher than 9,000 feet.

To get to Fishpole Lake, walk to the outlet of Iron Bog Lake, descend about 80 feet along the outlet stream, and you should find the trail. It's about a mile, and a 250-foot climb, to Fishpole Lake. Including Fishpole, the Fishpole cirque contains four lakes.

The country around these lakes is meadow and open forest of whitebark pine and Douglas fir. Wildflowers are abundant before September. Large, rugged peaks rise behind the lakes.

The best month for the hike is probably July, because domestic sheep begin to graze the area in July, gradually moving higher and reducing the wildlife and camping pleasure. However, the hike is usually accessible from late June through September.

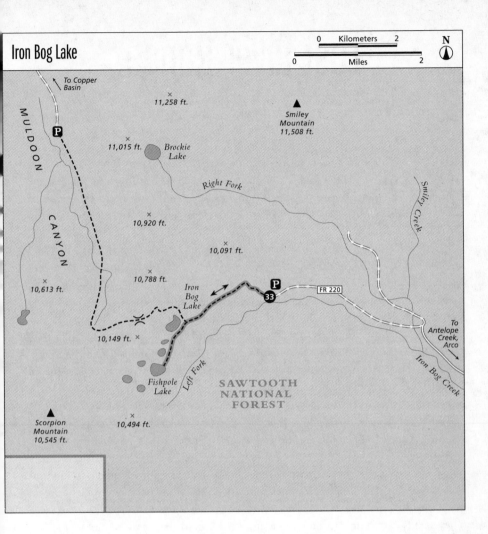

Options: A trail climbs from Iron Bog Lake about 400 feet over a pass into the head of Muldoon Canyon, a long, moist-bottomed, but almost nonforested canyon ringed by scenic peaks. Muldoon Canyon is an alternative route to Iron Bog Lake. You approach it from Copper Basin. However, it involves using four-wheel drive or walking several miles on a jeep road that is mostly in the sun. Even if you don't come up Muldoon Canyon, the short hike to its open and ruggedly scenic head from Iron Bog Lake is very worthwhile, both for the view and the chances of seeing wildlife.

—Ralph Maughan

Miles and Directions

0.0 Start at the trailhead (7,600 feet).

1.6 Reach Iron Bog Lake (9,067 feet). Option: Hike about 1 mile to Fishpole Lake (9,258 feet).

3.2 Arrive back at the trailhead.

Lost River Range

ountains of contorted sedimentary rock, the Lost River Range is by
far Idaho's highest. Running southeast to northwest, it parallels the
neighboring Lemhi Mountains, separated from them by the broad
Little Lost River Valley on the south and the Pahsimeroi Valley on
the north.

Borah Peak (12,662 feet) and Leatherman Peak (12,228 feet), Idaho's first and
second highest peaks, dominate the middle of the range. Only the nearby Pioneer
Mountains and the Lemhi Range have 12,000-footers (and then only one each).
Besides Borah and Leatherman, the Lost Rivers count seven others more than 12,000
feet. Only Mount Breitenbach, at 12,140 feet, is officially named. Lost River Mountain (12,078 feet), Mount Idaho (12,065 feet), and Donaldson Peak (12,023 feet)
have been surveyed and tentatively named. But Mount Church (12,220 feet plus),
although tentatively named, has not been officially surveyed. Finally, Peak 12,010 and
Peak 12,003 are not only unnamed but also not officially surveyed—a nice thought
in this time when everything seems overexplored and overdeveloped.

The range also hosts scores of peaks that are over 11,800 feet, but when you're
standing at the foot of them, 11,800 and 12,000 feet don't look much different.

Although the colorful Challis Volcanics have buried the low northern end of the
range and have also washed up on the mountains' east side, the high core of the Lost
Rivers is relentlessly limestone—ancient sea deposits compressed into rock and then
pushed by innumerable earthquakes until they rose more than 2 miles above sea level.
They stand warped, folded, and broken in the dry, cold air of east-central Idaho.

The Lost River Range has still fewer hiking trails than its longer neighbor, the
Lemhi Range, and—other than climbers seeking the summits of Leatherman and
Borah, a few hunters, and stray recreationists—these heights see only cowhands, and
too few of those because overgrazing is a problem. One exception is King Mountain
on the range's southern end. It is one of the prime hang-gliding sites in the United
States.

The west-facing side of the Lost Rivers rises very abruptly, presenting a bold and
austere mountain front towering 5,000 feet above some of the largest alluvial fans in
the West. Many people travel US 93, which follows the Big Lost River Valley here, but
few reach the mountains, because the access roads are poor and the canyons rough,
rugged, and choked with brush.

The east-facing side of the range, on the other hand, contains long canyons, which
harbor much more flowing water, some hiking trails and easy routes, and a few lakes

The Lost River mountain front. PHOTO BY LUKE KRATZ

near the crest, where the altitude and snowmelt overcome the tendency of water to drain into the limestone. These lakes are rare, but they are among the most beautiful in Idaho.

The Lost Rivers are split into four sections by low passes, unlike the parallel Lemhi Mountains, which have no such passes. The first section begins southeast of Arco near Howe. Often called the Arco Hills, these "hills" rise to 9,045 feet at Jumpoff Peak. With no hiking trails and absolutely no water, this rarely visited area contains many interesting cliffs and rock formations. To the north, Arco Pass separates the Arco Hills from the next section of the range.

Next comes King Mountain, the first big mountain in the range. At 10,612 feet, King Mountain is one of the few named peaks in what has become known as the 95,000-acre King Mountain Roadless Area. Despite the great height of these mountains, where one would expect water, there is not even a reliable spring. Instead, you'll find little-known country of big mountains and canyons lined with incredible cliffs, rock fins, caves, and other geological oddities.

A good dirt road goes over Pass Creek Summit (only 7,600 feet) and eastward down Wet Creek. This canyon route marks the next division of the Lost Rivers. Here, the really high Lost Rivers begin. This middle portion of the range was proposed for classification as the 115,000-acre Borah Peak Wilderness by the forest service back in the 1970s, and again by the Challis National Forest Plan a decade later. Though it contains no commercial timber, no minerals, no dam sites, no proposed ski areas, and the highest mountains in Idaho, anti-wilderness diehards have blocked its classification and protection. Your voice is needed in the campaign to protect this area.

North of the Borah Peak proposed wilderness, a deep trough cuts across the range. Here, at Doublespring Pass (8,318 feet), another good dirt road crosses the mountains. It leads from the upper part of Big Lost River Valley over to the Pahsimeroi Valley. The last and northernmost portion of the range is often called the Pahsimeroi Mountains. It, too, is a little-traveled area of high limestone peaks and sparse water. Just north of Grouse Creek, the Pahsimeroi Range fades and is buried by the Challis Volcanics, taking on a rolling rather than a rugged appearance. This is a very pretty area in late June, before the livestock trample it.

From south to north, the major canyons in the Lost Rivers include Ramshorn, Cedarville, Cabin Fork and North Fork of Cedarville, Van Dorn, Basin Creek, Elbow, Pass Creek, Wet Creek, Big Creek, Lower Cedar, Upper Cedar, Long Lost Creek, Dry Creek, East and West Forks of the Pahsimeroi, Mahogany Creek, Willow Creek, Doublespring Creek, Christian Gulch, and Grouse Creek. Roads fill Pass Creek, Willow Creek, and Doublespring Creek, leaving little room for hiking. The rest of the canyons offer good, but sometimes rough, hikes—mostly either on a jeep trail or cross-country. Reliable water can be found in Basin Creek, Big Creek, Bear Creek, Lower and Upper Cedar, Long Lost and Dry Creeks, the forks of the Pahsimeroi, and Mahogany and Grouse Creeks.

By and large, road access to the canyons is plentiful but of poor quality. Drive carefully, and carry maps, a shovel, and a spare tire. My truck had to be pulled out of a mud hole in normally waterless Ramshorn Canyon while I was doing research for this edition. A sudden rainstorm turned the road into a quagmire.

Wildlife in the Lost Rivers is varied but not particularly abundant. Most common are antelope, deer, and elk. A reintroduced herd of bighorn sheep is faring well. Cougars are common but rarely seen. As with the Lemhi Mountains, these mountains have been managed for livestock use rather than multiple use, unlike the law dictates. The prevalence of rock, however, keeps the absolute number of cattle down.

On October 28, 1983, the earth at the base of Mount Borah split, leaving a fault scarp 10 miles long from north to south. The scarp is still visible today. The earthquake was the biggest (7.3 on the Richter Scale) in the lower forty-eight in twenty-four years. Those exploring the range found a few rockslides and some rearrangement of the trails. Because the earthquake caused the valley to drop, the Lost River Range's relief may be 15 to 20 feet greater than before the quake.

—Ralph Maughan

34 Bear Creek Lake

This is a short hike into a small lake among big—really big—mountains.

Start: 12 miles northeast of Mackay; 90 miles northwest of Pocatello
Type of hike: Out-and-back
Distance: 5.2 miles
Approximate hiking time: 2 days
Difficulty: Moderate
Best season: Late June–October
Trail surface: Dirt and rock
Land status: Salmon-Challis National Forest
Canine compatibility: On leash
Fees and permits: None

Maps: USGS Mackay, Methodist Creek, and Massacre Mountain; Middle Fork, Challis, and Lost River Ranger Districts–Challis National Forest map
Trail contact: Lost River Ranger District; (208) 588-3400
Parking and trailhead facilities: The trailhead has room for about four vehicles, although you can park in several other places a few hundred yards back down the road. In fact, this option may be prudent if the road is muddy, even if you have a four-wheel-drive vehicle.

Finding the trailhead: From US 93 8 miles south of Mackay (19 miles north of Arco), turn off at a clump of houses called Leslie. Here a gravel road travels northward for about 2 miles and then turns northeast heading toward a low spot (an obvious canyon) in the Lost River Mountains. The good gravel road enters this tight canyon, which is called Pass Creek Gorge. The dramatic rugged scenery of the gorge's limestone walls lasts for 2 miles. Suddenly the gorge opens into a broad canyon, where cows graze the pastureland. About 2 more miles brings you to the Bear Creek side road (to the left). This road is 9.5 miles from the US 93 exit at Leslie.

This road heads northward over stream gravel toward a canyon with an impressive walled entrance–Bear Canyon. The portal cliffs rise 600 vertical feet. The road passes through scrubby aspen, past informal campsites, and then into open forest. The trailhead is 1.2 miles from the start of the Bear Creek side road. Don't take a road to the right (it goes right down to the creek) at about the 1-mile mark. I did that my first time in Bear Creek and spent an hour wading through stinging nettle, cow pies, and swamp. Keep left and drive up a short, steep hill, navigate a rough road, and park in the shade where the road ends at the trailhead, just below the big cliffs. You don't need four-wheel drive, but high clearance helps. Be very cautious if the road is muddy. GPS: N43 59.26' / W113 28.86'

The Hike

The easy-to-follow trail strikes out straight ahead up-canyon; it begins to climb very steeply, but the climb is brief. It then follows the left side of the canyon for about 0.3 mile and suddenly drops down about 40 feet and crosses Bear Creek, which will probably be dry by midsummer. The topographic map shows the trail crossing the creek several times, but it is wrong.

Now on the creek's right side, you'll walk through a level, open forest a short distance to the forks of the canyon—Methodist Gulch to the left and Bear Creek to

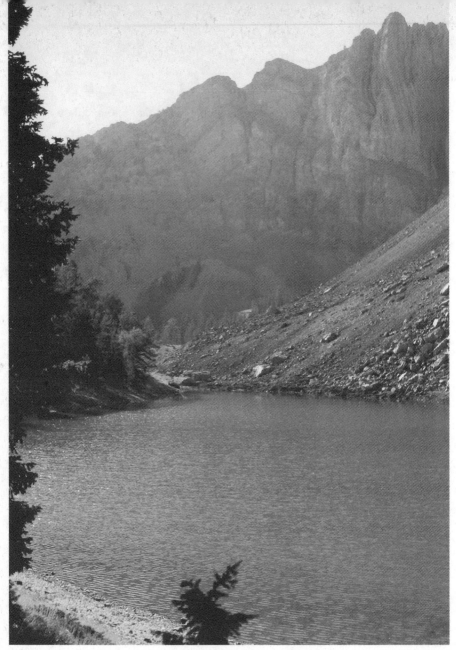

Cliffs of "giant's taffy" overlooking Bear Creek. PHOTO BY LUKE KRATZ

the right. Huge peaks appear up Methodist Gulch, but their full magnitude is frustrat-ingly hidden by nearby trees and a bend in Methodist Gulch.

At the forks ignore a faint (and unmapped) trail to the left, and follow the main trail. It climbs steeply up the mountainside on the right. Climb about 300 feet in 0.25 mile through a Douglas fir forest growing on the dry, rocky mountainside. Next you'll break out into the open. Bear Creek below usually has water year-round at this point, and across Bear Creek you can see the decaying remains of an old horse road once used for logging.

After climbing about 0.5 mile (and 500 feet) from the forks, you come to a faint sign on a fir that points uphill to the right and reads Wet Creek. Don't follow it. Instead, take the obvious left fork of the trail, which continues up Bear Canyon. Bear Canyon Trail does not appear on the Methodist Creek USGS quadrangle. It is shown on the older 15-minute Mackay quadrangle, however.

Soon you arrive at springs where Bear Creek's waters appear from the limestone rubble of the creekbed. Beyond this point the bed is usually dry. Except for one short section, stay to the right of the creekbed.

After a waterless 0.5 mile or so, the creek reemerges. Then, just past a small, startlingly green meadow, the trail climbs straight up the hillside to Bear Creek Lake. It's about 0.5 mile, and a tough 300-foot climb, to the lake. The trail twists and winds and can be a bit obscure here, so watch carefully. You may find that it disappears completely, but that's OK. You will find the lake if you keep your eyes on the giant peak ahead and just angle to the right.

Just before the lakeshore, emerge onto a limestone shelf surrounded by glorious peaks, including what I call the "Bear Creek Pinnacles" to your south. This is the south wall of Bear Canyon. These twisted rocks flow toward the sky like taffy from a giant's kitchen. The pinnacles are similar in appearance to the much-photographed, much-climbed Dolomites in the Italian Alps, and they guard a green alpine meadow where Bear Creek begins its tumbling descent in the grass and boulders. If you walk over to the base of the pinnacles (a 10-minute walk on a faint trail), you reach the meadow beneath these crags. Up-canyon from here, you can see lofty and unnamed Peak 11,138 and two other peaks, one about 11,200 feet and the other about 10,900 feet. The various pinnacles are approximately 9,800 to 10,000 feet.

The main trail proceeds to the lakeshore. The shore appears to be rocks and dirt but is really deep mud. Walk carefully as you approach the lake's jade waters. There are no fish in Bear Creek Lake since it loses much of its water by September and therefore is too shallow for fish to winter over.

Just a few yards to your right, over a minor hill, is a beautiful, green, flat meadow (it's a pond in early June). The giant peak that you have been hiking toward rises as a long wall behind the lake. Northeast of the lake, a long talus gulch slides down from a pass. You can scramble up the gulch for access to Wet Creek (no water!), or you can use it as a scrambling route to the crest of the mountain range. At the pass at the top of the gulch is an interesting area of grassy limestone plateau, complete with wildflowers and ephemeral ponds, all high above timberline.

—Ralph Maughan

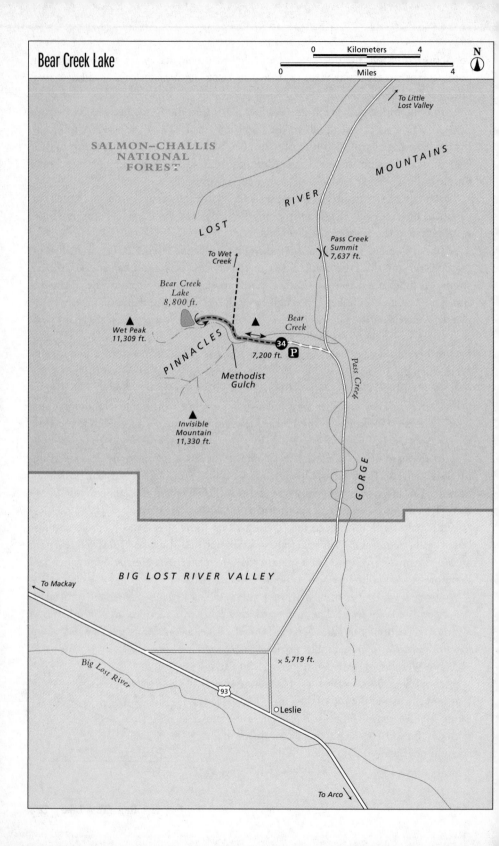

Miles and Directions

0.0 Start at the Bear Creek trailhead (7,200 feet).

0.4 Cross Bear Creek (7,420 feet).

0.7 At the fork of Methodist Gulch–Bear Creek, stay right (7,600 feet).

1.2 At the Wet Creek–Bear Creek trail junction, stay left on the Bear Creek Trail (8,000 feet).

2.5 Reach the shelf above Bear Creek Lake (8,850 feet).

2.6 Reach Bear Creek Lake (8,800 feet). Retrace your steps.

5.2 Arrive back at the trailhead.

35 Merriam Lake

Merriam is one of Idaho's most beautiful lakes, set in a large cirque and dominated by Mount Idaho, at 12,065 feet, Idaho's seventh-tallest peak.

Start: 16 linear miles northwest of Mackay and 75 miles south of Salmon, at the crest of the Lost River Range in the proposed Mount Borah Wilderness
Type of hike: Out-and-back. Could be a day trip were it not for the time-consuming drive to the trailhead.
Distance: 4 miles
Approximate hiking time: 2 days
Difficulty: Moderate due to steepness
Best season: Mid-July–late September
Trail surface: Dirt and rock
Land status: Salmon-Challis National Forest
Canine compatibility: On leash
Fees and permits: None
Maps: USGS Burnt Creek, Elkhorn Creek, and Leatherman Peak ID
Trail contact: Challis Ranger District; (208) 879-4100

Special considerations: As with most accesses to the east side of the Lost Rivers, the road to the trailhead is long and harsh. You must take a high-clearance vehicle; four-wheel drive is recommended. The trailhead is approximately 25 miles from US 93. Allow at least an hour and a half for the drive. The road becomes increasingly worse as it approaches the trailhead. The first 0.5 mile of the hike is not very accurately portrayed on the Burnt Creek USGS quadrangle.
Parking and trailhead facilities: Undeveloped and without potable water, the trailhead is often busy because it also serves as the trailhead for Pass Lake as well as Leatherman Pass, which many people use to access Leatherman Peak from the back side.

Finding the trailhead: From Challis, drive south along US 93 over Willow Creek Summit, and then 7.8 more miles to May-Patterson (Doublespring Pass) Road, on the left. From Mackay, drive northward on US 93 about 26 miles to this turnoff.

At 2.4 miles on May-Patterson Road, there is a picnic area with interpretive displays describing the effects of the great earthquake of 1983. This area is near Mount Borah, at 12,662 feet the highest mountain in Idaho, and adjacent to a portion of the earthquake scarp. Drive 5 more miles on a fairly good gravel road to Doublespring Pass (8,318 feet). Continue over the pass and down broad, dry Doublespring Creek Canyon for 3 more miles. Turn right at the sign indicating Horseheaven Pass.

For the Pahsimeroi Valley access, drive to the almost-ghost town of May; then cross over the valley to the county road that goes up its west side. This road leads up into Doublespring Creek, and 35 miles from May it reaches the Horseheaven Pass turnoff. Drive up a short, steep hill and follow the dirt road to Horseheaven Pass (7,925 feet), which is really a broad rangeland divide between the Lost Rivers and an outlying mountain. This area is frequented by pronghorn antelope.

Seven miles past the turnoff from May-Patterson Road, you reach a junction. The road to the left leads to the Pahsimeroi Valley; keep to the right. In another mile the road comes to a four-way junction just before Mahogany Creek. Continue straight ahead at the junction, and drop down to cross Mahogany Creek. Go up the creek for 0.1 mile; then turn onto the road at the left to go up a steep, short hill. The road then makes a broad 180-degree turn around the hill and enters the broad valley that contains the headwaters of the Pahsimeroi River.

After about 2.5 miles on an increasingly rocky road, you'll pass a line shack and a corral. Just beyond, the road forks. The left fork follows the East Fork of the Pahsimeroi, in which amazing cliffs and folded rocks are visible. Continue to the right up the valley of the West Fork of the Pahsimeroi. Another 3 miles on the twisting and rocky road brings you to the trailhead. GPS: N44 07.75' / W113 43.62'

The Hike

The permeable limestone core of the Lost River Range is hostile to the formation of lakes, despite the mountains' great height. The few lakes that do exist in these crags are both fertile and scenic. Merriam Lake is possibly the most beautiful. Set in a glacier-carved cirque at 9,600 feet, Merriam reflects the image of picturesque Mount Idaho at the basin's head and is flanked by mountains higher than 11,000 feet on both sides.

The signed trailhead begins on the right (north) bank of the West Fork of the Pah-simeroi. It immediately crosses a smaller tributary stream that runs into the Pahsimeroi at a ninety-degree angle from the hills on the north side of the canyon. This tributary shares the wide gravel trail for a short distance before it meets with the West Fork.

At approximately 0.2 mile the trail forks. This junction is marked by a sign that points left to a trail that crosses the West Fork of the Pahsimeroi and right to Merriam Lake. Stay right.

Just past this trail junction, the West Fork of the Pahsimeroi (which runs from the south from its headwaters near Leatherman Pass) meets with the tributary that drains Merriam Lake to the west. The trail remains adjacent to this tributary for the remainder of the hike.

Merriam Lake Trail is, in general, well trodden and easy to follow with the aid of blazes on trees. Regular trail maintenance is evident by the removal of downed tim-ber, erected erosion control measures, and bridges over wet meadows.

The trail climbs moderately for 1.5 miles, gaining 650 feet in elevation and wind-ing through alpine meadows and conifer forests teeming with deer and elk. Here it nears the tributary that drains Merriam Lake (but it never crosses to the left bank of the tributary). Soon after, the trail crosses a small, spring-fed stream and then climbs 800 feet quite steeply, first through forest and then switchbacking up an open slope of quartzite outcrops. On the left side of the trail, the tributary that departs Merriam Lake falls abruptly over staircases of quartzite.

Finally, at 2 miles, you are rewarded for the steep climb with a view of majestic Merriam Lake. The lake sits on a shelf of less erosive quartzite and is surrounded on the north by a spattering of alpine conifers

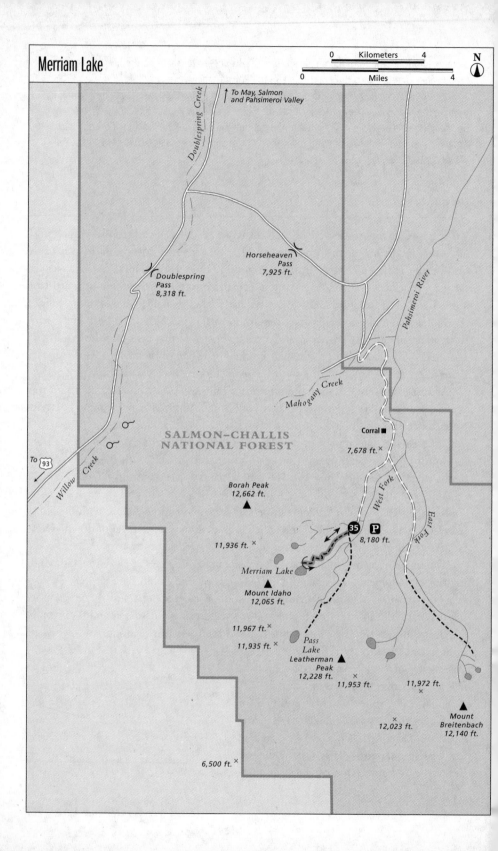

Merriam Lake

Kilometers 0 — 4

Miles 0 — 4

Doublespring Creek

To May, Salmon and Pahsimeroi Valley

Horseheaven Pass 7,925 ft.

Doublespring Pass 8,318 ft.

Pahsimeroi River

Mahogany Creek

SALMON–CHALLIS NATIONAL FOREST

Corral ■

7,678 ft. ×

To 93

Willow Creek

Borah Peak 12,662 ft. ▲

West Fork

East Fork

35 P 8,180 ft.

11,936 ft. ×

Merriam Lake

Mount Idaho 12,065 ft. ▲

11,967 ft. ×

11,935 ft. ×

Pass Lake

Leatherman Peak 12,228 ft. ▲

11,953 ft. ×

11,972 ft. ×

12,023 ft. ×

Mount Breitenbach 12,140 ft. ▲

6,500 ft. ×

and on the south by a talus slope of sedimentary rock. The huge peak that dominates the view up the basin is the 12,065-foot Idaho Peak. A surprising number of visitors think this peak is Mount Borah. Mount Borah, however, is a good 2 miles to the north and is not visible.

Although this trail is hard to access, it is quite popular, so don't be disappointed if you are not alone. There is more solitude above the lake in a rock garden and alpine meadow setting. Please use a stove rather than scavenging the meager woods for a campfire.

For the fly fisher, the banks of the lake on the right (north) and left (south) sides are steep, and fish can be visually tracked. The trail along the north side is moderately wooded, making cast-

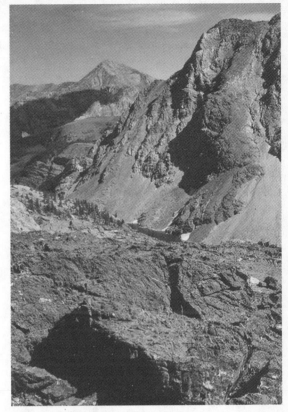

Merriam Lake among towering giants.
PHOTO BY RALPH MAUGHAN

ing somewhat difficult. Around the west side of the lake, near the inlet, the bank and lake bottom are shallow, and wading is possible. Fish are small, stocked rainbow/cutthroat hybrids, and are very plentiful. Their size, on average, is less than 10 inches, with the largest probably no longer than 18 inches.

If you follow the lake's inlet stream upward, you will pass delightful cascades, wildflower-filled meadows, and a few small ponds. Eventually you reach an upper jade-colored lake, set in an alpine rock basin at 10,220 feet. There are no fish here. The sharp peak rising to the lake's northwest is 11,936 feet high and, as is usual for many lofty peaks in these mountains, has no name.

From Merriam Lake, you can also climb the ridge to the lake's northwest. From the top, you look straight down to a no-name lake in a nameless canyon. To the southwest you look across 11,000-foot-high side ridges of bare rock, with the high point of Leatherman Peak in the distance. This ridge is a good location for hunting fossils (Paleozoic coral).

Options: Because of the long, brutal drive to the trailhead, consider also hiking to Pass Lake on the same trip. Spend a night at each lake. At the Pass Lake Trail junction, take a left and climb 4 miles to Pass Lake at 10,000 feet (use the same topos as for Merriam Lake).

—Ralph Maughan, Gwen Gerber, and Doug Gail

Miles and Directions

0.0 Start at the signed trailhead (8,160 feet).

0.2 At the Pass Lake junction (8,240 feet), stay right.

2.0 Reach Merriam Lake (9,590 feet). Retrace your steps.

4.0 Arrive back at the trailhead.

Lemhi Mountains

More than 100 miles long as the crow flies, longer still with the kinks stretched out, the Lemhi Range rises out of the arid lava of the Snake River Plain and advances northwest to central Idaho.

These mountains, which form a high, continuous ridge, are relatively arid in their southern reaches despite the fact that numerous peaks thrust up above 11,000 feet. Towering Diamond Peak, for example, reaches 12,197 feet, making it the third tallest in Idaho. Nevertheless, you can climb it without an ice ax in late June.

The Lemhi Mountains lie in a rain shadow, and the moisture of Pacific storms is dissipated first by the many mountain ranges of central Idaho. In the southern Lemhis, the precipitation that does fall percolates rapidly through the limestone and dolomite that constitute the mountains' vertebrae, and there is a general absence of lakes and creeks.

One ought not be misled by the arid beauty of the southern Lemhis, however. June storms can dump as much snow as a winter blast, and summer thunderstorms can be violent. In 1987 a tornado even touched down in Sawmill Canyon.

Northward these mountains shrink to a "mere" 10,000 to 11,000 feet but compensate for the lower elevation as their girth spreads to 15 or 20 miles. Here, the sedimentary rock formed under ancient seas gives way to harder rock. As you travel from south to north, dolomite first appears, then changes to an assortment of quartzites through which a number of mineral-bespeckled intrusions have pushed. These quartzites are some of the oldest exposed rocks in Idaho. Adding color, the quartzites of the northern Lemhis are covered in places by the chocolate, red, black, brown, gray, and maroon of the younger Challis Volcanics, the result of a vast outpouring of volcanic activity twenty-five to fifty million years ago. These volcanics washed over and covered large parts of east-central Idaho.

Thanks to the harder rock, water stays on the surface in the northern Lemhis. Cirque lakes huddle beneath peaks, and permanent creeks run down almost every canyon.

Despite years of prospecting, sporadic timber cutting, and little official attention to recreation, almost 500,000 acres of roadless land in these mountains has been identified by the forest service as suitable for congressional wilderness designation. Most of the roadless land is in two large blocks: a 187,000-acre roadless area in the southern Lemhis and more than 300,000 acres in the northern Lemhis.

The Southern Lemhis in mid-June. PHOTO BY LUKE KRATZ

Idaho environmentalists have long proposed that Congress designate 130,000 acres in the south and 180,000 acres in the north of this range as the Lemhi Wilderness. The southern roadless area is sometimes referred to as the proposed Diamond Peak Wilderness in reference to the giant pyramidal peak that rises 5 miles west of Lone Pine. The forest service did propose a small wilderness in the north during the late 1970s but, under pressure, changed its mind. In the early 1990s the Caribou–Targhee National Forest finally recommended to Congress that about half of the southern Lemhis—at least the half of the southern half of that forest—be designated wilderness. The proposal has languished because Idaho politicians don't support wilderness protection anymore. Meanwhile, the Caribou–Targhee has done nothing to protect the area from off-road vehicle abuse. Please come experience this amazing area and show your support for its protection!

Four great high desert valleys flank the Lemhi Mountains. To the north are the Pahsimeroi and Lemhi Valleys, lying on the west and the east sides of the Lemhis, respectively. To the south is the Little Lost River Valley, on the southwest side, and the Birch Creek Valley on the southeast. The streams draining these valleys flow into the volcanic rock of the Snake River Plain and disappear.

These four valleys support the majority of Idaho's pronghorn antelope. You may see them as they speed with seemingly little effort over the desert and open mountain slopes. With massive lungs, they sometimes will race alongside your vehicle and even overtake it on a gravel road to pass in front of you. In addition, it is common to see deer and even elk patrolling the valley floor and foothills. Here truly, the deer and the antelope play. Even black bears are sometimes seen in the valleys.

The typical Lemhi Range hike proceeds like this: A dirt road leaves the highway and gradually deteriorates into a jeep track near the mouth of, or a little way up, a canyon. Intelligence gets the best of inertia, and you park. Wearing your pack now, you follow the track, which deteriorates further, and then you set out cross-country. This usually isn't difficult, for in many places these mountains, like the nearby Lost River and Beaverhead Mountains, have little underbrush.

Be sure to take the prescribed USGS topographic maps along. The maps are usually as much for navigating the maze of dirt roads in the valleys as for orienting yourself once you're in the mountains. Shovels will prove a useful accessory, since minor wash-outs are frequent on these unmaintained roads, which cross over the big alluvial fans that have been built by thousands of years of runoff spilling from canyons to desert.

Nights are cold until after July 4. Once spring is past, storms are brief but can be violent: wind with lots of dust, heavy rain, and lightning (remember, much of this is open country). The often numerous mosquitoes of the June rangeland fade as the summer progresses, to be replaced by biting flies the remainder of the season.

Motorcycles and ATVs are becoming common, especially on weekends. You will rarely find them far back in the mountains, although they are penetrating the northern Lemhis to a greater distance than in the south. Worse, the Salmon–Challis National Forest even let an ATV trail be built over the crest of the mountains from Patterson Creek.

Lack of water can be a problem when hiking the Caribou–Targhee National Forest (southeast) side of these mountains. The South Fork of Pass Creek is the only reliable source, although scenic Rocky Canyon often has a small creek until midsummer. On the other hand, the southwest side has small creeks in most of the major canyons. Water is common in the northern part of the range.

In addition to the deer, elk, and antelope mentioned, there are quite a few black bear, cougar, and bobcat, as well as a growing herd of bighorn sheep from a transplant, and a large mountain goat population. Moose were recently transplanted into the Sawmill Canyon area. Occasionally a member of the growing Idaho wolf population may wander through, but there seems to be no reproducing population of wolves yet.

Public interest in the Lemhi Mountains grew throughout the 1980s and 1990s. We hope the day is near when politicians will be required to direct the forest service and the Bureau of Land Management to manage these superlative mountains and valleys for recreation and wilderness, rather than for subsidized grazing and logging.

—Ralph Maughan

36 Big Creek-Big Timber Creek Loop

There are lofty mountains and high meadows with spacious views on this long loop trail with many additional opportunities.

Start: 95 miles northwest of Idaho Falls and 10 miles west of Leadore
Type of hike: Loop
Distance: 37.2 miles
Approximate hiking time: 5–7 days plus
Difficulty: Strenuous
Best season: July–September
Trail surface: Dirt and rock
Land status: For the Big Creek and Snowbank Trail portions: Challis Ranger District. For the Big Timber Creek portion: Leadore Ranger District. Both are in the Salmon–Challis National Forest.
Canine compatibility: On leash recommended
Fees and permits: None
Maps: USGS Big Creek Peak, Iron Creek Point, Sheephorn Peak, and Yellow Peak ID
Trail contact: Challis Ranger District; (208) 879-4100. Leadore Ranger District; (208) 768-2500

Special considerations: Early hikers (late June) should be prepared for difficult fords and, on the high passes, a foot or more of snow. There can still be slab avalanches this time of year. Bring wading shoes.
Parking and trailhead facilities: North Fork Trail leaves from Big Creek Camp, which is a small campsite with a couple of picnic tables at the confluence of the North and South Forks of Big Creek. There is room for only three vehicles. The trail's beginning is signed and obvious.

The South Fork of Big Creek Trailhead is 0.2 mile back up the road and about 70 feet uphill, in a wide-open spot with an impressive view of both North and South Big Creek Canyons and Flatiron Mountain, which rises between them. Parking space is ample.

Finding the trailhead: Drive 19 miles north from Idaho Falls on I-15. Then turn left (west) onto ID 33. Continue 17 miles to Mud Lake; from here, it is another 28 miles on ID 33 to the small town of Howe. At Howe, turn right (north) off the highway and follow the county road that goes up the Little Lost River Valley all the way to the valley's end at Summit Reservoir. Cross the low divide here, and drop down into the Pahsimeroi Valley. About 57 miles north of Howe, a sign reads Big Creek Trail. Take a left onto the dirt road here, and drive 3.5 miles to Big Creek. The road ends at the small Big Creek Camp near the forest boundary, where Big Creek forms from its north and south forks.

The other access points to the loop are from Iron Creek Trail in Sawmill Canyon, and Big Timber Creek Trail, with access from Leadore. Iron Creek Road is graveled and located just 2 miles up Sawmill Canyon beyond Mill Creek Road. GPS: N44 23.08' / W113 25.71'

The Hike

This is a tremendous loop in a mountain range that has few loop trails. If you can't spend most of a week, you will also enjoy hiking portions of the loop. In total it has 12,500 feet of relief. You hike over three divides and through a variety of mountain scenes. You will not encounter many other people, but the area is better known now than when the first edition of *Hiking Idaho* was published.

Much of the loop is open to off-road vehicles and motorcycles, and you will certainly encounter a few. The South Fork of Big Creek was closed to machines after a big battle. The North Fork of Big Creek is open to them, including ATVs, but gets no ATV use because the trail is too rocky and narrow for them. The Snowbank Trail portion gets the most machine use.

The entire loop is within the area proposed by Idaho conservationists as the Lemhi Range Wilderness.

Commonly seen are deer, elk, mountain goats, antelope, coyotes, and black bears. Moose are occasional. Cougar are abundant, but rarely seen. The profuse whitebark pine in the northern Lemhi would make for outstanding grizzly bear habitat, but there are probably no grizzly bears.

You can begin the hike from either fork. This description describes the loop going clockwise, starting up the North Fork of Big Creek and ending at the South Fork of Big Creek.

Proceeding up the North Fork of Big Creek, it is 6.6 miles from the trailhead to the Park Fork of Big Creek. The trail leaves the trailhead campground and goes north along the right bank of the North Fork. For a mile, it's rocky but fairly easy, passing through conifer, aspen, and cottonwood, with some mountain mahogany present. Near the mouth of trailless West Fork of Big Creek, you reach the first of two fords of the North Fork. The water can be fast and deep, and fortunately, as of the summer of 2000, there was a log bridge upstream for hikers.

Once across, you make a steady, but easy, climb for almost another mile to the second crossing. There will probably be another hiker's log bridge here, too. If no log, this is also a major ford in early season.

There is a small meadow at the second crossing and two more meadows in the next 2 miles. At 4.5 miles you enter the Big Creek burn from the mid-1990s. Up-canyon past the meadows, the trail climbs to what appears to be a large, low glacial moraine, and it stays on this moraine for about a mile. Ford two small tributaries as you cross over talus and glacial cobblestone stretches. Glimpses of large, unnamed peaks up-canyon reward your efforts.

The trail approaches the North Fork closely as you near the Park Fork tributary. You can ford the Park Fork where the trail crosses (it's about 12 feet wide here), or you can search upstream for a log. The Park Fork ford is not bridged, but it is not difficult except in June.

The trail then goes between the Park Fork and the North Fork for about 0.2 mile, leading to their confluence. Here the left fork of the trail continues up the North Fork, giving access to Devils Basin and Big Eightmile Creek (see Options). Take the right fork instead, and head up the Park Fork of Big Creek.

It's about 4 miles and 2,000 feet of relief from the bottom of the Park Fork to Yellow Pass (its unofficial name). The first 0.5 mile of the ascent is a steep, switchbacking, 500-foot climb, paralleling the Park Fork, which thunders down the mountain in June and early July. The gradient then declines. Scout the mountain slopes on the left (north) for mountain goats as you listen to the pikas calling from the talus slides. The trail goes through fir forest interspersed with huge, scenic boulders.

The trail keeps to the north side of the creek until you are about a mile below Yellow Pass. After a jump of the Park Fork, the trail to Yellow Pass turns southward at the junction with the trail to the Middle Fork of Little Timber Creek. Just before reaching this spot, you have the opportunity to make a cross-country hike to Park Fork Lake. Head to the northwest and climb 300 feet to this small lake, located at 9,300 feet in a glacier-cut bowl of intruded igneous rock of the Park Fork Stock.

After crossing the Park Fork, you climb quite rapidly toward Yellow Peak (10,968 feet), which probably was named after the slightly yellow quartzite boulders on its slopes. After just 0.25 mile the trail forks. The left fork soon forks again, with one fork leading over to Park Fork Lake and then to Yellow Lake. The second fork goes to the Middle Fork of Little Timber Creek, and the third goes to Rocky Canyon (a tributary of Big Timber Creek). Ignore all this unless your destination is not Yellow Pass. Take the trail to the right. This junction has signs giving destinations. The sign pointing out the trail to Yellow Pass is south and downhill—a bit confusing.

Follow the trail southward to the obvious pass. At Yellow Pass (9,702 feet), you are rewarded with a spectacular view of Flatiron Mountain (11,019 feet) and Big Creek Peak (11,350 feet) to the southwest. An extra hour will allow you to scramble to the top of Yellow Peak for a panorama of mountains grander still.

At Yellow Pass, you cross the crest of the Lemhi Range. The trail drops steeply and is faint in places until, after a descent of 1,000 feet in a distance of 1.3 miles, you reach Big Timber Creek Canyon. From here the trail is good and easy, and you roll down the canyon for about 4 miles until you reach Cabin Creek, which you will go up to continue the loop. Many elk and mule deer frequent this large drainage. The low whistles and grunts of the elk add to the wilderness atmosphere in this land of striking high mountain scenery and subalpine meadows, which break up the stands of quaking aspen and conifer.

After passing four major side drainages that drop off Flatiron Mountain and Big Creek Peak, enter a large meadow that lies directly below Junction Peak (10,620 feet) and opposite the Cabin Creek and Squirrel Creek side canyons. Signs in the meadow help you locate this important junction. Take Cabin Creek Trail (Trail 127) to continue the loop. Squirrel Creek is a scenic and interesting side option.

The meadow is a large area of hunting and other camps, and it is about 20 miles from here down-canyon to the town of Leadore. The trail that continues down Big Timber Creek from the junction is a good alternative access trail to and from the Big Creek–Timber Creek Loop. It is 6 miles down Big Timber Creek from Cabin Creek to FR 105, which comes up from Leadore.

The climb to Cabin Creek Pass (its unofficial name) gains 1,600 feet in about 4 miles. The trail stays close to Cabin Creek for the first 1.5 miles; then the grade increases, and the trail follows a fork of Cabin Creek, switchbacking to the pass, which is a small saddle at 9,282 feet. At the pass, walk westward along the divide, and you will soon find yourself on Snowbank Trail, where there are likely to be trail machines on weekends. You can hike the trail on this divide either east or west. The route to the east leads to Timber Pass, where you can descend Trail Creek north back to Big Timber Creek or head south via Timber Creek, in the head of Sawmill Canyon, to FR 105. However, to continue the loop, follow the trail to your right.

The ridge on which Cabin Creek Pass sits marks the southern boundary of the wilderness proposed by Idaho environmentalists. Southward, you will see a proliferation of logging roads and the scar of the Little Lost Fire, which burned 9,000 acres in the head of Sawmill Canyon during the drought summer of 1988. Despite this view and possible dirt bikes, the Snowbank Trail is picturesque, especially the first several miles past Cabin Creek Pass. There are some high-elevation camping spots about a mile past Cabin Creek Pass.

Snowbank Trail climbs and then contours high above Sawmill Canyon, giving inspiring views of the canyon. As you reach the high point of the trail, you gain excellent views of Bell Mountain and Diamond Peak far to the southeast, and also of the unnamed and rarely visited symmetrical peaks and cirque basins to the south of the South Fork of Big Creek. High marshy meadows intermingle with well-weathered conifers as the trail bumps along just below the ridgeline. This ridgeline, unlike the others visited while hiking this loop, is composed of colorful volcanic rocks rather than quartzite, dolomite, or limestone.

You'll follow Snowbank Trail for 7 miles to its junction with Iron Creek Trail (another good access trail onto the loop). The trail drops off the ridgeline and rolls through a few small side drainages to Redrock Creek, named for the color of the rock in the area. Past Redrock Creek, the trail climbs and then continues to contour around the upper slopes of Sawmill Canyon. About a mile south of Redrock Creek, you cross an area clear-cut about 25 years old. A volcanic column looms above.

Continue contouring around the upper slopes of Sawmill Canyon and one of its major tributaries, Iron Creek. Massive Bear Mountain (10,744 feet) and pointed Iron Creek Point (10,736 feet) dominate the view as you round a spur and head generally southwest around the top of Iron Creek. From the spur, an easy 1.5 miles brings you to a four-way trail junction, which is signed and obvious. Take the trail that goes upward over the pass to the west. This is the South Fork of Big Creek Trail. Heading down is Iron Creek Trail. Continuing toward Iron Creek Point is an extension of Snowbank Trail.

The climb out of Iron Creek into the South Fork is about 400 feet. If the trail is faint due to the "trail-eating" meadows, just head for the obvious divide above you. The views here of Diamond Peak, Bell Mountain, and the other Lemhi peaks rival any views in Idaho.

Switchback down into the South Fork of Big Creek canyon through a mixture of ancient, fire-ravaged ghosts of whitebark pine and new growth. Iron Creek Point rises behind you, and the trail's grade decreases as you come to a place of multiple springs, the birthplace of the South Fork of Big Creek.

The canyon remains narrow, and you'll cross the creek perhaps ten times in small jumps as the trail descends through thick fir forest. The need to cross talus slopes occasionally slows you down. After crossing a tributary from the north, the trail remains on the right side of the stream.

A major tributary (incorrectly named the South Fork of Big Creek on older maps) flows in from the northeast about 3 miles from the trail junction back at Iron Creek. Still the canyon remains narrow, and soon another major tributary flows in from the north. Some interesting avalanche chutes spill from the high, unnamed ridge to the south of the creek. The canyon now widens, but the trail traverses talus slides above the marshy, willow- and alder-choked flood plain.

The canyon continues to widen and narrow as you walk downstream, and the trail always stays on the north side of the creek.

About 2.25 miles past the second tributary, you reach a wide, green area supported by upslope springs and kept in place by beaver dams. There are good camping sites here. The trail turns left just beyond the beaver dams at a sign that simply says "Trail." It then fords the South Fork and climbs up around and through the buttresses above the South Fork. Then it contours midway around a steep tributary of the South Fork before reaching the trailhead 2.75 miles from the ford.

Options: To make another possible loop, from the confluence of North Big Creek and the Park Fork, rather than going up the Park Fork, continue up the North Fork to Devils Basin and a pass at 9,850 feet into Big Eightmile Creek. Drop down steeply to the east, into the gentle uplands at the head of Big Eightmile Creek. When the grade levels out, head east-by-southeast—that is, contour around the base of Peak 10,601. Eventually turn southeast and climb over obvious Pass 9,892. Drop down toward the Lake Fork, but not into it. Instead contour northeastward to the large cirque that holds Yellow Lake.

From Yellow Lake a trail leads southwest over a pass that is 10,200 feet into the headwaters of the Park Fork. Here you can go back down the Park Fork to complete the loop or continue over Yellow Pass and down Big Timber Creek.

Big Creek-Big Timber Creek Loop

| 0 | Kilometers | 6 |
| 0 | Miles | 6 |

N

SALMON–CHALLIS
NATIONAL FOREST

Yellow Lake

Park Fork Lake

Park Fork

Yellow Pass

To Lemhi Valley, Leadore

Yellow Peak
10,968 ft.

Junction Peak

West Fork Big Creek

North Fork Big Creek

North Fork Trail

Big Timber Creek

Big Creek Peak
11,350 ft.

Squirrel Creek

Cabin Creek

Cabin Creek Trail

To Pahsimeroi Valley

Big Creek Camp Trailhead

FR097

36

P

6,540 ft.

To May, Salmon

South Fork

Springs

South Fork Big Creek

Flatiron Mountain
11,019 ft.

Snowbank Trail

Slide Creek

South Fork Trail

Springs

10,504 ft.

10,738 ft.

Iron Creek Point
10,736 ft.

Iron Creek

Bear Mountain
10,744 ft.

PAHSIMEROI VALLEY

County Road

LITTLE LOST VALLEY

To Howe

SAWMILL CANYON

To Howe

Another option is to make a side loop from Squirrel Creek to Falls Creek and back down to Big Timber Creek (or vice versa). Both the Devils Basin–Yellow Lake Loop and the Squirrel Creek–Falls Creek Loop are very scenic. The Devils Basin Loop should only be attempted after mid-July.

—Ralph Maughan

Miles and Directions

0.0 Start at the Big Creek Camp Trailhead (6,590 feet).

1.3 Cross the North Fork of Big Creek via ford or bridge (6,760 feet).

2.2 Reach the second ford/bridge over the North Fork of Big Creek (6,950 feet).

6.6 Ford the Park Fork (7,581 feet).

9.9 At the trail junction, go south for Yellow Pass (9,144 feet).

10.8 Cross Yellow Pass (9,702 feet).

12.2 Reach Big Timber Creek Canyon (8,800 feet).

16.4 Reach the meadow with trails up Squirrel and Cabin Creeks (7,610 feet). Take the Cabin Creek Trail (Trail 127).

20.5 Reach Cabin Creek Pass (9,282 feet).

21.3 Pass the high point on Snowbank Trail (9,680 feet).

24.5 Cross Redrock Creek (8,150 feet).

25.5 Pass beneath a volcanic column (8,300 feet).

28.0 Arrive at a four-way trail junction (8,700 feet). Take the South Fork of Big Creek Trail.

28.5 Pass into the South Fork of Big Creek canyon (9,170 feet).

31.7 Pass a major tributary to South Fork of Big Creek (7,460 feet).

32.0 Pass a second major tributary (7,405 feet).

34.3 Ford the South Fork and begin to climb (7,005 feet).

35.2 Reach the high point of the climb (7,640 feet).

37.2 Arrive at the trailhead 0.2 mile above Big Creek Camp (6,664 feet).

37 Buck and Bear Valley Lakes

There are two clusters of cirque lakes with excellent fishing amid the grandeur of the northern Lemhi Mountains. The lakes are beneath the pyramidal Lem Peak (10,986 feet), in an area abundant with wildlife, including mountain goats.

Start: About 25 miles south-southeast of Salmon in the proposed Lemhi Wilderness
Type of hike: Out-and-back, with the opportunity to spend several days visiting different mountain lakes
Distance: 11 miles
Approximate hiking time: 2–5 days
Difficulty: Easy to moderate (due to elevation gain) to the trailed Buck and Bear Valley Lakes
Best season: July–late September
Trail surface: Dirt and rock
Land status: Salmon–Challis National Forest
Canine compatibility: On leash
Fees and permits: None
Maps: USGS Hayden Creek and Lem Peak ID; Salmon National Forest map

Trail contact: Leadore Ranger District; (208) 768-2500
Special considerations: The road to the trailhead is easily passable by sedan; however, the condition of the last few miles, which are dirt, is worse in the early summer and after a rain.
Parking and trailhead facilities: At the trailhead for pack animals, you'll find a latrine, potable water, and several developed campsites especially equipped for pack animals. At the hiker's trailhead there is also a latrine, as well as a water pump, picnic tables, and some minimal camping. The trailhead has a register and is well marked.

Finding the trailhead: From the junction of US 93 and ID 28 in Salmon, Idaho, drive 26 miles south on ID 28. Approximately 1 mile north of the unincorporated crossroads of Lemhi, turn to the west (right) onto a paved county road, Hayden Creek Road, leading up Hayden Creek. The road is signed, indicating the direction of Hayden Creek Road, Basin Creek, and Bear Valley Creek. If you are coming from the south, from Mud Lake, drive north on ID 28 for approximately 95 miles through Lemhi, and turn left on Hayden Creek Road, which is also signed from that direction.

After 3.5 miles on Hayden Creek Road, reach the Basin Creek intersection, where the road turns into gravel; go left here, remaining on Hayden Creek Road. The road then gradually narrows, as does the canyon, and remains about 100 feet above the stream on a cut in the steep canyon sideslope. At 8 miles you enter the Salmon–Challis National Forest. Just beyond the forest boundary, reach another fork in the road. The Hayden Creek Road (FR 008) continues to the left. To reach the trailhead, take the right fork (FR 009). A sign indicates that this is the way to Bear Valley Lake Trail. Remain on FR 009 all the way to the trailhead. It's a generally good dirt road as it climbs and winds tortuously above Bear Valley Creek, crossing several creeks. It finally ends at the well-developed trailhead just past tributary Short Creek. At 12.4 miles you reach the trailhead for pack and saddle horses, and at 13.2 miles you reach the end of the road and the trailhead for hikers. GPS: N44 47.56' / W113 46.77'

The Hike

Both the Buck and the Bear Valley Lakes nestle in the heart of the proposed Lemhi Range Wilderness. They are situated at the north end of the high Lemhi peaks. This hike describes the trail to Bear Valley Lake, the largest of the lakes. The options describe three alternatives for hikes along the way, including one to Buck Lakes.

Unfortunately, according to the forest service travel plan, both Buck and Bear Valley Lake Trails are still open to motor vehicles. Fortunately, during my trip to Bear Valley Lake in the autumn of 2000, the trails showed no sign of motor vehicle use.

Bear Valley Trail begins 100 yards below and east of the parking area. Cross over Bear Valley Creek on a good bridge and begin to hike westward up Bear Valley Canyon. The trail immediately splits; a sign indicates Basin Creek Trail to the right and Bear Valley Lakes, 5.5 miles to the left. Go left. Bear Valley Trail remains along the north side of the creek, near the canyon bottom, and is easy to follow.

The first portion is fairly level and traverses open country but soon enters forest. Here, just inside the forest, in 1989, coauthor Ralph Maughan surprised a young cougar at close range. After 2.5 miles of gradual uphill, you approach Buck Creek Canyon, visible through the forest to the left. The trail up Buck Creek is marked with a sign on a tree on the right side of the trail. This sign indicates that Buck Valley Lakes are 2 miles to the left and Bear Valley Lakes to the right (sometimes these signs are taken down in the winter, and in early summer they might not be back up).

Bear Valley Trail continues to wind through the trees and climbs, rather steeply in places, up Bear Valley. At 4 miles from the trailhead, the trail splits again. A sign indicates the Bear Valley High Trail (Trail 178) to the right and the trail to Bear Valley Lakes—1.5 miles to the left. Stay left. After another 0.5 mile you reach the signed Upper Bear Valley Lakes junction. The left fork crosses Bear Valley Creek on two consecutive bridges and continues on to Bear Valley Lake. Between this junction and Bear Valley Lake, there are two turnoffs to the left, which are less obvious and unmarked. These trails eventually merge and meet up with a jeep trail that climbs up Allison Creek on the other side of the mountain range.

Bear Valley Lake is 1 mile, and a 500-foot climb, past the Upper Bear Valley Lakes junction. It leads to the largest of the lakes, which occupies a large cirque at the head of Bear Valley Creek, 5.5 miles from the trailhead. The cirque's western bank is splattered with alpine conifers, while its other banks jut steeply toward the sky. At 9,135 feet, the translucent waters of Bear Valley Lake reflect the surrounding 600- to 900-foot-high rocky cliffs.

0   Kilometers   4

N

0   Miles   4

Options: Upper Bear Valley Lakes: To visit the Upper Bear Valley Lakes, take a right at the junction 4.5 miles from the trailhead. This junction is signed and points toward the Upper Bear Valley Lakes. It is approximately 1 mile, and a 400-foot climb, to the largest of the upper lakes. The highest Bear Valley Lake lies at 9,240 feet and is another mile (and a 350-foot climb) from the first of the Upper Bear Valley Lakes. There is plenty of room here and a fine view of Lem Peak.

Buck Lakes: Buck Lakes Trail (Trail 081) is not on the USGS topographic map. It leaves Bear Valley Creek Trail 2.5 miles past the trailhead, at approximately 7,680 feet, after you have begun to climb steeply and have partially passed the mouth of Buck Creek Canyon. Take a right at the signed Buck Lake junction to immediately cross Bear Valley Creek on several logs upstream from its union with Buck Creek. The route switchbacks through the forest, keeping to the west side of Buck Creek. After a little over a mile, you'll cross a small creek, the outlet of the first Buck Lake. This is really just a pond 400 feet above you on the mountainside. Next, the trail climbs to Lake 8,474, the largest of the Buck Lakes. The next lake is only 0.5 mile above Lake 8,474, but it's a steep, 500-foot, cross-country pull through timber and deadfall. The route is to follow the inlet creek up the mountainside; camping here is limited. The highest Buck Lake sits at 9,456 feet, with its back to the base of rubble-strewn Lem Peak, which is almost 11,000 feet high. Not only is the route difficult to this prize lake, but there also is just one marginal spot for a tent.

Bear Valley High Trail/Basin Creek Trail: To make a loop trip and hike along the northern ridges of Bear Valley, you can hike to or from the Bear Valley Lakes on the High Trail. To take the High Trail to the lakes, take a right at the intersection just past the trailhead that points in the direction of Basin Creek Trail. This route is about 1.5 miles longer and has significantly more elevation gain and loss. I chose not to take this route; therefore, I am unsure of its condition. Approximately halfway along this route, the trail forks and either continues north to McNutt Creek and then Basin Creek, or remains on the northern ridgeline of Bear Valley. Stay left at this intersection. The High Trail meets up with Bear Valley Trail at the junction 4 miles from the Bear Valley Trailhead and is signed from this junction as Bear Valley High Trail.

—Gwen Gerber

Miles and Directions

0.0   Start at the Bear Valley Trailhead (6,800 feet).

2.5   Pass the Buck Lakes Trail junction (7,680 feet).

4.0   Pass the Bear Valley High Trail junction (8,400 feet).

4.5   Reach the Upper Bear Valley Lakes junction (8,650 feet).

5.5   Reach Bear Valley Lake (9,195 feet). Retrace your steps.

11.0   Arrive back at the trailhead.

38 Mill Creek Lake and Firebox Summit

This scenic lake looks as though it's alpine but opens early in the season.

Start: 90 miles northwest of Idaho Falls
Type of hike: Out-and-back, with options to explore the Lemhi crest area
Distance: 4.6 miles to Mill Creek Lake and back; 8.4 miles to Firebox Summit and back
Approximate hiking time: 2-plus days
Difficulty: Moderate to the lake; moderately strenuous to Firebox Meadows due to a trail that is faint in some crucial places
Best season: July–August
Trail surface: Dirt and rock
Land status: Salmon-Challis National Forest
Canine compatibility: On leash
Fees and permits: None
Maps: USGS Gilmore and Big Windy Peak; Middle Fork, Challis, and Lost River Ranger

Districts-Challis National Forest map
Trail contact: Lost River Ranger District; (208) 588-3400
Parking and trailhead facilities: The trailhead has a few picnic tables, with three or four places to camp under a forest canopy. They are right by Mill Creek, the only source of water. Several undeveloped campsites are downstream but nearby. Unfortunately, in recent years large recreational vehicles have taken to using the shaded trailhead as a camping spot, and hikers find it monopolized by campers who are not interested in using the trail. The forest service plans to eliminate this problem by moving the trailhead downstream.

Finding the trailhead: Leaving the hamlet of Howe on the county road, drive north in the Little Lost River Valley for 36 miles. At 36 miles, a generally well-signed and well-maintained gravel road exits to the right (east) for Sawmill Canyon. Follow this road across Mud Flats, and 7 miles from the intersection you will cross Sawmill Creek. Now drive up into Sawmill Canyon, a large, south-ward-draining stream valley. After a mile, you enter the Salmon-Challis National Forest. Continue about 3 more miles on the gravel road (which can be very washboarded) to the bridge over Mill Creek. A hundred yards past the bridge, turn right (east) on the dirt road at a meadow that blazes with larkspur and wyethia in June. Go 1.2 miles to the end of the road. GPS: N44 22.07' / W113 21.73'

The Hike

When winter's ice still grips most high mountain lakes, Mill Creek Lake, in the rugged Lemhi Mountains, is usually suitable for a hike and overnight camping.

Dammed by a landslide, the lake lies in a short, rocky canyon. The rocks and cliffs enclosing the lake may cause you to think the surroundings are more alpine than they really are.

A faint trail above the lake leads to Firebox Meadows and Firebox Summit. This beautiful meadow and forest country, which is important elk range, contrasts sharply with the rocky lake environs below.

You can usually reach the lake by mid-June, although July and August are the best months to visit.

You will easily find the trail. It is obvious, marked with a sign that reads "Closed to Motor Vehicles." Set out into the forest for the peaceful, 2.3-mile, 1,200-foot climb to the lake. At first you'll walk easily through a gentle, open forest. There are some small meadows, some large, often leaning, old-growth Douglas fir, and an unnamed rivulet of Mill Creek, which you soon cross. Then, after 0.5 mile, cross Mill Creek on a good bridge.

Across the bridge, the forest becomes denser. The trees have smaller trunks, and the forest floor is rocky, with little vegetation. The trail begins to climb a bit, and soon you are in a small canyon. The grade increases, and the trail now keeps about 50 to 75 feet above rushing Mill Creek. After about 0.75 mile, you come to the base of a big rockslide that has filled the canyon. The trees thin out as the trail switchbacks up the slide. Below, Mill Creek pours as a full-blown stream out of the slide's base. The hard rock of the rockslide is quartzite, part of the Kinnikinnick Formation.

A few big, old Douglas fir have struggled to make a living out of the harsh conditions of the slide. These trees are hundreds of years old. Their ancient branches frame the view down the canyon of the Lemhi foothills and, farther to the west, Idaho's highest mountains, the Lost Rivers.

When the switchbacks of this well-maintained trail end, there's a brief reprieve through a level section. Here, in early summer, you pass a small lower lake (not on the map) and a small, very pretty meadow stream that meanders over the top of the slide to feed the lake. These waters are the children of spring and disappear as the season progresses. From this spot, there is one more steep pitch to the lake.

Mill Creek Lake's water level varies. Naturally, it is highest after a winter of heavy snow. The lake supports a good population of fat cutthroat trout. I've been most successful with wet flies and streamers.

You'll find campsites at both ends of the lake, but the north and south sides of the lake are too steep to camp on. Much of the time you'll find a spring flowing just below a rockslide that rests above the lake's east side. The trail around the lake goes follows its east (right) side. Although one hiking guide says there is a trail around both sides of the lake, the left side is far too steep for a trail.

To find the trail around the lake, from the lakeside you must climb 30 feet backward on the trail. A marker points to the trail's continuation. It follows the crest of the rockslide and then a cutbank above the lake and then into the steeply sloped forest, gradually descending to near the inlet of the lake.

If you wish to hike beyond the lake, a trail climbs at a gradual rate up Mill Creek Canyon through a dense, rocky, and uninteresting forest. The trail remains on the right side of Mill Creek. After 0.5 mile you come to a meadow with springs. Here the canyon bends around to the north.

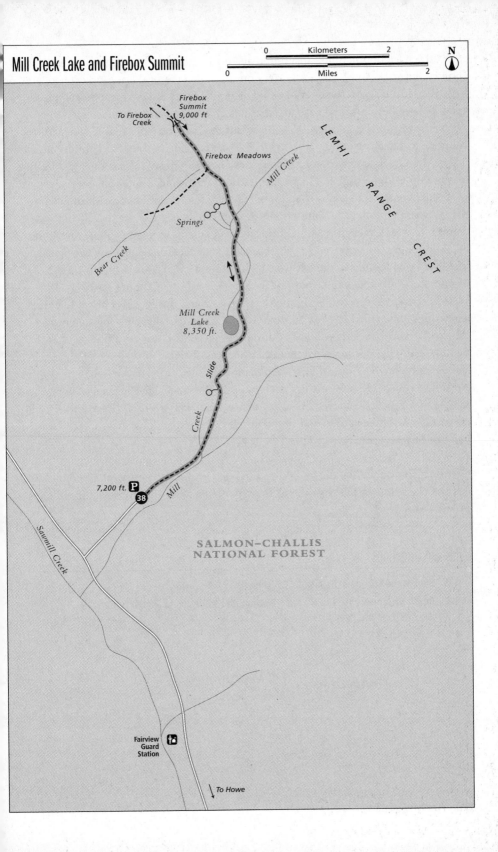

Mill Creek Lake and Firebox Summit

0 ___ Kilometers ___ 2
0 ___ Miles ___ 2

N

Firebox
Summit
9,000 ft
To Firebox
Creek

Firebox Meadows

LEMHI

Mill Creek

RANGE

CREST

Springs

Bear Creek

Mill Creek
Lake
8,350 ft.

Slide

Creek

7,200 ft. P
38

Mill

SALMON–CHALLIS
NATIONAL FOREST

Sawmill Creek

Fairview
Guard
Station

To Howe

At the meadow, the trail's tread immediately fades, as is so often the case in such country, but it goes just inside the trees on the right side of the meadow. There are large, but old, blazes on the trees marking the route. The tread does reappear in places, and logs have been sawed. These together help you keep on the trail.

At the top of the meadow, it is important that you find the trail if you wish to continue to Firebox Summit at 9,000 feet. Make certain you find the leftmost channel of Mill Creek at the top of the meadow. The trail crosses this channel and heads leftward up into the timber. The tread is obvious once you're in the timber.

From here, the trail is easy to follow all the way to pleasant Firebox Meadows. This is a fairly large meadow. It is important for your return trip to note that the meadow drains into Bear Creek, not Mill Creek. Pass over an almost imperceptible divide just before reaching the lower end of Firebox Meadows. Fortunately, at the divide there is a signed trail leading to the left (west). This is Bear Creek Trail, which is on the old 15-minute USGS quadrangle but not the new 7.5-minute Gilmore quad.

The trail keeps just to the right of the meadow and finally passes into a few trees and crosses unheralded Firebox Summit, where a faint trail descends through dry forest into Firebox Creek. If you walk out onto the meadow, you get a fine view of the Lemhi Crest. The meadow is surrounded by lodgepole pine, subalpine fir, Engelmann spruce, and whitebark pine. Elk are abundant until the cattle arrive.

When you head back, be very sure you find the trail. Don't just walk down the middle of Firebox Meadows, because you are very likely to reach Bear Creek Trail rather than Mill Creek Trail and find yourself quite a way down Bear Creek before you realize your error.

Options: You can follow the trail down Firebox Creek. I did not check its condition, nor the condition of the Bear Creek Trail, which may have been rehabilitated after 30 years of neglect.

—Ralph Maughan

Miles and Directions

0.0   Start at the Mill Creek Trailhead (7,240 feet).

2.3   Reach Mill Creek Lake (8,330 feet). **Option:** Hike 1.9 miles to Firebox Summit (9,018 feet). Retrace your steps.

4.6   Arrive back at the trailhead.

39 Nez Perce Lake

Nez Perce Lake is noted for its solitude and the chance to catch Arctic grayling, a rare species in the Rocky Mountains.

Start: 7 linear miles southeast of Leadore, beneath 10,465-foot Sheephorn Peak
Type of hike: Out-and-back on a relatively short, steep trail
Distance: 5.6 miles
Approximate hiking time: 2 days
Difficulty: Moderate with a steep climb
Best season: July–late September
Trail surface: Dirt and rock
Land status: Salmon-Challis National Forest
Canine compatibility: On leash
Fees and permits: None
Maps: USGS Purcell Spring and Sheephorn Peak ID

Trail contact: Leadore Ranger District; (208) 768-2500
Special considerations: Although the road to the trailhead, when dry, is passable with a passenger car, four-wheel drive is recommended.
Parking and trailhead facilities: This is an informal, unmarked trailhead. It is recommended that you park your vehicle along the road before you enter the forest, because the road becomes exponentially worse. At Nez Perce Spring, a four-wheel-drive road continues through the trees for another 0.5 mile but is very rough.

Finding the trailhead: Drive south on ID 28 from Leadore. After about 6 miles, turn west (right) onto a well-maintained gravel road. The road is marked with a BLM sign indicating the route to Timber Creek and Cold Springs.

Coming north from the town of Mud Lake, take ID 28 for about 69 miles to the gravel road, which is also signed from this direction.

The gravel road crosses Texas Creek (the headwaters of the Lemhi River) and forks at approximately 1 mile. At this intersection, stay left; a sign indicates you are heading in the direction of Cold Springs. At approximately 3.8 miles the road forks again, just before arriving at a ranch at the base of a butte. Turn right here. This road, in poorer condition, climbs a short distance through a gap between the edge of the mountain range and the small butte. Just short of 5 miles, pass Purcell Spring on the right. The road soon turns into dirt and its condition deteriorates, especially if it is wet. At approximately 6.2 miles, reach another intersection; bear right. This fork will soon take you to a gate that leads you into the Salmon-Challis National Forest. At approximately 7.5 miles, as you enter a conifer forest, you reach Nez Perce Spring, which may be dry in late summer. The spring, just to the right of the road, bubbles out of the earth here and travels to meet a tributary of Nez Perce Creek. GPS: N44 31.35' / W113 20.99'

The Hike

Seldom-visited Nez Perce Lake is reached by a short hiking trail that is closed to trail machines. The trail is steep but not difficult to follow. It is 2.8 miles, and a climb of about 1,700 feet, to the lake. The hike starts past Nez Perce Spring and is a four-wheel-drive road for the first 0.5 mile. As the road nears its end, a sign nailed to a

Nez Perce Lake. PHOTO BY LUKE KRATZ

tree on the left side of the road indicates the direction of Nez Perce Trail and Nez Perce Lake—2.2 miles ahead. Just past this sign, the four-by-four road ends, and a sign indicates that the area beyond is closed to motor vehicles.

The trail immediately climbs a steep embankment. An alternative route leaves the trail to the right and switches back to join up with the main trail. Within the first 0.5 mile, you cross a small tributary of Nez Perce Creek (which may be dry in late summer) and switchback to climb a ridge between two tributaries to Nez Perce Creek. Thankfully, 1.2 miles after leaving the road, the trail levels out and actually drops about 100 feet. The remaining mile to the lake is not as steep, and it travels between a high ridge to the south and a major tributary to Nez Perce Creek to the north. Cross this tributary at 0.25 mile from the lake. It has reliable water all year, although the creek in some places runs beneath the sedimentary rocks.

Nez Perce Lake occupies a small cirque below Sheephorn Peak (10,465 feet). It is fed by several springs and contains water year-round. Its water level declines slowly over the summer, exposing its rocky banks. There are no fire rings at the lake; please keep it that way and use your stove. Deer and elk are frequently seen in the area, and, if you are fortunate, a mountain goat may be spotted on the flank of Sheephorn Peak. As I was having lunch and relaxing on a warm rock, a billy and a nanny sauntered along the shoreline on the opposite bank.

Nez Perce Lake has been stocked with Arctic grayling, which have been known to grow quite large. It is also filled with freshwater shrimp, which

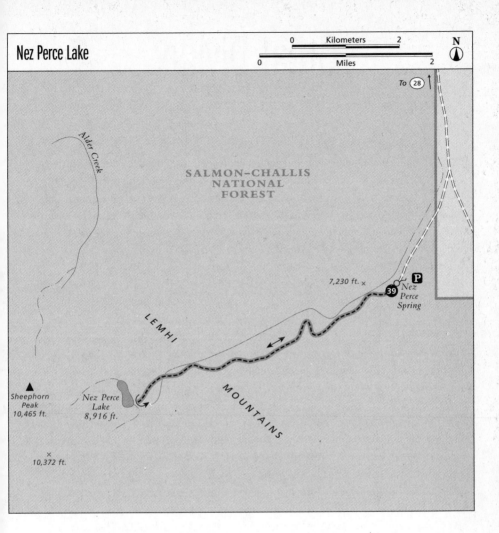

Nez Perce Lake

are good for growing fat fish but make hooking a grayling more difficult. Trout in this small lake sometimes are winter-killed.

Nez Perce Trail is a good choice if you are looking to stay away from the crowds and enjoy a lake that graciously rewards you with its charm after a steep journey.

—Gwen Gerber

Miles and Directions

0.0 Start at Nez Perce Spring (7,120 feet).

0.5 Reach the end of the four-wheel-drive road (7,350 feet).

2.5 Make a stream crossing (8,600 feet).

2.8 Reach Nez Perce Lake (8,840 feet). Retrace your steps.

5.6 Arrive back at the trailhead.

Great Divide

The Idaho-Montana border is borne on the back of the Continental Divide for several hundred miles. Idaho and Montana are the only two states whose mutual boundary is marked by such a big mountain range. The divide runs from Yellowstone National Park northwestward, turning north into Montana only as it approaches the Bitterroot Mountains. Beyond Chief Joseph Pass, the divide stays in Montana, and the Idaho-Montana boundary becomes the Bitterroot Divide.

Despite its prominence on maps, this area has been hiked or backpacked little compared with other parts of Idaho. Trails are relatively scarce, but much of the country is open, making trails unnecessary. The situation is changing, however.

In 1989 the Continental Divide National Scenic Trail was dedicated from Canada to the west boundary of Yellowstone National Park. Today the trail is roughly 3,000 miles long; the Idaho border portion of the trail is roughly 180 miles.

Long neglected by forest service management, the Great Divide has seen little recreation but also only scattered development. Six important roadless areas along the Great Divide are being proposed for wilderness designation by Idaho and Montana conservationists. These six units of the Great Divide Wilderness are—from northwest to southeast—Anderson Mountain, West Big Hole, Italian Peaks, Garfield Mountain, Centennial Mountains, and the Lionhead.

The Great Divide is also divided into three mountain ranges, each separated by a low pass. From Lost Trail Pass north of Salmon southeast to Monida Pass, where I-15 crosses, the range is called the Beaverhead Mountains. From Monida Pass east to Red Rock Pass are the Centennial Mountains, and from Red Rock Pass to Reas Pass, next to Yellowstone, are the Henrys Lake Mountains.

This chain of mountain ranges is environmentally important because it provides a corridor for wildlife migration from Yellowstone to central and northern Idaho and to western Montana. It is politically significant, too, in the sense that folks in Idaho and Montana have been kept socially and economically separated by this range, compared with states that have a flat boundary.

Wildlife is abundant in the remote areas of the Great Divide: deer, elk, moose, pronghorn antelope, coyote, eagle, and black bear are common. Grizzly inhabit the Henrys Lake Mountains, and one occasionally may wander all the way from Yellowstone to central Idaho. Wolves have been tracked many times in the area, although no packs existed there as of the year 2001.

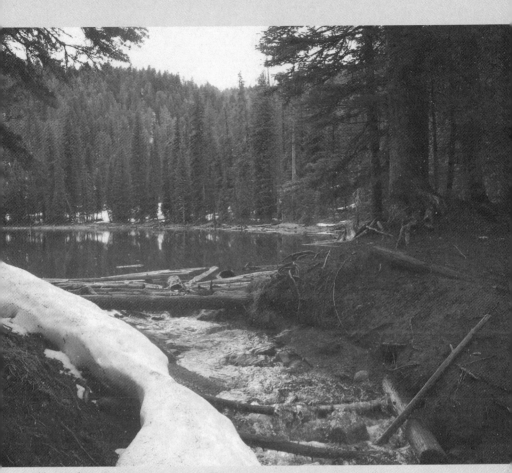

Aldous Lake in spring. PHOTO BY LUKE KRATZ

The major threats to the area are below-cost logging (particularly in the northern Beaverhead Mountains and on the Idaho side of the Centennials), scattered mining, overgrazing by livestock and, increasingly, off-road vehicles scarring the open grassy slopes so common in these mountains.

The public lands on the Idaho–Montana portion of the Continental Divide are under the jurisdiction of the following agencies: Caribou–Targhee National Forest, Beaverhead National Forest, Salmon–Challis National Forest, Idaho Falls District Bureau of Land Management (BLM), Dillon District BLM, and Salmon District BLM.

—Ralph Maughan

40 Salamander Lake Loop

Salamander Lake hosts beautiful meadows and good wildlife habitat flanking the Continental Divide.

Start: 76 miles north-northeast of Idaho Falls in the mountains behind the almost-ghost town of Kilgore on the Idaho-Montana border
Type of hike: Loop near the Continental Divide in a "low" spot of the Centennial Mountains, with the opportunity for day hikes from a multi-day base camp
Distance: 9-mile loop with shorter options
Approximate hiking time: 2–3 days
Difficulty: Moderate, with difficulty mostly due to trails that disappear when crossing meadows
Best season: Early June–mid-October
Trail surface: Dirt and rock

Land status: Caribou–Targhee National Forest
Canine compatibility: On leash
Fees and permits: None
Maps: USGS Winslow Creek ID; Dubois and Island Park Ranger Districts, Caribou–Targhee National Forest map
Trail contact: Dubois Ranger District; (208) 374-5422
Parking and trailhead facilities: There is parking for about six vehicles 100 yards beyond the undeveloped trailhead, which is obvious and leads up Trail Creek. No potable water or sanitary facilities are available.

Finding the trailhead: From Idaho Falls, drive north on I-15 for 48 miles to Dubois. From Dubois, on the east edge of town, bear left at the flashing yellow light onto CR A2. About 27 miles later turn left (north) on a paved road signed for Kilgore. After you pass through Kilgore, take a left at the T intersection. The road becomes gravel here. At 0.3 mile past the T intersection, take a right and cross Camas Meadows. After 5.8 miles you enter the Caribou–Targhee National Forest and 0.5 mile later come to the junction of FR 026 and FR 027. Bear to the left onto the good, graveled FR 026. About 0.75 mile past this junction, take Cottonwood Creek Road (FR 029) to the right. This is a decent dirt road when dry, but becomes poor after a soaking rain. It is not quite 2 miles from here to the trailhead. GPS: N44 31.16' / W111 55.38'

The Hike

There are several broad, low spots in the Centennial Mountains. In these areas, the distance to the Continental Divide is not so strenuous. This hike describes one such spot with the good fortune to have retained an extensive trail system. These trails may be used to make a number of loop hikes (a rare situation in the Centennials where, in the past, trail systems have often been neglected or destroyed by logging). So far the area described here has remained intact due to lack of high-value timber combined with topography frequently changed by creeping soil and small landslides.

All of these trails are closed to motor vehicles, and a sign so indicates at the beginning. Trail Creek Trail climbs moderately through small meadows and mixed conifer forest and runs a short distance from the creek for about 0.5 mile to a sign that points to Lake Creek to the left and Trail Creek to the right. Take a right. Lake Creek Trail is the trail you will return on to complete the loop described.

After another mile of moderate uphill, the trail intersects again. A sign indicates Salamander Lake to the left and Trail Creek to the right; stay right. About 0.25 mile past this junction, the trail descends slightly to cross Trail Creek (just a hop on rocks in mid-July). It then climbs briefly, levels out, and drops to cross a major tributary of Trail Creek.

After this crossing, the trail climbs fairly steeply uphill. As you climb, you begin to enter larger and larger meadows and gain a view of the mountainside ahead. Vegetation in the meadows is typical of the 7,500- to 9,000-foot elevation all along the Continental Divide in this locale: beautiful, tall, and generally fleshy forbs, such as monkshood, western coneflower, sticky geranium, wild carrot, lupine, bluebells, cow parsnip, and tall cinquefoil, but little grass. The midsummer growth rate of the forbs is such that they hide the tread of any trail through a meadow not traveled more frequently than every week or so. Be sure to follow the blazes on the trees.

At about 8,500 feet, you arrive at the highest elevation of the loop when you cross a meadow on a shelf that sits between two tributary drainages of Trail Creek. Off to the left are views of the Trail, Salamander, and Lake Creek Valleys. This meadowland, with clumps of subalpine fir and whitebark pine, continues until the trail descends sharply to a pond (which is sometimes dry by late summer).

The trail then drops about 200 feet, rather steeply, to Salamander Lake at 4.2 miles. This is a small, shallow lake surrounded on the south by a lush meadow and on the north by a conifer forest. Springs keep this lake full year-round. It is a pretty location.

Moose frequent this lake and so do a few fish; however, due to the nature of the shoreline, wading is not an option because of the soft earth.

The trail keeps to the left (south) side of the meadowy lakeshore. Below the lake's outlet is an important trail junction. Here a sign indicates "Trailhead" straight ahead and Divide and Lake Creek to the right. To reach the divide and the large loop described here, take the right fork of the trail and quickly reach a bridge over Salamander Creek. From this bridge, follow the blazes across the forbs to the obvious trail that enters the forest and climbs 100 feet to a ridgeline. Here you enter a large meadow, and you can see into Montana.

The trail immediately disappears in the tall forbs of the meadow, but trail markers point in the right direction. There are about half a dozen of these markers, occurring

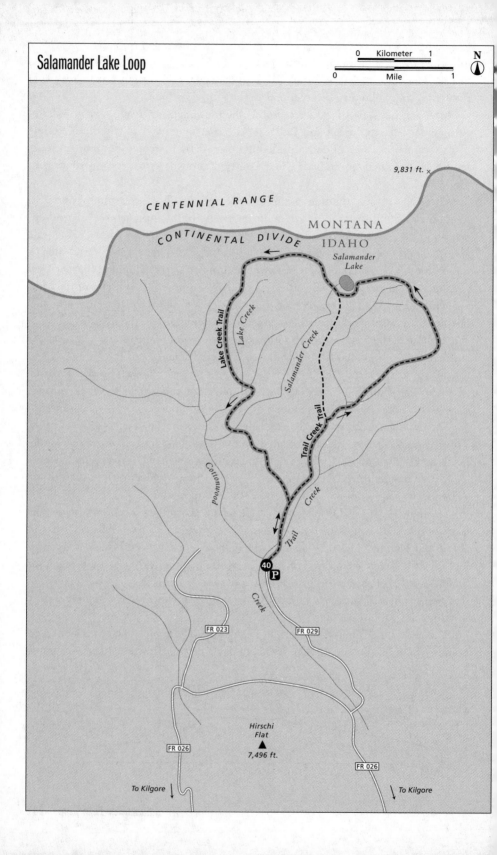

every couple hundred yards, to lead you across the meadow and down into the drainage of Lake Creek. The trail never actually climbs to the Continental Divide. However, at 4.8 miles, there is a sign placed at a ninety-degree angle to the trail indicating the Divide Trail, with no arrow and no obvious trail junction. This sign also indicates Salamander Lake in the direction from which you came.

After about 0.3 mile, following the arrow-imprinted trail markers, the route swings down into the headwaters of a creek and a streamside meadow. From this point on, follow the blazed trees whenever the tread becomes faint.

Soon the trail leaves streamside and climbs a short distance to a ridge. Amble down this pleasant ridge between Lake Creek (to the left) and Cottonwood Creek (to the right). Both canyons remain largely out of sight. At 6.8 miles you drop down and, in quick succession, cross Lake Creek and one of its tributaries. You climb briefly to another ridge. After about 0.3 mile you descend from this ridge to cross Salamander Creek. A sign reading "Divide" points in the direction you came from and also points to "Lake Trail" to the right. The sign doesn't point to the plainly obvious trail to the left that crosses Salamander Creek on a bridge and goes up a little hill on the other side. This junction is 1.5 miles from your vehicle. The trail is sometimes faint as it climbs over a broad ridge and descends to Trail Creek, completing your loop.

The entire loop is good habitat for moose, elk, deer, and an occasional bear, and is gorgeous in late spring and early summer, when the wildflowers are in bloom. This area is an extremely important wildlife corridor between Yellowstone National Park and the wilderness of central Idaho. Let's hope this rare and beautiful area will remain as it is.

Options: To take a quick route to Salamander Lake, turn left at the trail junction at 1.5 miles. This route is 1.25 miles shorter; however, it does not offer the same views. It is a steady climb up the ridge between Salamander Creek and Trail Creek. You can also choose to return by this route from Salamander Lake by turning left at the trail junction at 4.4 miles (in the direction indicated by the sign pointing toward the "Trailhead"). This choice will get you back to the trailhead almost 2 miles sooner than the large loop described above.

The Divide Trail: The Divide Trail is directly adjacent to the northern portion of the Salamander Lake Loop and is easy to find. To reach the divide, leave your route at the sign indicating the Divide Trail at 4.8 miles, at an angle of between forty-five and ninety degrees. Simply keep walking until you are on the divide (about 1,000 feet due north). Once you are on the Divide Trail, you can walk as far as you wish in either direction; watch where you came from, however, since the divide is fairly gentle here and has a large number of big, similar meadows.

—Gwen Gerber

Miles and Directions

0.0 Begin at the Cottonwood Creek Road trailhead (7,040 feet).

0.5 Reach the Lake Creek Trail junction (7,240 feet). Go right on the Trail Creek Trail.

1.5 At the Salamander Lake Trail junction (7,500 feet), go right.

4.2 Reach Salamander Lake (8,150 feet).

4.4 At the Trailhead/Lake Creek junction (8,120 feet), stay right on Lake Creek Trail.

4.8 Pass the sign for the Continental Divide Trail (8,280 feet).

6.8 Cross Lake Creek (7,380 feet).

7.5 Pass the trail junction and cross Salamander Creek (7,300 feet).

9.0 Arrive back at the trailhead

DEHYDRATION

Have you ever hiked in hot weather and had a roaring headache and felt fatigued after only a few miles? More than likely you were dehydrated. Symptoms of dehydration include fatigue, headache, and decreased coordination and judgment. When you are hiking, your body's rate of fluid loss depends on the outside temperature, humidity, altitude, and your activity level. On average, a hiker walking in warm weather will lose four liters of fluid a day. That fluid loss is easily replaced by normal consumption of liquids and food. However, if a hiker is walking briskly in hot, dry weather and hauling a heavy pack, he or she can lose one to three liters of water an hour. It's important to always carry plenty of water and to stop often and drink fluids regularly, even if you aren't thirsty.

41 Webber Creek

The trail up Webber Creek explores a small area of tremendous peaks along the Continental Divide. It is also a good area for wildlife observation.

Start: 65 miles northwest of Idaho Falls in the Italian Peaks (the highest portion of the Beaverhead Range)
Type of hike: Out-and-back, with the opportunity for longer trips requiring a shuttle
Distance: 18 miles
Approximate hiking time: 2–5 days
Difficulty: Moderate if at least 2 nights are devoted to the trip
Best season: July–October. The lower canyon is accessible in mid-June
Trail surface: Dirt and rock
Land status: Caribou-Targhee National Forest
Canine compatibility: On leash

Fees and permits: None
Maps: USGS Heart Mountain and Scott Peak ID; Dubois and Island Park Ranger Districts, Caribou-Targhee National Forest map.
Trail contact: Dubois Ranger District; (208) 374-5422. Island Park Ranger District; (208) 558-7301
Parking and trailhead facilities: There is a small, unimproved campground at the trailhead with space to park, although it's a squeeze for horse trailers. The trail (Trail 111) is obvious and leaves directly at the upstream end of the campground.

Finding the trailhead: From Idaho Falls, drive north on I-15 for 48 miles to Dubois. Leave I-15 at Dubois by turning onto ID 22. Travel west for 6 miles to a paved county road that leaves to the right (north) from ID 22. The road makes three or four right-angle turns. Don't let this lead you to believe you are off track. Travel through farmland and into the scenic basalt canyon of Medicine Lodge Creek. The yellow flowers covering almost everything in early summer are one of the most noxious weeds known—leafy spurge—and this is one of the worst infestations in Idaho. It began in the early 1990s and is spreading.

The road is paved for about 20 miles, then becomes good gravel. Continue up the gravel road to the signed Webber Creek Road (FR 196) on the left. This is 22.5 miles from ID 22.

It's 5 miles up FR 196 to the Webber Creek Trailhead. The road varies from good gravel at the beginning to two tracks at the trailhead. A sedan can make it if the road is dry or damp, but it does get very slippery in a few spots after substantial rain. GPS: N44 21.81' / W112 41.30'

The Hike

The Italian Peaks, culminating in 11,200-foot-plus Scott and Webber Peaks, are the highest in the Beaverhead Range, which forms the Idaho-Montana border for about 200 miles.

In the Italian Peaks, mountain goats and bighorn sheep ply the cliffs. Elk graze the high meadows, and deer graze the forest. An occasional moose wanders by. Raptors search the land from the sky. Every so often there are reports of grizzly bear and wolves. This is wild territory.

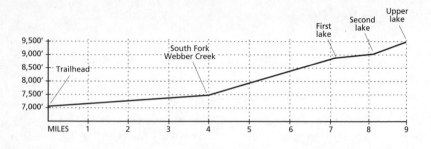

Begin by hiking from the trailhead into a narrow, densely forested canyon with a damp riparian zone. There are some cliffs near the trail, as well as a few sagebrush-dominated meadows. After 3.5 miles the canyon begins to open. Willow and beaver ponds line the stream bottom, and the gray, rugged Italian Peaks appear at the head of the canyon. The massive ice-carved mountain to the left is Webber Peak, nearly 11,300 feet. In the center, partially hidden by a lower pinnacled mountain, is Scott Peak, with a similar elevation. At about 4 miles you reach the confluence of the South and North Forks of Webber Creek. A trail—Myers Creek Trail—goes up the South Fork, a possible option.

Continue up the North Fork. The peaks draw near, and after about 1.5 miles you begin the climb into the North Fork's glacial valley. Here you come to a trail junction after climbing 900 feet in 1.5 miles. The right-hand trail (Trail 111) climbs out of the canyon and eventually leads to Divide Creek or Deadman Creek in Montana. This, too, is another hike option.

Up the left fork (Trail 034), imposing mountains rise on both sides of the canyon in stepped cliffs and awesome fluted pinnacles. In places the strata show in giant folds of limestone. The right wall is the Continental Divide. The trail is gentle, and you actually lose elevation getting to the first lake, which you reach quickly, but then you begin to climb. The uppermost lake is a climb of about 600 feet from the trail junction. It sits tightly against great mountain walls.

These cyan-colored lakes are not for anglers. Because the rock is porous, the lakes lose much of their water by autumn. They are a place to stay overnight and admire the hidden valley sandwiched between a great Idaho ridge and a Montana ridge of the Italian Peaks.

The forest service has long supported designating the core of the Italian Peaks as wilderness. The 1996 Targhee National Forest Plan reaffirmed this decision by closing most trails to summertime motor vehicle use, with only a few exceptions. Most of the opposition to protection comes from groups that claim to represent off-road vehicle interests. Report violations of the closures to the Dubois Ranger District. Get a photo and license plate number(s) if possible.

Options: Myers Creek Trail (Trail 113) leads southward up the South Fork of Webber Creek and over the north shoulder (9,220 feet) of rugged Heart Mountain (10,402

Webber Creek

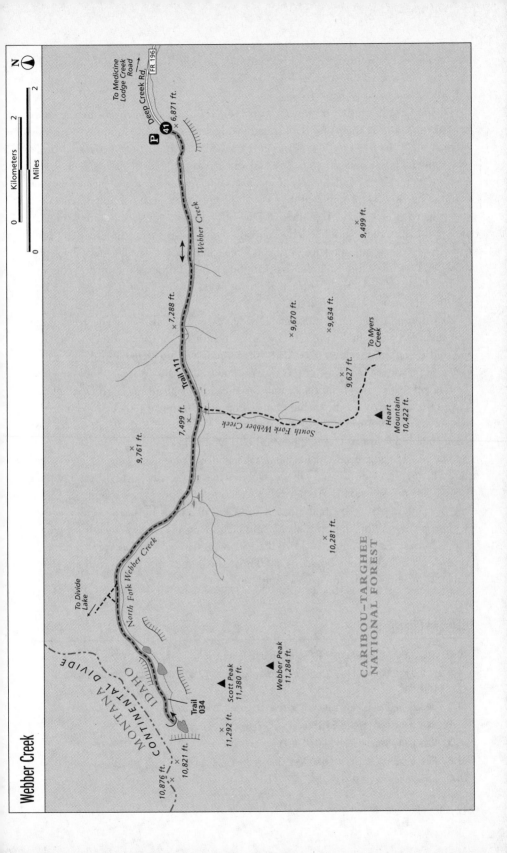

To Medicine
Lodge Creek Road

FR 196

Deep Creek Rd.
P 41
× 6,871 ft.

Webber Creek

× 7,288 ft.

Trail 111

× 9,499 ft.

× 9,670 ft.

× 9,634 ft.

To Myers
Creek

× 9,627 ft.

7,499 ft. ×

South Fork Webber Creek

Heart
Mountain
10,422 ft. ▲

9,761 ft. ×

× 10,281 ft.

CARIBOU–TARGHEE
NATIONAL FOREST

North Fork Webber Creek

To Divide
Lake

Webber Peak
11,284 ft. ▲

MONTANA
CONTINENTAL DIVIDE
IDAHO

Scott Peak
11,380 ft. ▲

Trail
034

× 11,292 ft.

10,876 ft. ×
× 10,821 ft.

N

0   2
Kilometers

0   2
Miles

feet) before it drops into Myers Creek and ends at a dirt road (shuttle location). The dirt road is about 10 linear miles from the Webber Creek Trailhead, but the road for a shuttle is longer than that.

Divide Lake is another option. Continue on Trail 111, either bypassing the Webber Lakes or visiting them and then backtracking 2 miles. Trail 111 climbs to a grassy ridge at 9,200 feet, where elk are often seen. Then the trail continues north, drops into timber, and crosses the very head of the canyon of North Fritz Creek. Connecting Trail 112 descends steeply from this point. You could exit here to a shuttle. Continuing, however, complete the traverse of Fritz Creek, and then roll down a not-very-rugged stretch of the Continental Divide. The trail leads slightly into Montana, then into Idaho, and so on. The large canyon to your left is Deadman Creek in Montana. This is a beautiful side trip. Deadman Creek Trail leads to a 9,700-foot-high pass (between Deadman and Nicholia Creek), a fine place to observe mountain goats and the sheer north face of the Continental Divide at Italian Peak (for more information, see *Hiking Montana*, Globe Pequot).

As you walk along the Continental Divide, descending slowly, the character of the land changes rather quickly from rocky peaks and cliffs to open, meadowy mountains and mid-elevation meadows filled with tall, fleshy, flowering plants (forbs), such as are visible in Deadman Creek below. As is commonplace in this area, the visible track of the trail fades as you go from rocky forest to meadowy upland. To reach Divide Lake, stay on the divide. Avoid the inclination to drop into Deadman Creek or to climb the hills to your right. Aim for the slot at the base of the mountain that rises on the east (right) side of Deadman Creek. The slot holds Divide Lake.

The lake is barely inside Idaho, being separated from Montana by a 100-foot-high cliff, which is the Continental Divide. Divide Lake is a fertile body of water, with a rugged cliff on one side but otherwise surrounded by low, grassy mountains and a ring of conifers, giving an appearance reminiscent of a large meadow pond.

The last leg of this option is all downhill. Follow tiny Divide Creek from where it spills from the lake. It gurgles down the narrow, grassy canyon. The canyon deepens rapidly for a mile, but then broadens out. The trail emerges onto a jeep road just above Cow Camp, where you can leave a shuttle.

—Ralph Maughan

Miles and Directions

0.0   Start at the Webber Creek Trailhead (6,940 feet).

4.0   At the junction with the South Fork of Webber Creek (7,510 feet), stay right on the North Fork trail.

7.1   Reach the Trail 034 junction (8,900 feet); go left to Webber Lakes.

7.7   Reach the first lake (8,820 feet).

8.3   Reach the second lake (9,040 feet).

9.0   Reach the upper lake (9,560 feet). This is the turnaround.

18.0   Arrive back at the trailhead.

Middle Rocky Mountains of Eastern Idaho

The Rocky Mountains include perhaps a hundred mountain ranges, extending from the Yukon Territory on the north to New Mexico on the south. In the lower forty-eight states, they are often broken into three sections, or physiographic provinces (a fancy name for an awful lot of beautiful country).

The Southern Rockies run from northern Colorado to northern New Mexico. The mountains northwest of Yellowstone in Montana and Idaho are the Northern Rockies. In Idaho this includes primarily the Selkirk, Salmon River, Clearwater, Boulder, White Cloud, Pioneer, Smoky, and Soldier Mountains.

The Middle Rockies begin with the Wasatch and Uinta Ranges in Utah and bump northward along the Idaho–Wyoming border to just north of Yellowstone National Park. In Wyoming, some of these ranges are very well known: the Wind Rivers, Bighorn, Gros Ventre, Tetons, and Absaroka. The Middle Rockies of eastern Idaho include some fabulous country, and we have spent years enjoying them, but the names will not sound familiar to many: the Big Holes, Snake River Range, Caribou Range, Bear River Range, Aspen Range, Gray's Range, Pruess Range, Gannett Hills, and Webster Range.

Unlike the relentlessly granitic Wind Rivers or the pile of welded volcanic ash that is the Absaroka, all of the Middle Rockies in Idaho consist of soft sedimentary rock in what is known geologically as the Overthrust Belt, a place of amazingly broken and complicated geology. This is where gigantic forces pushed the rock layers eastward, one on top of another, until they overturned, hence the term *overthrust*. The result is that older limestone, shale, dolomite, siltstone, and so forth often rest on top of younger rocks thousands of feet below the older rock. There are many variations among the ranges. This is also earthquake country. The forces that made the mountains are not yet spent.

Throughout much of the area, the phosphoria formation from which phosphate fertilizer is made can be found. One result of this is very fertile mountains, with large herds of big deer and elk. Were it not for all the livestock, this could be the most productive wildlife area in the West.

Rocky outcroppings along thickly forested slopes in the Snake River Mountains.
PHOTO BY LUKE KRATZ

Eastern Idaho's Middle Rockies range from high, glaciated peaks, such as those found in the Snake River Range, to steep hills with rounded tops, such as the Gannett Hills. Because of the softness of the rock, mountain lakes are fewer in number than in the Northern Rockies. The topography, geology, and climate, however, produce the largest aspen forests in Idaho. Wildlife includes, as mentioned, elk and deer, but also moose, mountain goat, cougar, black bear, bobcat, wolverine, coyote, fox, and an occasional wolf or grizzly bear migrating from Wyoming.

Another feature of these mountains is their instability. Mudflows, landslides, and blowouts are common, as are avalanches wherever the topography is steep. Unlike central Idaho, where the forest understory is usually grouse whortleberry, huckleberry, or sagebrush, wherever it lacks enough water for a wet meadow, tall perennial flowers predominate along the Idaho–Wyoming border. Unlike the short flowers of alpine meadows, these are flower fields you can actually get lost in.

—Ralph Maughan

Big Hole, Snake River, and Caribou Mountains

These ranges hug the border of Idaho and Wyoming. The Big Hole and the Snake River Ranges are really the same mountain range, but an arbitrary division between them was made at Pine Creek Canyon. The Caribou Mountains are the next range to the west, separated from the former by Swan Valley and Palisades Reservoir.

The Big Hole–Snake River Range emerges out of the volcanic rock of the Snake River Plain, just south of Rexburg, Idaho. It begins as a generally forested, semicircular area of steep, but relatively low and intensively dissected mountains. Of course, this makes for many trail possibilities due to the number of canyons and ridges, and these mountains have a lot of trails. Unfortunately, most of them are not well maintained.

Farther to the southeast, the Big Hole–Snake Rivers rise about 1,500 to 2,000 feet higher than the northern section, topping out at more than 10,000 feet at Mount Baird. The general form of the mountains remains the same, however. Even more to the south, this range pushes on into Wyoming, where it is called the Salt River Range, with some peaks that top 11,000 feet. This fine area is described in *Hiking Wyoming* (Globe Pequot).

The Caribou Range is relatively unknown, despite its length, beauty, and abundant wildlife. These mountains parallel the Big Hole–Snake River and Salt River Mountains, which lie across the valley to the east. The topography is rather unique, consisting of numerous ridges interspersed with small, high-elevation stream valleys. The Caribous are not as high as the Big Hole–Snake River ranges, but they have more forest because fewer avalanches scour trees away.

These mountain ranges are very well watered compared with those in the Middle Rockies to their southwest, and especially the Basin and Range mountains even farther west. As a result, these mountains have many good fishing streams, although the natural instability of the Caribou Range makes fisheries vulnerable if roads are built or timber harvested.

These ranges, like all of the Middle Rockies of Idaho, are mountains built entirely of sedimentary rocks, pushed into complicated jumbles by thrust faulting. The material of these mountains (and of all mountains near the Wyoming border) was once many miles to the west. It was pushed eastward by the forces of continental drift.

This geology allows for hypothetical pockets of oil and natural gas. The oil industry has been exploring the Overthrust Belt of eastern Idaho for almost a generation, but this interest waned in the 1990s. All wells drilled failed to locate commercial quantities of oil or natural gas, but the oil companies used the area's potential to wage a strong campaign against wilderness designation. These mountains are managed much more for wildlife and recreation today than they were in the 1980s but are still vulnerable to drilling and mining pursuits.

These mountains are full of wildlife. Especially notable are the elk herds of the Caribou Range, but deer, mountain goats, bighorn sheep, and moose are also present. The population of mountain goats, which centers on the Mount Baird area, has

Beautiful waterfalls. PHOTO BY RALPH MAUGHAN

shown an impressive increase in numbers. Moose, once relatively rare, have also increased greatly.

The Big Hole and the Snake River Ranges abut a vast area of wild country to their north and northeast in Wyoming—the Greater Yellowstone country. You can hike from US 26, at the south end of the Snake Rivers, northward to the Tetons and Yellowstone National Park, and cross only one paved highway and one dirt road. The rest is wild. Moreover, the Big Holes, Snakes, and Salt Rivers provide an important corridor for big game to migrate from the Yellowstone country down to southwestern Wyoming, eastern Idaho, and northern Utah. In fact, this is how moose reinhabited Utah.

The entire area is geologically active, and tremors frequently shake the state border. Another large quake is possible at any time.

The Big Hole and Caribou Ranges, due to their relatively low elevations, provide early-summer hiking. The 220,000-acre roadless area in the core of the Snake River Range, which is named the Palisades Backcountry, is large enough to allow you a weeklong backpacking vacation. Several other roadless areas, more than 60,000 acres in size, are located in these two ranges.

Idaho and Wyoming environmentalists have been trying for years to protect these roadless areas as designated wilderness. They have been successful in keeping them roadless, but unless wilderness designation arrives soon, these pristine areas may fall to the oil companies and to the increasingly well-funded dirt bike and all-terrain vehicle lobbies.

—Ralph Maughan

42 Palisades Creek–Upper Palisades Lake–Waterfall Canyon

View exquisitely beautiful cliffs looming over a large stream, as well as wildlife due to no livestock grazing or motorized use, on this trip.

Start: About 45 miles east of Idaho Falls in the Snake River Range, near the Wyoming border
Type of hike: Out-and-back, with some possible strenuous loops in conjunction with other trails
Distance: 13 miles to Upper Palisades Lake and back
Approximate hiking time: 2–5 days
Difficulty: Moderate
Best season: Early June–mid-October
Trail surface: Dirt and rock
Land status: Caribou–Targhee National Forest
Canine compatibility: On leash recommended due to popularity of trail
Fees and permits: None
Maps: USGS Palisades Peak and Thompson Peak ID; Island Park, Ashton, Teton Basin, and

Palisades Ranger Districts; Caribou–Targhee National Forest map
Trail contact: Palisades Ranger District; (208) 523-1412
Special considerations: There are just two places along this trail where camping is permitted.
Parking and trailhead facilities: Seven campsites, potable water, latrines. The trailhead has room for about ten vehicles at the hiker's parking lot and is often filled to capacity. There are separate trailheads for hikers and horses, although they soon share the same trail. Walk to the east end of the campground (upstream), to the beginning of the trail for hikers.

Finding the trailhead: Drive about 52 miles from Idaho Falls, headed east on US 26. Continue through the small towns of Swan Valley and Irwin, and turn left onto a gravel road at the unincorporated community of Palisades. The sign reads "Palisades Creek, Forest Road 255." After 1.8 miles this gravel road ends at Palisades Campground, set in the mouth of the V-shaped opening to mountain beauty beyond. Parking for hikers is to the left just before the campground entrance and just before the bridge over Palisades Creek. The horse transfer area is on the other side of the bridge and to the right. GPS: N43 23.73' / W111 12.91'

The Hike

Walk past the forest service information sign and into the narrow mouth of the canyon. Palisades Creek splashes beside the trail (earlier in the season, it thunders). The creek never gets very low because much of its flow comes from year-round springs emerging far up the canyon and up its tributaries. Fortunately, the creek is bridged all the way (except for the remote upper canyon, which is not described in this hike). You will cross six bridges.

Despite the rugged, steep walls of the canyon, its bottom is forested, shaded by both conifers and deciduous trees. From its beginning at the campground, Palisades Canyon is 2,000 feet deep. Farther upstream it's well over 3,000 feet deep.

The horse trail quickly joins the hiker's trail. The trail follows the creek closely, passing under Douglas fir and towering cottonwoods. After 1.3 miles, near the first bridge, the canyon opens into a large amphitheater. Here, temporarily out of the forest that fills the canyon, you can see the great cliffs lining the side slopes. Look for mountain goats.

After the first bridge, the trail climbs about 75 feet up the north side of the canyon, and the trail proceeds 3 more miles (sometimes following the stream, other times climbing again to about 75 feet above it) up the generally narrow canyon to a landslide that impounds Lower Palisades Lake.

Many people make a day hike to Lower Palisades Lake and back. You can tell when you are approaching the lake because you cross three bridges in fairly close succession, and also encounter a corduroy section of the trail over an area of springs just before the last of the three bridges.

A short, switchbacking climb up the slide brings you to the lake. Here you'll find the first of two legal camping areas. The area is nice and flat, but it has no water and appears generally overused. The second campsites are 1.4 more miles farther, at the confluence of Chicken Springs Canyon. Moose live in the area from the lower lake on. The fertile lake waters have pretty good fishing for cutthroat trout. Better fishing lies ahead at Upper Palisades Lake.

To continue, cross the bridge at the lake's outlet, and walk up the north side of the canyon past the lake and the low willow marsh at its head. Continue to pretty Chicken Springs Canyon, where water splashes over logs at its mouth before flowing into Palisades Creek. There is a sign here, and a bridge leads across Palisades Creek to a pleasant camping area.

A sign at Chicken Springs reads "Palisades Creek Trail 084; Upper Palisades Lake 1.2 miles; Palisades Campground 5.4 miles." Another sign reads "Chicken Springs Canyon Trail 092, Thompson Creek Trail 1.7 miles, Atkinson Peak 3.9 miles, Rainey Creek 6.5 miles." Chicken Springs Canyon is a pleasant walk. The springs rise about 0.75 mile up the canyon. This trail gives access to the other trails mentioned. They are steep and faint, but also very scenic.

Back on Palisades Creek Trail, 0.6 mile past Chicken Springs and after crossing the creek, the trail immediately begins climbing uphill on a giant landslide that fell off the mountain ages ago, filling the mouth of the canyon that holds Upper Palisades Lake. The trail switchbacks easily up this slide to Upper Palisades Lake, a 375-foot climb. Halfway to the lake, the lake waters emerge from the slide as a large, beautiful spring cascading down into the forest toward Palisades Creek. This spring is a major reason Palisades Creek runs high and clear year-round.

As you approach the lake, notice the bulges of earth in the tops of the avalanche runs in the mountains surrounding the lake. The earth remains unstable in this area.

The lake itself is deep and cool, with numerous coves. Abundant cutthroat trout live in the fertile waters that filter down from the limestone and phosphate rock of the mountains. The trail for hikers stays about 50 feet above the east shore of the lake.

Upper Palisades Lake. PHOTO BY LUKE KRATZ

About 100 yards above this trail is the horse trail. Since the mountain slope plunges steeply into the lake's water, hikers and horse parties won't want to share the same path.

A lightning fire in 1994 burned much of the Upper Palisades Lake area. The trails were rebuilt and are in good condition. As you walk along, see if you can spot the fire scars. The burn has healed very well despite its intensity. The trail contours a steep slope above the east side of the lake until it reaches the lake's inlet, where there are many campsites and the junction of trails from three canyons that rise above the inlet: Vacation, Dry, and Waterfall. It is important that you find the trail up Waterfall Canyon if you plan to hike up there (see Options).

Probably ninety-nine out of every hundred people who continue go up Waterfall Canyon Trail, but Trail 084 does continue up Palisades Creek. However, it is faint and wet, and it fords Palisades Creek twenty-two times. Though diminished in size, Palisades Creek is still substantial. It's hard to cross until mid-July. This is important, because you quickly come to the first of the twenty-two fords! The upper canyon is full of moose, elk, and black bear. The difficult access makes it a real wilderness experience.

Palisades Creek Trail has a long season due to its relatively low elevation. The forest canopy keeps the heat down in midsummer. Autumn is very beautiful because the cottonwoods turn yellow and the mountain maple turns red. This is probably the most heavily used hiking trail in the Snake River Range. It is closed to motorized vehicles but open to foot, horse, and bicycle traffic.

Options: The classic option is to continue up Waterfall Canyon Trail from Upper Palisades Lake. A quarter mile above the lake inlet, you come to the well-marked Vacation Canyon junction. Keep to the right and make sure you are on the Waterfall Canyon Trail. Continue, and cross the creek. Near the creek, the trail to the left goes up Dry Canyon. Continue to the right. The trail is easy to follow. It was substantially rebuilt after the fire, although none of Waterfall Canyon itself burned. The trail begins to climb, and soon you approach a clear, splashing, spring-fed stream in the forest. This is near the unnamed (but marked on the map) Waterfall Canyon spring. Waterfall Canyon recapitulates Upper Palisades Lake and its spring. The trail then climbs 300 feet up a steep slope into Waterfall Canyon.

Waterfall Canyon was left hanging above the lake by a glacier. Its mouth is filled with a moraine, which is also, perhaps, part landslide. At the end of the 300-foot climb in early July, I found that the trail dropped down and disappeared into a deep snowmelt pond, with a snowmelt stream running into it. I skirted the pond, going cross-country. Only two days later, on my return, the pond was just a puddle inches deep and the snowmelt stream dry. This and other water from the canyon obviously comes out at Waterfall Canyon spring.

The trail climbs above the pond, wandering through patches of forest and meadow. In early summer water still runs in the creek in places, but where it is dry, water surely runs underground not far below. The trail is broad and easy to find, but strewn with a lot of deadfall at certain points.

As you near the top of the canyon, a spectacular cascade plunges 920 feet down the east wall of the canyon. Its waters flow into a pond. Early in the season, a second waterfall adorns the opposite canyon wall. It has much less volume and is perhaps 200 feet high, but very pretty. The roar of the falls was so great I could not camp here, at what I will call "Waterfall Meadows." Would it damage my hearing to listen, to feel the roar all night long?

Beyond the falls, the trail becomes faint due to annual snowmelt outwash that runs over its tread. Later in the summer it is obscured by tall flowers.

As the canyon narrows, move to the right and cross the creek (or creekbed later in summer). The trail suddenly appears and climbs 300 feet very steeply up a cirque wall carved by ancient glaciers. It is shaded by some giant conifers as you step upward. You then come to ledge overlooking a gorge. In July a side tributary makes a double waterfall down into the awesome gorge.

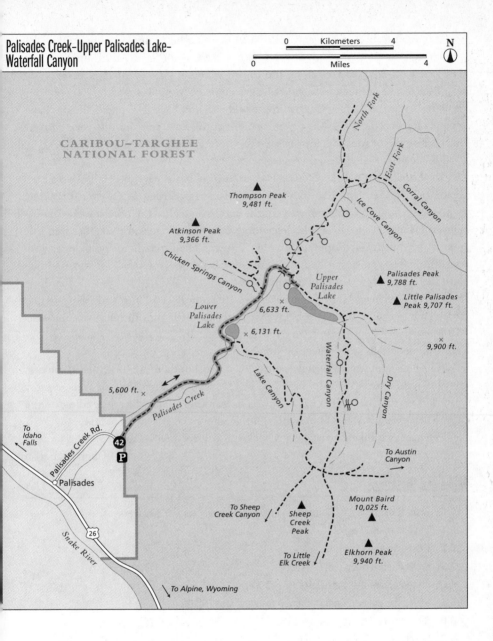

The trail slowly climbs away from the creek, and you are past the gorge and into a small basin.

The stream, which may not have water in late summer, forks in this small basin. The trail follows the right fork up into a large basin just below the highest peaks of the Snake River Range. From mid-July to late August, this is a vast field of tall, flowering perennials. Their growth rate is so rapid that they may obscure the trail, which is plainly obvious just after the snow melts in late June or early July.

At 6 miles from the bridge over Palisades Creek, where you started up to the lake, you'll reach the junction with Sheep Creek–Lake Canyon Trail. At this junction, the trail fork to the east snakes along the top of Waterfall Canyon. It then passes right over Peak 9,630 and forks into either Dry Canyon or Austin Canyon (if you continue farther eastward). The Dry Canyon route will take you back to Upper Palisades Lake, completing a scenic loop. Note that Dry Canyon lacks water until its very bottom, but is quite pretty. Austin Canyon Trail takes you down into Big Elk Creek.

The uplands are exquisitely beautiful.

The Sheep Creek–Lake Canyon fork of the trail heads westward. Climb to a high divide at 9,600 feet and pass south of an unnamed peak that is just over 9,900 feet high. Here you gain a sublime view of the Tetons and all of the other nearby mountains. You can elect to go south, descending into Sheep Creek, or take the trail that goes to the northwest, dropping into Lake Canyon. The latter choice provides a grand loop that takes you down to Lower Palisades Lake. Sheep Creek Canyon is closed until July 15 to protect the mountain goats.

The Lake Canyon Trail down to Lower Palisades Lake is faint and overgrown as it descends from the basin just below the high divide. It runs through wet meadow and forest that is kept fairly open by winter's avalanches. In the mid-reaches of Lake Canyon, sheer cliffs arise where mountains goats are commonly seen.

No permanent stream runs down Lake Canyon, but there are snowmelt rivulets in the cliff-walled basin near the high divide. They run until mid-July in average snow years. Hikers have described Lake Canyon as beautiful to horrible, depending on the year, whether any water was present, and the amount of avalanche debris.

The nice exit hike down Sheep Creek Canyon requires a shuttle.

—Ralph Maughan

Miles and Directions

0.0 Start at the Palisades Campground trailhead parking area (5,500 feet).

0.1 The hikers' trail begins.

0.2 The horse trail joins.

1.3 Cross the first bridge (5,720 feet).

4.0 Arrive at Lower Palisades Lake (6,131 feet).

5.4 Reach the Chicken Springs Canyon camping area (6,200 feet).

6.0 Cross the bridge over Palisades Creek to Waterfalls Canyon Trail (6,245 feet).

6.5 Reach Upper Palisades Lake (6,633 feet). Retrace your steps. The upper end of Upper Palisades Lake is 1 mile beyond. **Options:** From the upper end of the lake you can start climbing into Waterfall Canyon. After 0.8 mile you will reach the top of the climb into Waterfall Canyon (7,220 feet). After another 1.5 miles you reach Waterfall meadow (7,520 feet). It's another 0.8 mile to the gorge overlook, with double falls in early season (8,240 feet). Another 1.4 miles will take you to the Dry Canyon or the Little Elk–Sheep Creek–Lake Canyons Trail junction (8,840 feet).

13.0 Arrive back at the trailhead.

43 South Fork of Tin Cup Creek to Lau Creek

A shuttle hike or loop is available along three different creek drainages and through lush meadows. This hike also serves as an entrance point to a wild, roadless area in the Caribou Mountains.

Start: 40 miles east of Soda Springs along ID 34

Type of hike: Shuttle hike with options. It is easiest if one group parks at the trailhead while the other parks at the terminus, at Pine Bar Campground trailhead.

Distance: 6 miles (add 2.5 miles on the road if you don't use a shuttle)

Approximate hiking time: 2 days

Difficulty: Easy to moderate due to route-finding

Best season: Spring to early fall

Trail surface: Dirt and rock; can be muddy near crossings

Land status: Caribou National Forest

Canine compatibility: Voice command

Fees and permits: None

Maps: USGS Tincup Mountain ID; Montpelier and Soda Springs Ranger Districts–Caribou National Forest map

Trail contact: Montpelier Ranger District; (208) 847-0375. Soda Springs Ranger District; (208) 547-4356.

Special considerations: Mosquito repellent will be needed.

Finding the trailhead: Drive east on ID 34 from Soda Springs to Freedom, Wyoming, beyond the towns of Henry and Wayan. After 30 miles you begin to descend along Tin Cup Creek. Look for the sign on the right indicating Pine Bar Campground; continue driving another 2.5 miles to the well-marked access to the South Fork of Tin Cup Creek. There is ample parking space. GPS: N42 58.6' / W111 09.95'

The Hike

The trail begins after you cross the bridge over Tin Cup Creek at its confluence with the South Fork of Tin Cup Creek. Continue hiking on the trail along the right side of the South Fork of Tin Cup. This riparian or riverland area is a delicate home to many plant and animal species. Beavers are commonly seen in the creek, busy at work. Sheep are grazed periodically in this general area but keep along the drier hillsides.

After 2 miles of hiking up and down through forests and clearings parallel to the creek, an easy crossing puts you on the left side of the creek. Shortly after this comes the trail junction to Brush Creek. At this point you could return the way you came for a nice day hike, continue on the South Fork Trail for more options deep into this roadless area, or make the right up Brush Creek, following this trail description.

The trail along Brush Creek can be a bit "flaky." As long as you follow the drainage, remaining on the right side and uphill from the creek, the trail will always reappear. Also look for markings on the trees. I've included some GPS points in Miles and Directions to get you back to the trail, to avoid any frustration. A mile up Brush Creek,

Gorgeous wildflowers are abundant in the Lau Creek drainage. PHOTO BY LUKE KRATZ

nice clearings and level places to camp open up. The trail then weaves in and out of thickly wooded areas and swampy meadows, adding variety. After 2 miles the trail begins a slight ascent and moves away from the creek. The trail heads north, climbing onto a forested plateau and then into a high clearing with patchy dark blue Engelmann spruce groves; you can see that this must be the apex. Begin the descent of Lau Creek.

The trail from here on out is quite good as it drops down through beautiful rolling hills and meadows filled with colorful wildflowers. After 2.5 miles from the top, you can see the drainage opening up into Tin Cup Creek. When the creek gets closer, stay on the main trail by keeping left, so you can reach the bridge across Tin Cup without getting scoured by nettles and other cross-country creek-hiking hazards. After crossing the bridge to the Pine Bar trailhead, you can rendezvous with the shuttle vehicle or walk/jog 2.5 miles down ID 34 back to the start.

Options: The South Fork Trail continues for more than 10 miles and turns into the North Fork of Hyde Creek. Along the way there are many junctions with trails up other drainages, including Deer Creek, Crooked Creek, and Stump Creek. These are all nonmotorized trails.

South Fork of Tin Cup Creek to Lau Creek

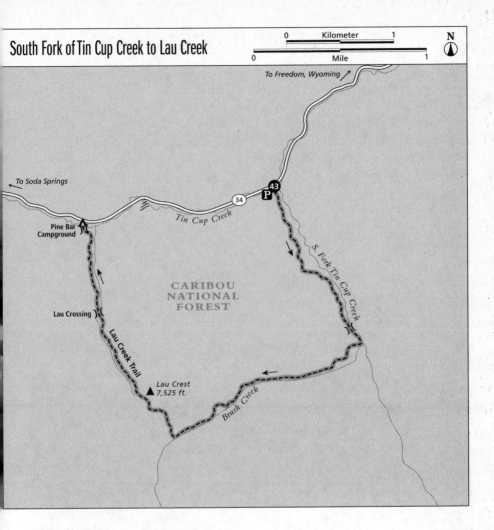

Miles and Directions (estimates)

0.0 Begin at the South Fork of Tin Cup Creek Trailhead (6,136 ft.).

2.1 Cross the South Fork.

2.3 Turn right at the junction, heading up Brush Creek. GPS for locations to pick up the trail: N42 56.98' / W111 9.03', N42 56.9' / W111 9.27', N42 56.83' / W111 9.98'

3.3 Reach the camping area (N42 56.83' / W111 10.32'). GPS to pick up the trail: N42 56.82' / W111 10.4'

3.7 Veer north to ascend to the Brush Creek/Lau Creek saddle.

4.2 Descend into the Lau Creek drainage.

6.0 Arrive at the Pine Bar Campground. Retrieve your shuttle vehicle, or walk 2.5 miles back to the Tin Cup Creek trailhead.

Bear River Mountains

The Bear River Mountains—an extension of Utah's famed Wasatch front—dominate the skyline of the Cache Valley. They host a variety of terrain and are one of the most prominent areas for wildflowers in the Rocky Mountains. Many of the limestone and dolomite peaks are over 9,000 feet, providing subalpine areas rarely found in southeastern Idaho. Unfortunately, a majority of the trails on the Idaho side are open to off-road vehicles, offering little opportunity for the hiking purist. The majority of the trail to Worm Creek is "hiker only," and initial segments for motorcycles are rarely used.

Southeastern Idaho splendor. PHOTO BY LUKE KRATZ

44 Worm Creek

Access a remote, scenic area in southeast Idaho.

Start: 20 miles west of Montpelier, 100 miles south of Pocatello
Type of hike: Lollipop loop
Distance: 10.4 miles
Approximate hiking time: 2 days
Difficulty: Strenuous up to the ridge above the horse flats; moderate to easy on the loop
Best season: Late June–September

Trail surface: Dirt and rocks; narrow trail
Land status: Cache National Forest
Canine compatibility: Voice command
Fees and permits: None
Map: USGS Paris ID
Trail contact: Montpelier Ranger District; (208) 847-0375

Finding the trailhead: From Montpelier, take US 89 through the towns of Ovid and Paris, then on to Bloomington. At the sign reading "Bloomington Canyon," turn west toward the mountains. This road leaves pavement after a little over a mile and enters national forest land at 4.6 miles. It's a good road, but watch for rocks and oncoming traffic—it gets narrow in places. After 7 miles the road forks. Take the left fork, FR 409, up toward Bloomington Lake for less than 0.5 mile, then make a left onto FR 457. Follow this road for 0.5 mile to its end near the South Fork of Bloomington Creek, and park at the trailhead. GPS: N42 10.43' / W111 33.05'

The Hike

For the first 0.5 mile, the trail follows the South Fork of Bloomington Creek. Watch for resident moose lurking in the willows and trout darting between pools. This used to be a road but has been blocked off with large boulders. At the first junction, head through the forest, crossing a small bridge, and begin the ascent up the ridge above Horse Flats. This section of the hike is available for motorcycle use, but the narrow trail would seem too steep and difficult to negotiate through its rocks and tree roots.

After an uphill hike of 1 mile (seeming like 5) with two switchbacks, you reach the ridge overlooking Horse Flats to the east. On the other side are beautiful views of Paris Peak and the surrounding Bear River Mountains. Here, at nearly 8,400 feet, a trail to the right continues along the ridge. Follow this trail instead of descending down into the broad valley of Horse Flats. For 1.6 miles meander along the ridge until you reach Worm Lake, catching occasional distant views of Idaho and Utah's well-visited Bear Lake area.

Worm Lake can be little more than a giant puddle depending on when you visit. It does have a beautiful backdrop of lush pine forests and green-walled alpine cliffs. At the lake, the trails begin to fizzle; keep to the left side to begin the loop. After picking up this trail, head east down to the spring of Worm Creek. Follow this for over a mile until you reach a campsite area near a draw. If you reach large cliffs over Worm Creek

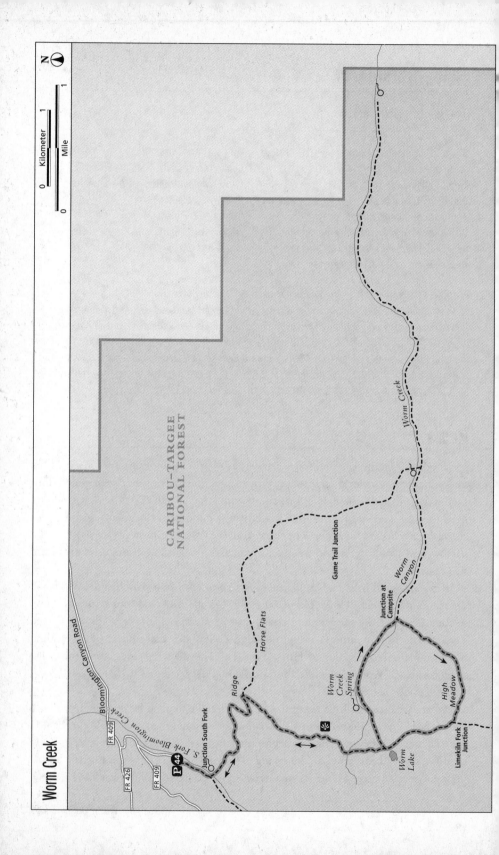

Worm Creek

CARIBOU–TARGEE
NATIONAL FOREST

Bloomington Canyon Road

FR 409
FR 426
FR 409

P 44

S. Fork Bloomington Creek

Junction South Fork

Ridge

Horse Flats

Game Trail Junction

Worm Creek
Spring

Junction at
Campsite

Worm Canyon

Worm Creek

Worm
Lake

High
Meadow

Limekiln Fork
Junction

N

0   Kilometer   1

0   1
Mile

Canyon (though they are worth checking out), you've gone too far; you'll need to retrace your steps to the camp area.

The trail junction is faint, but turn right up the draw, and pick up the trail again. As you continue ascending, to your left you may catch a glimpse of the rock formations above the forest. Deer are very common here.

Finally at the top, there is a great open area. The trail disappears here, but you can pick it up again if you remain near the forest edge instead of crossing the open meadow. The rest of the way simply loops you back to southern part of Worm Lake, where you can take the trail back down the mountain to arrive back at the trailhead.

Options: Another way to access the loop part of this lollipop hike is to begin from Worm Creek Road, and follow the creek itself for 4 miles until it reaches the junction at the camp area.

You cannot be in the area without visiting scenic Bloomington Lake. Continue up FR 409 to the trailhead; it's an easy 0.5-mile hike to this pristine gem of a lake.

Miles and Directions

0.0 Begin at the trailhead on the South Fork of Bloomington Creek (7,444 feet).

0.6 Reach the junction at the South Fork of Bloomington Creek. Go left.

1.5 Reach the ridgetop trail junction. Go right.

3.1 Reach Worm Lake and the trail heading east to Worm Creek Springs.

4.4 Reach the campsite area. Go right to complete the loop.

6.6 Keep right (north) at the meadows.

7.2 Return to Worm Lake on south side.

7.3 Head back from Worm Lake, retracing your steps.

8.9 Reach the ridgetop trail junction.

10.4 Arrive back at the trailhead.

Basin and Range

All of Nevada, western Utah, southeast Oregon, southern Arizona, a bit of California, a bit of Idaho, and much of northern Mexico are part of the Basin and Range Province. This is not a governmental subdivision. It is a land of broad, mostly arid valleys separated by hundreds of long, narrow, and often high mountain ranges. As one person put it, the map of Nevada looks like hundreds of caterpillars crawling to the south. The caterpillars are the ranges, and between them are the big basins.

The heart of the Basin and Range is the Great Basin—that part of America where rivers flow but never reach the sea. They flow into places like the Great Salt Lake, the Carson Sink, Mono Lake, and Pyramid Lake. All drainage is internal.

Part of southern Idaho is on the margins of the Basin and Range, and a smaller part is in the Great Basin, that portion drained by the Bear River, which oddly enough flows mostly through the Middle Rockies before it dies in the Great Salt Lake.

Idaho's Basin and Range mountains are generally considered to be, going from west to east, the Albion Range, the Jim Sage and Cotterel Range, the Black Pine Range, the Sublett Range, the Deep Creek Range, the Samaria Mountains, and the Clarkston Range. While they share some of the characteristics of the Middle Rockies, most also put the Bannock Range, Pocatello Range, Portneuf Range, and Fish Creek Range into Idaho's part of the Basin and Range Province.

Idaho's tall Lemhi and Lost River Ranges have many of the characteristics of Basin and Range mountains. They are narrow, uplifted fault blocks, with normal faults at their base (none of that tricky overthrust stuff, or big old batholiths). However, they are separated from the rest of the Basin and Range by the anomaly of the Snake River Plain. Due to proximity, we list these two ranges as being within the Northern Rockies.

—Ralph Maughan

Albion Range

The Albion Range is the westernmost of Idaho's slice of the Basin and Range Province. The Goose Creek Mountains (South Hills), to the west, are part of the Columbia River Plateau and are geologically much different from the Basin and Range Province or the Rocky Mountains.

The Albion Range rises southeast of the town of Burley and due east of Oakley. It is the highest mountain range south of the Snake River, culminating at 10,339-foot Cache Peak. The range consists of two big mountains connected by a lower ridge (crossed at Elba Pass). On the north is Mount Harrison and, to its south, massive Independence Mountain, of which Cache Peak is the highest point.

An impressive cirque was carved by glaciers into the northeast side of Mount Independence. It holds four lovely lakes, accessible only by trail. This hike is described in this section.

Mount Harrison has a road-accessible subalpine lake, as well as a fire lookout and the Pomerelle Mountain Resort (ski area), which is notable for having plenty of snow even when other resorts lack snowpack.

At the southern end of the range, soft granite has been exposed to the elements and eroded into numerous odd-shaped monolithic domes, pinnacles, and huge boulders. This area, called the City of Rocks, is a national reserve created by Congress. This designation gives the area protection from vandalism and promotes the development of hiking trails, sanitation facilities, and camping and picnicking facilities. The City of Rocks National Reserve is a splendid area for rock climbing or an easy family outing in the fall or late spring. We describe this fascinating rock garden in this section.

—Ralph Maughan

The Albion Mountains. PHOTO BY JOHN KRATZ

45 Independence Lakes

This route leads to four scenic subalpine lakes high on Independence Mountain. Grand views are available of Mount Harrison, Elba Basin, Cache Peak, and the Jim Sage Mountains.

Start: 35 road miles southeast of Burley
Type of hike: Out-and-back
Distance: 4.4 miles
Approximate hiking time: 2 days
Difficulty: Moderate
Best season: Mid-July–August
Trail surface: Dirt and rock
Land status: Sawtooth National Forest
Canine compatibility: On leash recommended
Fees and permits: None
Maps: USGS Cache Peak ID; Twin Falls and Burley Ranger Districts–Sawtooth National Forest Map

Trail contact: Burley Ranger District; (208) 678-0430
Special considerations: Water is scarce below the lakes.
Parking and trailhead facilities: There is a spacious trailhead with an outhouse, bulletin board, stock-loading ramp, and walk-in picnic area surrounded by a fence to keep the omnipresent cattle at bay. Park and open the gate to the campground (close it to keep the cows out), cross Dry Creek on a good bridge, and walk through the campground to the broad trail. You are now on your way.

Finding the trailhead: Drive about 20 miles south of Burley on ID 27 to the small town of Oakley. Turn left onto 2000 South from Oakley's Main Street (which is also ID 27). Take this paved county road directly east toward Independence Mountain. The road is paved for 6 miles. As the pavement ends, a sign indicates that the rough gravel road ahead leads to Independence Lakes. The road, which seems to have been covered with inordinately rough gravel, climbs more than 2,000 feet steeply. It switchbacks 5 miles up to Elba Pass (7,106 feet). The road surface improves after 2 miles, when you enter the Sawtooth National Forest.

At Elba Pass there is a fine view of the South Hills to your west, as well as part of Mount Harrison to the left and massive Independence Mountain at two o'clock.

The road forks at the pass. Do not continue across the pass, but take the road to the right. A sign indicates that the Independence Lakes Trailhead is 4 miles. Head over a rise and down the other side, and come to a fork after about a mile. Keep to the right. After about 1 more mile, you come to Potholes Junction. Here, take the fork to the left and continue to the trailhead. The road climbs through some aspen, with good views of Mount Harrison to the north. About 0.3 mile from the trailhead, you come to the horse transfer trailhead. Pass it by, and follow the road as it swings downhill to end at Dry Creek (which has water).

Elba Pass can also be accessed from the east by turning onto CR 1950 South at Elba. This road eventually becomes FR 548. The pass is 10 miles of gravel road, then dirt road, from Elba. GPS: N42 13.11' / W113 40.39'

The first Independence Lake. PHOTO BY LUKE KRATZ

The Hike

The broad and easy trail, which is closed to motorized vehicles, climbs gently across the forested north face of Independence Mountain toward Green Creek, staying far above Dry Creek. There are breaks and meadows in the fir, spruce, and aspen forest with outstanding views to the north and northeast.

I approached the trail with trepidation because of all the cattle gathered at the fence around the picnic area. I thought this perhaps would be a trek through environmental degradation, but there were few cows on the mountain itself, perhaps because the sparse understory consists mostly of inedible or toxic native plants like penstemon, lupine, western coneflower, and astragalus (the locoweed genus).

Shortly before you begin the climb up into the cirque that holds the lakes, the trail passes just above a small forest fire burn, and there is a trail junction. To the left is the Rangers Trail (not on the map), which drops into Green Creek. Keep to the right, and begin to climb steeply toward the lakes.

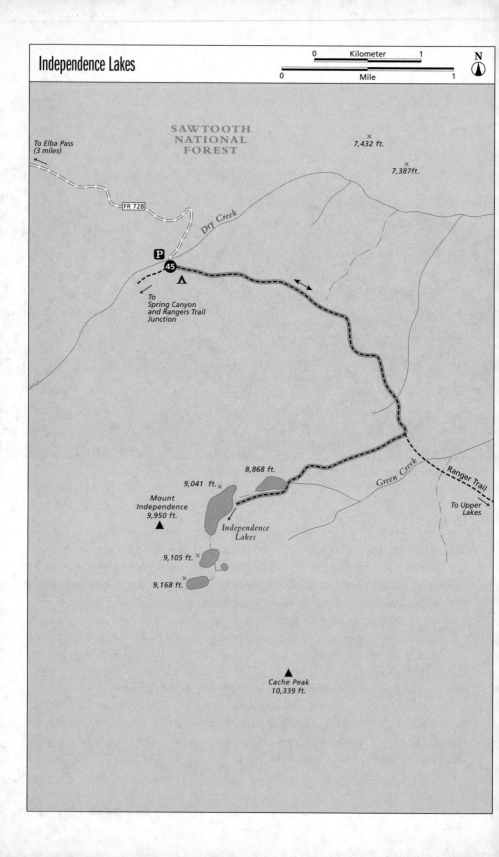

The trail never drops into Green Creek, but keeps on a shelf just to its right (west). There are many forks in this broad trail, but they are all switch-back cutoffs. After climbing 900 feet, you suddenly come upon the first lake, which is large, shallow, and partially filled with marsh grass. It has plenty of small fish, however. Behind the lake is the steep cirque wall just below Independence Peak. This impressive wall continues up the entire west side of the cirque. The cirque is very rocky, with boulders of granitic rock and beautiful white quartzite of the Eureka Formation (metamorphosed white sandstone).

The trail continues to the second lake, which appears to be by far the largest on the topo, but in fact is not by the end of the summer. This lake is deep, however, and has large trout.

There is no trail to the upper two lakes. The route is over and through many granitic gray boulders. Although the lakes are fishless, this hike over the rocks is worthwhile because the upper two lakes are beautiful, especially the very last, which is large but shallow, with very clear water. Sunlight through the clear water does beautiful things to the moderately large, flat, submerged rocks.

Cache Peak, which is the highest point on Mount Independence, rises just east of the lakes, but that side of the cirque wall is not as impressive as the west side. Cache Peak, which tops out at 10,339 feet, is also the highest mountain in Idaho south of the Snake River.

The only downside is the fact that a few cows do make it to the lakes. Complain to the Sawtooth National Forest, for this mountain has no real food for them, and it shows bad public priorities, given the popularity of this trail and these lakes.

Options: You can scramble to the top of the mountain from the head of the cirque, although this is not easy. From the top, you have a wonderful 360-degree view of all the mountains and valleys of southern Idaho and of the City of Rocks National Reserve just to the south, plus the bold Raft River Range just inside Utah. Walk around the ridge to climb either Cache Peak or the somewhat lower Independence Mountain (9,950 feet).

—Ralph Maughan

Miles and Directions

0.0 Start at the trailhead at Dry Creek (7,720 feet).

1.2 Reach the junction with the Rangers Trail (8,100 feet).

2.0 Arrive at the lower lake (8,868 feet).

2.2 Reach the second lake (9,041 feet).

4.4 Arrive back at the trailhead.

South Hills

The South Hills, also known as the Twin Falls Hills, Goose Creek Mountains, and Cassia Mountains, don't look like much from the interstate near Twin Falls—just some small, dome-shaped rises to the south. Most hikers turn north toward Sun Valley and the Sawtooth National Recreation Area. But get down in them, and you will find lovely nooks of desert streams, cliffs, volcanic formations, and mountain vistas well worth your time. In late spring and early summer, there are numerous species of birds, and the 25-acre Shoshone Wildlife Pond supports nesting waterfowl and wading birds.

The paved Rock Creek Road is the main entry to the South Hills and leads to the Magic Mountain Resort ski area. Along the way are seven developed campgrounds, plus the beautiful Harrington Fork Picnic Area, a perfect stopping-off point in early or late season. In addition, there are another eleven campgrounds and two more picnic areas beyond Magic Mountain or requiring different access.

These hills are the playground for Twin Falls, and most folks consider a gas-powered vehicle the equipment of choice. Consequently, trails good for hikers are hard to find, and the Twin Falls–Burley District of the Sawtooth National Forest has put 99.9 percent of its emphasis on off-road-vehicle trail development. There are signs that this is starting to change with increased use by mountain bikers and cross-country skiers. Hikers, too, should weigh in and let the district know that more of this handsome country should be devoted to self-propelled traffic. The district has constructed the Rim View Trail, which is open to foot and horse traffic only. We give access information to this trail in the options portion of the description of the Third Fork Rock Creek–Wahlstrom Hollow Loop.

—Jackie Johnson Maughan

Aspen forests are common along slopes in the south. PHOTO BY LUKE KRATZ

46 Third Fork Rock Creek–Wahlstrom Hollow Loop

Follow an extraordinary desert stream to mountain habitat with volcanic rock formations and beaver ponds in this area of the South Hills.

Start: 31 miles south of Twin Falls
Type of hike: Loop
Distance: 9 miles
Approximate hiking time: 2 days
Difficulty: Moderate for first half; moderately difficult for second
Best season: May–June and September
Trail surface: Dirt and rock
Land status: Sawtooth National Forest
Canine compatibility: On leash
Fees and permits: None
Maps: USGS Pike Mountain, Rams Horn Ridge, and Trapper Peak ID; Twin Falls and Burley Ranger Districts–Sawtooth National Forest map
Trail contact: Twin Falls Ranger District; (208) 737-3200; www.fs.usda.gov/sawtooth

Special considerations: This area sees desert to mountain weather. Bullsnakes (common) and rattlesnakes (uncommon) are found here. There is an elevation gain of 2,000 feet if you do both sides of the loop. Flying and biting insects plus heat make this a poor midsummer hike.

Parking and trailhead facilities: The trailhead is easy to miss. It is on the left (east) side of the road, but the only sign reads "trailers." The trailhead has ample parking and a latrine. Third Fork is not a good place to camp, and there are a number of better developed sites within easy driving distance. Among these are Steer Basin, Lower and Upper Penstemon, and Pettit.

Finding the trailhead: From the south end of Twin Falls, turn left (east) onto Kimberly Road. After 5 miles, jog to the right (south) to enter Kimberly. (Do not take ID 50, which is to the left.) Then, shortly, a sign directs you onto US 30. After 3 miles you will see a sign marking Rock Creek Canyon, CR G3. Continue for a very short way to reach the turnoff to Rock Creek, which is marked by a sign and a filling station and is just on the outskirts of Hansen. As you drive due south up the paved Rock Creek Road, the South Hills rise directly in front of you. This is open range country, and there might be livestock on the road. After about 18 miles, you will reach the first of four campgrounds preceding the Third Fork Trailhead, which is at mile 23. GPS: N42 15.12' / W114 14.85'

The Hike

This lovely piece of terrain has been dismissed by some because of use by off-road vehicles. However, on a busy Memorial Day weekend, we found only a few motorized bikers and a few mountain bikers on the Third Fork portion of the loop. We saw many, many ATVs and motorcycles going up the Rock Creek Road, but this trail doesn't appear to be a favorite. After the marshes on the Wahlstrom Hollow portion, we saw no one except a couple of equestrians. There has been a rumor that the Third Fork portion of this hike is slated for ATV development. Please contact the ranger district to protest the ruining of this one of only three or four trails not already devoted to mechanized use.

The South Hills were created by volcanic action, and this hike takes you through welded volcanic ash deposit formations (tuff) that have eroded into hoodoos and pinnacles. These ash deposits are capped with black basalt cliffs at the top of the loop. Consequently, there is not only interesting geology but a variety of flora and fauna, as you start out in willows and sage, top out in subalpine fir, descend through aspen and past beaver ponds, then drop back to the trailhead through red rock and hoodoos.

Going clockwise, cross a bridge over Third Fork and start out on a sagebrush bench close to the creek. The rise is gentle as you travel through aspen and willow and, in season, a riot of birdcalls, including those of lazuli buntings and yellow warblers. There are bridges over Second Fork and where the trail crosses Third Fork near Cotton Creek, 2.5 miles in. Here, you will have climbed 400 feet from the 5,200-foot trailhead. Ahead is unnamed Peak 7,068, and to your left is Cotton Ridge.

Now the canyon begins to narrow, and the elevation gain becomes more pronounced as you swing gradually to the west and climb 240 feet in 0.75 mile. Lupine and penstemon are abundant in June, as is the sound of hummingbirds. The trail continues to curve west along a 200-foot basalt cliff face to reach the A. H. Creek Trail junction in 0.75 mile. Now comes the most difficult portion of the hike, as you leave this meadowy junction to continue to your right (northwest), climbing up the aspen-covered hill some 800 feet to the pass. The trail, rather than going straight up A. H. Creek as shown on the Trapper Peak and Pike Mountain USGS quads, has been rebuilt into three long switchbacks. The upper portion here is open and unshaded.

Once on top, it's easy to lose the trail because it isn't shown on the Pike Mountain quad, and it is intersected by a road and Trail Canyon Spring Trail. To keep your bearings, do not turn left onto the road or the other trail, or right onto the road. Instead, bear straight ahead and north-northwest to find the trail as it drops slowly off the top and descends on the right (east) side of the creek in Wahlstrom Hollow. You will descend 260 feet in slightly less than a mile. Off to your west is a series of marshy beaver ponds.

If you do get sidetracked and onto the road, it's okay. Simply follow it to the west (left) for 0.75 mile. From there, it will intersect with the road down (to your right and going north) to the Wahlstrom Hollow beaver ponds. Just past the ponds, the road peters out, crosses the stream, and joins the trail.

Once the trail meets the stream, it drops steeply 800 feet in just over a mile. The country changes dramatically as it enters red rock formations and the canyon. The

Third Fork Rock Creek-Wahlstrom Hollow Loop

Kilometer

0   1

0   1

Mile

N

To ③⓪
(23 miles)

P ㊷ Third Fork
Trailhead

× 6,000 ft.

Rock Creek Road

× 6,763 ft.

Third Fork Rock Creek

Second Fork

To Rock Creek
Ranger Station
(6 miles)

Wahlstrom
Hollow

× 6,737 ft.

Beaver
Ponds

Cotton Creek

× 7,080 ft.

× 7,068 ft.

FR 523

FR 116

A. H. Creek Pass Hoodoos

Spring ○

FR 523

A. H. Creek

two stream crossings are not bridged but are small enough not to require wading. In the last 2 miles, the trail continues its downward drop, and you will also encounter scree and some unstable footing. The hoodoos and other rock formations make this part of the hike quite stunning. The canyon is generally narrow, and getting out of the way of horse traffic can present a challenge. Mountain bikers and motorcyclists do not appear to use this part of the loop because it is narrow, steep, and rocky.

You are likely to see bullsnakes in the lower elevations of the entire hike. These harmless reptiles are protectively patterned to look like rattlers, but their heads are much smaller in proportion to their bodies, and, of course, they don't have a rattle.

Options: Rim View Trail is 9.5 miles one way as it follows the Rock Creek Canyon rim. Open to foot and horse traffic only, it offers excellent views and enough water for overnight excursions. Since it is a through hike, a shuttle is required. This trail is not shown on the Sawtooth Forest map or the Pike Mountain USGS quad. Access to its two trailheads (Rim View and Third Fork–Rim View) from Rock Creek Road is not marked.

Starting at the Rim View Trailhead will save you a 2,000-foot climb out of the canyon, but there is still significant elevation gain and loss up and down the rim. To find the trailhead, take FR 500 where it leaves Rock Creek Road just before (north of) the ski area. In about 3 switchbacking miles is the 7,200-foot trailhead on the right (north) side of the road.

The Third Fork–Rim View trailhead (5,200 feet) is located on the right (west) side of Rock Creek Road, directly across the road from Third Fork Campground.

—Jackie Johnson Maughan

Miles and Directions

0.0 Start at the Third Fork trailhead (5,200 feet).

2.5 Cross the Third Fork near Cotton Creek (5,600 feet).

4.0 Reach the A. H. Creek trail junction (6,000 feet). Stay right.

5.5 Reach the A. H. Creek–Wahlstrom Hollow pass (6,800 feet).

6.0 Pass the beaver ponds (6,400 feet).

7.5 Walk among the red rock hoodoos and pinnacles (5,600 feet).

9.0 Arrive back at the trailhead (5,200 feet).

APPENDIX A:
CONSERVATION ORGANIZATIONS AND RESOURCES

Committee for Idaho's High Desert
PO Box 2863
Boise, ID 83701
(208) 384-1715

For Wolves
Wolf Recovery Foundation
PO Box 444
Pocatello, ID 83204
forwolves.org

Friends of the Clearwater
PO Box 9241
Moscow, ID 83843
(208) 882-9755
friendsoftheclearwater.org

Greater Yellowstone Coalition
13 South Wilson, Ste. 2
Bozeman, MT 59715-4610
(406) 586-1593
greateryellowstonecoalition.org

Hells Canyon Preservation Council
PO Box 2768
La Grande, OR 97850
(541) 963-3950
hellscanyon.org

Idaho Conservation League
Boise Office
PO Box 844
Boise, ID 83701
(208) 345-6933
(208) 344-0344 (fax)
Street address: 710 North 6th St.
Boise, ID 83702
idahoconservation.org

Idaho Conservation League
Idaho Office
162 North Woodruff Ave.
Idaho Falls, ID 83401
(208) 522-7927
idahoconservation.org

Idaho Conservation League
Ketchum Office
PO Box 2671
Ketchum, ID 83340
(208) 726-7485
(208) 726-1821 (fax)
Street address: 110 West 5th St., Ste. 201
Ketchum, ID 83340
idahoconservation.org

Idaho Conservation League
Sandpoint Office
PO Box 2308
Sandpoint, ID 83864
(208) 265-9565
(208) 265-9650 (fax)
Street address: 102 South Euclid, Ste. 207
Sandpoint, ID 83864
idahoconservation.org

Idaho Rivers United
PO Box 633
Boise, ID 83701
(208) 343-7481
(800) 574-7481 (toll-free)
www.idahorivers.org

The Nature Conservancy
nature.org

Roadless Land
roadlessland.org

Sierra Club Idaho Chapter
503 West Franklin St.
Boise, ID 83701
(208) 384-1023
www.idaho.sierraclub.org

Sierra Club Outings
85 2nd St., 2nd Floor
San Francisco, CA 94105-3441
(415) 977-5630 (24-hour voice mail)
sierraclub.org/outing

The Lands Council
25 West Main St., Ste. 222
Spokane, WA 99201
(509) 838-4912
landscouncil.org

Western Watersheds Project
PO Box 1770
Hailey, ID 83333
(208) 788-2290
westernwatersheds.org

Wild Rockies
wildrockies.org

Wilderness Society, Idaho Office
710 North 6th St., Ste. 102
Boise, ID 83702-5544
(208) 343-8153
www.wilderness.org/idaho

Wildlands CPR
Wildlands CPR is the only national
conservation group in the United States
that specifically targets off-road vehicle
abuse of public lands and actively promotes wildland restoration, road removal,
and the prevention of wildland road
construction.
www.wildlandscpr.org

Wolf Recovery Foundation
PO Box 44236
Boise, ID 83711-0236
(208) 363-0203
wolfrecoveryfoundation.com

APPENDIX B:
ADDRESSES OF LAND MANAGEMENT AGENCIES FOR HIKE INFORMATION

Boise National Forest

Cascade Ranger District
PO Box 696
540 North Main
Cascade, ID 83611
(208) 382-7400

Emmett Ranger District
1805 ID 16, #5
Emmett, ID 83617
(208) 365-7000

Idaho City Ranger District
PO Box 129
3833 ID 21
Idaho City, ID 83631
(208) 392-6681

Lowman Ranger District
7359 ID 21
Lowman, ID 83637
(208) 259-3361

Mountain Home Ranger District
2180 American Legion Blvd.
Mountain Home, ID 83647
(208) 587–7961

Caribou–Targhee National Forest

Ashton Ranger District
PO Box 858
46 ID 20
Ashton, ID 83420
(208) 652-7442

Dubois Ranger District
98 North Oakley
Dubois, ID 83423
(208) 374-5422

Island Park Ranger District
PO Box 220
3726 ID 20
Island Park, ID 83429
(208) 558-7301

Montpelier Ranger District
322 North 4th St.
Montpelier, ID 83254
(208) 847-0375

Palisades Ranger District
3659 East Ririe Hwy.
Idaho Falls, ID 83401
(208) 523-1412

Soda Springs Ranger District
410 East Hooper Ave.
Soda Springs, ID 83276
(208) 547-4356

Teton Basin Ranger District
PO Box 777
Driggs, ID 83422
(208) 354-2312

Westside Ranger District
4350 Cliffs Dr.
Pocatello, ID 83204
(208) 236-7500

Hells Canyon National Recreation Area

Riggins Office
PO Box 832/US 95
Riggins, ID 83549
(208) 628-3916

Idaho Panhandle National Forests

Idaho Panhandle National Forest Headquarters
3815 Schreiber Way
Coeur d'Alene, ID 83815
(208) 765-7223
www.fs.usda.gov/ipnf

Bonners Ferry Ranger District
Route 4/PO Box 4860
Bonners Ferry, ID 83805-9764
(208) 267-5561

Coeur d'Alene River Ranger District
Fernan Office (208) 664-2318
Silver Valley Office (208) 783-2363

Priest Lake Ranger District
32203 ID 57
Priest River, ID 83856-9612
(208) 443-2512

Sandpoint Ranger District
1500 US 2, Ste. 110
Sandpoint, ID 83864-9509
(208) 263-5111

St. Joe Ranger District
St. Maries Office
PO Box 407
St. Maries, ID 83861-0407
St. Maries Office (208) 245-2531
Avery Office (208) 245-4517

Nez Perce–Clearwater National Forests

Nez Perce–Clearwater National Forest Supervisor's Office
903 3rd St.
Kamiah, ID 83536
(208) 935-2513

Grangeville Office
104 Airport Rd.
Grangeville, ID 83530
(208) 983-1950

Lochsa Ranger District
502 Lowry St.
Kooskia, ID 83539
(208) 926-4274

Moose Creek Ranger District
Fenn Ranger Station
831 Selway Rd.
Kooskia, ID 83539
(208) 926-4258

Nez Perce Ranger District
Route 2/PO Box 475
Grangeville, ID 83530
(208) 983-1963

North Fork Ranger District
12730 ID 12
Orofino, ID 83544
(208) 476-4541

Palouse Ranger District
1700 ID 6
Potlatch, ID 83855
(208) 875-1131

Powell Ranger District
192 Powell Road
Lolo, MT 59847
(208) 942-3113

Red River (Elk City) Ranger District
300 American River Rd.
Elk City, ID 83525
(208) 842-2245

Salmon River Ranger District
Slate Creek Ranger Station
304 Slate Creek Rd.
White Bird, ID 83554
(208) 839-2211

Payette National Forest

Payette National Forest
500 North Mission St.
McCall, ID 83638
(208) 634-0700

Council Ranger District
PO Box 567
2092 US 95
Council, ID 83612
(208) 253-0100

Krassel Ranger District
500 North Mission St.
McCall, ID 83638
(208) 634-0600

McCall Ranger District
102 West Lake St.
McCall, ID 83638
(208) 634-0400

New Meadows Ranger District
PO Box J/3674 US 95
New Meadows, ID 83654
(208) 347-0300

Weiser Ranger District
851 East 9th St.
Weiser, ID 83672
(208) 549-4200

Salmon–Challis National Forest

Salmon–Challis National Forest Supervisor's Office
1206 South Challis Street
Salmon, ID 83467
(208) 756-5100

Challis–Yankee Fork Ranger District
HC 63, Box 1669/US 93
Challis, ID 83226
(208) 879-4100

Leadore Ranger District
103 Ranger St./PO Box 180/ID 28
Leadore, ID 83464
(208) 768-2500

Lost River Ranger District
716 West Custer/PO Box 507
Mackay, ID 83251
(208) 588-3400

Middle Fork Ranger District
HC 63, Box 1669/US 93
Challis, ID 83226
(208) 879-4101

North Fork Ranger District
11 Casey Rd./PO Box 180
North Fork, ID 83466
(208) 865-2700

Salmon/Cobalt Ranger District
311 McPherson St,
Salmon, ID 83467
(208) 756-5200

Sawtooth National Forest

Sawtooth National Forest Supervisor's Office
2647 Kimberly Rd. East
Twin Falls, ID 83301-7976
(208) 737-3200

Fairfield Ranger District
PO Box 189/102 1st St. East
Fairfield, ID 83327
(208) 764-3202

Ketchum Ranger District
PO Box 2356/206 Sun Valley Rd.
Ketchum, ID 83340
(208) 622-5371

Minidoka Ranger District
2306 Hiland Avenue
Burley, ID 83318
(208) 678-0430

Sawtooth National Recreation Area

Sawtooth National Recreation Area Headquarters (Sawtooth NRA)
5 North Fork Canyon Rd.
Ketchum, ID 83340
(208) 727-5000
(800) 260-5970 (toll-free)

Sawtooth National Recreation Area—Stanley Office
HC 64, Box 9900
Stanley, ID 83278
(208) 774-3000

Other Offices

Bruneau Dunes State Park
27608 Sand Dunes Rd.
Mountain Home, ID 83647
(208) 366-7919
http://parksandrecreation.idaho.gov/parks/bruneau-dunes

City of Rocks National Reserve
PO Box 169
Almo, ID 83312
(208) 824-5910
www.nps.gov/ciro

Craters of the Moon National Monument & Preserve
PO Box 29/US 93 (18 miles west of Arco)
Arco, ID 83213
(208) 527-3257
www.nps.gov/crmo

Malad Gorge State Park
1074 East 2350 South
Hagerman, ID 83332
(208) 837-4505

Bureau of Land Management (BLM)

Idaho State Office
1387 South Vinnell Way
Boise, ID 83709
(208) 373-4000

Bruneau BLM Field Office
3948 Development Ave.
Boise, ID 83705
(208) 384-3300

Burley BLM Field Office
15 East 200 South
Burley, ID 83318
(208) 677-6600

Challis BLM Field Office
1151 Blue Mountain Rd.
Challis, ID 83226
(208) 879-6200

Cottonwood BLM Field Office
1 Butte Dr.
Cottonwood, ID 83522
(208) 962-3245

Four Rivers BLM Field Office
3948 Development Ave.
Boise, ID 83705
(208) 384-3300

Jarbidge BLM Field Office
2536 Kimberly Rd.
Twin Falls, ID 83301
(208) 735-2060

Owyhee BLM Field Office
20 First Ave. West
Marsing, ID 83639
(208) 896-5912

Pocatello BLM Field Office
4350 Cliffs Dr.
Pocatello, ID 83204
(208) 478-6340

Salmon BLM Field Office
1206 South Challis St.
Salmon, ID 83467
(208) 756-5400

Shoshone BLM Field Office
400 West F St.
Shoshone, ID 83352
(208) 732-7200

Upper Snake BLM Field Office
1405 Hollipark Dr.
Idaho Falls, ID 83401
(208) 524-7500

HIKE INDEX